Virginia Woolf

TO THE LIGHTHOUSE

Virginia Woolf

TO THE LIGHTHOUSE

[Edited with Introduction, Author's Information, Complete Text, Summary and Analysis and Study Questions]

Mansi Sachdeva
B.A. English (Hons), Delhi University;
M.A., M. Phil. (English), IGNOU

ANMOL PUBLICATIONS PVT. LTD.
NEW DELHI - 110 002 (INDIA)

ANMOL PUBLICATIONS PVT. LTD.

H.O.: 4374/4B, Ansari Road, Darya Ganj,
New Delhi-110 002 (India)
Ph.: 23278000, 23261597

B.O.: No. 1015, Ist Main Road, BSK IIIrd Stage
IIIrd Phase, IIIrd Block
Bangalore - 560 085 (India)
Visit us at: www.anmolpublications.com

First Published, 2009

PRINTED IN INDIA

Printed at Balaji Offset Press, Delhi.

Contents

Preface

Virginia Woolf (1882-1941) in full Adeline Virginia Woolf, original surname Stephen.

British author who made an original contribution to the form of the novel also distinguished feminist essayist, critic in The Times Literary Supplement, and a central figure of Bloomsbury group.

Highly poetic and densely allusive, To the Lighthouse is a self-reflexive, feminist künstlerroman. Woolf conceived its triadic structure as "two blocks joined by a corridor" Part One, "The Window" is linked via Part Two, "Time Passes", to Part Three, "The Lighthouse". Each part is subdivided into numbered sections varying in length.

Author

Chapter 1

Introduction

Highly poetic and densely allusive, To the Lighthouse is a self-reflexive, feminist künstlerroman. Woolf conceived its triadic structure as "two blocks joined by a corridor": Part One, "The Window" is linked via Part Two, "Time Passes", to Part Three, "The Lighthouse". Each part is subdivided into numbered sections varying in length.. Set in a holiday house on the Hebridean island of Skye, Part One examines the domestic, sexual, political, philosophical and aesthetic tensions in the lives of Mr and Mrs Ramsay, a philosopher and his wife of renowned beauty, and their numerous children and guests, as they take their holiday one summer around 1910.

It culminates in a banquet to celebrate the engagement of two guests, Paul and Minta. Part Three returns to the house during a summer after the Great War, when the certainties and pleasures of the pre-war world have crumbled (along with Paul and Minta's marriage). In each summer, one of the guests, Lily Briscoe, hemmed in by patriarchal contempt for women's artistic abilities, and by Mrs Ramsay's forceful marital ideology, attempts a painting, which serves as self-reflexive reference point for the novel itself. Indeed, it closes with an account of her final visionary brush-stroke in an elegiac moment of lyric consolation. Lily's rejection of Mr Ramsay's amorous approaches, combined with his children's defiance, suggest an unsettling, if not an overcoming, of patriarchy.

The middle section, "Time Passes" covers the intervening years, focusing on the object world of the house, and its environs, in decline and under repair, as a metaphor for the losses and changes in personal terms for the individuals in the novel as well as and in wider social, and political terms. This highly experimental piece of writing, published separately to begin with, has been understood to reflect on the social and political upheavals occurring during the war period through the lens of further turbulence in the 1920s.Shockingly, major events, such as the death of Mrs Ramsay, the central figure in Part One, the death of her son in the war, and of her daughter in childbirth, are communicated in brief, stylised, parenthetical statements inserted into Woolf's sustained lyrical description of time passing in the house. Woolf's theory of androgyny has been pressed into critical service for readings of this part of the novel, where the Great War's unsettling of gender politics is suggested by a cataclysmic "down-pouring of immense darkness" in which "not only was furniture confounded; there was scarcely anything left of body or mind by which one could say 'This is he' or 'This is she.'". We might ask of this writing Auerbach's simple, but perceptive, question: "Who is speaking in this paragraph?" Woolf has pushed free-indirect discourse to the limits in describing the forces at work in an empty house.

Woolf emphasised the lyric qualities of her fiction when she was "making up 'To the Lighthouse'", and had the "idea that I will invent a new name for my books to supplant 'novel'. A new – by Virginia Woolf. But what? Elegy?". To the Lighthouse was conceived in part as an elegy on her dead parents, and is in some respects autobiographical: "This is going to be fairly short: to have father's character done complete in it; & mothers; & St Ives; & childhood; & all the usual things I put in – life, death &c.

But the centre is father's character, sitting in a boat, reciting We perished, each alone, while he crushes a dying mackerel" But it would be diminishing to transpose the novel's Hebridean setting simply as Cornwall, the location of Woolf's childhood family holidays, or to read the eponymous lighthouse as simply Godrevy lighthouse, which was visible from the Stephen's Cornish retreat. Woolf's friend Violet Dickinson was reprimanded by Woolf herself for such a transposition: "I'm so glad that you like some of the Lighthouse. Is it Cornwall? I'm not as sure as you are."

The novel offers by no means a realist account of its Hebridean setting, but makes many references to Scottish texts, including, for example, David Hume's enlightenment philosophy, and Boswell's and Johnson's accounts of their tour of the Hebrides, and the story of the events of the '45 (Prince Charlie and Flora Macdonald.) Such texts were the staple of her father's library.

Woolf felt, nevertheless, that in writing To the Lighthouse she had exorcised the ghosts of her parents. Vanessa Bell thanked her sister for her accurate portrayal of their mother, which she found "more like her to me than anything I could have conceived as possible". ReadingTo the Lighthouse involves the reader remaining open to both the autobiographical and the fictional at the same time. "Nothing is only one thing" in this text, as one of its characters, James, concludes when in sight of the lighthouse. And To the Lighthouse is a densely allusive text, brimming with allusions to and citations of many other poetic and literary texts: Shakespeare, Milton, Marvell, Tennyson, Scott, Virgil, and so on. During the first part, Mr Ramsay charges around the garden reciting Tenntson's "The Charge of the Light Brigade" while Mrs Ramsay is reading to her son the Grimms fairy tale, "The Fisherman and His Wife", which is a cautionary tale against over-ambitious wife. At the close of the first part, she is reading Shakespeare's sonnets, while Mr Ramsay reads a novel by Walter Scott.

The dense, self-conscious, layering of metaphor and symbolism in To the Lighthouse requires many levels of interpretation. The reader is constantly invited to ponder how the lighthouse itself, for example, might be understood. "I meant nothing by The Lighthouse" Woolf wrote to her friend Roger Fry, the formalist aesthete: "One has to have a central line down the middle of the book to hold the design together. I saw that all sorts of feelings would accrue to this, but I refused to think them out, and trusted that people would make it the deposit for their own emotions. I can't manage Symbolism except in this vague, generalised way. Directly I'm told what a thing means, it becomes hateful to me." Such discussion shows how far Woolf has moved the genre of her novel towards poetry. The normal frames of reference for fiction, such as plot and character, have given way to consideration of poetic device and philosophy. Like much of its contemporary poetic elegy, too, To the Lighthouse, speaks more generally of the dead of the Great War, and of the passing of one way of life to a radically different one, practically and philosophically, a transition made possible by the social and political changes accompanying the war.

Mrs Ramsay represents the social adhesive of the pre-war years, and her triumphant banquet, implicitly celebrating the engagement of Paul and Minta represents the continuity of her reactionary patriarchal family values. Mrs Ramsay is the mother and the wife who likes to say yes to her son and her husband. The first word of the novel is "Yes" and it is uttered Mrs Ramsay, to mollify her son: "'YES, of course, if it's fine to-morrow,' said Mrs Ramsay. 'But you'll have to be up with the lark,' she added. To her son these words conveyed an extraordinary joy". And Mrs Ramsay says "Yes" to her husband, too: "Her husband was so sensible, so just. And so she said, 'Yes; all children go through stages'"; "He would like a little solitude. Yes, she said. It annoyed him that she did not protest.". The closing words of Part One, "The Window", are hers unspoken, in victorious self-subordination, to her husband: "'Yes, you were right. It's going to be wet to-morrow.' She had not said it, but he knew it.

And she looked at him smiling. For she had triumphed again." Mrs Ramsay's "Yes" is deployed as an affirmation of patriarchal matrimony at every turn. Section 15 of "The Window", for example, comprises only one sentence, spoken by the patriarchal daughter Prue (who will die in childbirth in the parentheses of "Time Passes"): " 'Yes,' said Prue, in her considering way, answering her mother's question, 'I think did go with them.'. And it is interesting to watch how "yes" is deployed in the mouths of the surviving characters after Mrs Ramsay's death.

In To the Lighthouse, "yes" is also sometimes followed by "but"; and after Lily Briscoe implicitly refuses the widowed

Mr. Ramsay's mournful advances, she finally says yes, not to a man, but to her own art, in the closing paragraph of the novel, which is rhythmically punctuated by two yeses: "There it was—her picture. Yes, with all its green and blues, its lines running up and across, its attempt at something. With a sudden intensity, as if she saw it clear for a second, she drew a line there, in the centre. It was done; it was finished. Yes, she thought, laying down her brush in extreme fatigue, I have had my vision. Lily represents an alternative, creative, path for women, than the marriage prospectus set out by Mrs Ramsay. The marriage of Paul and Minta founders in the third part of the novel. The unmarried, independent, Lily, in many respects, "override" Mrs Ramsay's wishes at the same time as she memorialises her in her painting.

In the first part, Lily is interrogated by William Bankes, one of the Ramsays' guests, about her painting technique. Just as the painting may be understood as a self-conscious analogue for the novel in which it appears, so too does Lily's explanation serve as the novel's implicit aesthetic manifesto. Bankes asks Lily what she wished "to indicate by the triangular purple shape just there?" Lily explains her abstract coloured shape is "Mrs Ramsay reading to James She knew his objection that no one could tell it for a human shape. But she had made no attempt at a likeness, she said." Her defence makes clear that the painting, like the novel, is not a realist project. Mr Bankes ponders how "Mother and child then – objects of universal veneration, and in this case the mother was famous for her beauty – might be reduced to a purple shadow without irreverence."

The remarks in parenthesis show how patriarchy, in the form of Mr Bankes, has already positioned Mrs Ramsay as an aesthetic object prior to her appearance in the painting. Lily's post-impressionist technique of dreaming before nature may be understood to subvert this by adopting a non-mimetic aesthetic mode of expression, one that nevertheless correlates with the shape of mother and son on the step. Mr Bankes represents the reactionary views attributed to the man in the street who is baffled by modern art. He understands art in crudely monetary and mimetic, realist terms: "The largest picture in his drawing room, which painters had praised, and valued at a higher price than he had given for it, was of the cherry trees in blossom on the banks of the Kennet. He had spent his honeymoon on the banks of the Kennet, he said." His sentimentalism fits with the kind of greeting-card sentimentalism that Bloomsbury post-impressionism vehemently attacked. Lily's picture, she explains "was not of them not in his sense." In the third part of the book, Lily paints a fresh version of the same scene, except that Mrs Ramsay is absent, having died parenthetically in the middle part of the novel. Lily attempts both to represent the absent Mrs Ramsay and to overcome her absence and her influence.

Just as Mr Bankes is shocked by Lily's representation of Mrs Ramsay, so Woolf's readers may be shocked by the novel's representation of Mrs Ramsay's death: "[Mr. Ramsay stumbling along a passage stretched his arms out one dark morning, but Mrs. Ramsay having died rather suddenly the night before he stretched his arms out. They remained empty.]" This is the low point of "Time Passes". There are other deaths recorded here, each in parenthesis – the fall of a son in the Great War, the loss of a daughter in the pain of giving birth. But it is the death of the novel's central character, Mrs Ramsay, so casually reported, that most shocks. The notorious stumbling sentence in which the patriarch, Mr Ramsay, reaches out for his faithful wife only to clasp thin air, has given readers considerable trouble (especially as the first American edition gives a substantive variant). The passage may well allude to the story of Orpheus and Eurydice, a husband losing his wife at the gates of Hell. Mr Ramsay also seems to have learned the lesson of Andrew Marvell's carpe diem in "To His Coy Mistress": "The grave's a fine and private place,/But none, I think, do there embrace".

As well as overriding Mrs Ramsay's wishes, Lily is seen to override Mr Ramsay's wishes and his philosophy. Mr Ramsay is satirically depicted, in the first part of To the Lighthouse, exercising his disciplined Enlightenment mind as if it were a "keyboard" or an "alphabet". He finds himself stumbling at Q, which comes before his own initial: "He reached Q. Very few people in the whole of England ever reach Q But after Q? What comes next? Z is only reached once by one man in a generation. Still if he could reach R it would be something. Here at least was Q." He understands his "splendid" mind as part of a larger order of enlightened masculine subjectivity: "His own little light would shine, not very brightly, for a year or two, and would then be merged in some bigger light, and that in a bigger still". Lily puts forward an alternative model of intellectual endeavour by understanding enlightenment in non-linear terms as "little daily miracles, illuminations, matches struck unexpectedly in the dark."

Mrs McNab and Mrs Bast, the cleaning ladies who appear in the middle part of the novel, may also be understood as putting forward another alternative model for women's subjectivity. They labour to rescue the neglected summer house from disrepair: "Slowly and painfully, with broom and pail, mopping, scouring, Mrs McNab, Mrs Bast stayed the corruption and the rot, rescued from the pool of Time that was fast closing over them now a basin, now a cupboard; fetched from oblivion all the Waverley novels and a tea-set one morning; in the afternoon restorned to sun and air a brass fender and a set of tool irons." Woolf's rendering here of working-class women as chthonic goddesses, conferring life and fertility in the midst of decay, may also be understood as a political allegory describing the historical social transformations that occurred during and after the Great War.

The commercial success of To the Lighthouse was sufficient for Woolf to purchase a car on her proceeds, and the novel met with serious critical interest. The TLS found it as "elastic as a novel can be", but was doubtful over the achievement of the middle part. Rachel Taylor, reviewing for the Spectator, on the other hand, admired how "Time Passes" "in some passages chants heavily and dreamily like the prose litanies of Mallarmé". And the poet Edwin Muir, reviewing for the Nation and Athenaeum, admired "Time Passes" as work by "a writer of profound imagination", but worried "how this kind of imagination can be applied, as one feels sure it can, to the business of the novelist, the shadowing forth of human life, is still a problem to be solved.". Woolf's harshest critic, Arnold Bennett was baffled not by Woolf's rendering of character, but by her slender plot. "The scheme of the story is rather wilful", he opined, "—designed seemingly, but perhaps not really, to exhibit virtuosity. A group of people plan to sail in a small boat to a lighthouse. At the end some of them reach the lighthouse in a small boat. That is the externality of the plot." Bennett is merely highlighting what generations of readers of To the Lighthouse discover with more pleasure than he – that they are reading a novel not for any of the conventional expectations of plot or character, but for its ability to compress in its narrative all the lyric achievements of poetry, while simultaneously performing the work of prose in recounting profound historical changes.

To the Lighthouse is one of the most widely read and critically scrutinized of Woolf's novels and has been examined in relation to every modern phase of literary criticism from formalism to postmodernism and postcolonialism. Her early formulations of the work as an elegy on her parents lead many later critics to understand the novel as "frankly biographical". On the other hand, the aesthetic formalism of To the Lighthouse has also engaged a deal of formalist criticism. There have also been numerous readings of the novel and its imagery as enigmatic, mystical, and nebulously symbolic. The novel's playfulness with typographical presentation (its famous brackets, in particular) prompt one to ask how such a novel as To the Lighthouse might ever be successfully translated to the medium of film, without losing its important qualities as written text. (There has been one unsatisfactory television version, for example.) And we might also consider the attempts of various critics and writers to describe and even produce visual art that might be said to embody the aesthetic of Lily Briscoe's painting, or indeed to reproduce it (the work of the Australian artist, Suzanne Bellamy is particularly interesting).

Chapter 2

Biography

Virginia Woolf-in full Adeline Virginia Woolf, original surname Stephen

British author who made an original contribution to the form of the novel-also distinguished feminist essayist, critic in The Times Literary Supplement, and a central figure of Bloomsbury group. Virginia Woolf's books were published by Hogarth Press, which she founded with her husband, the critic and writer Leonard Woolf. Originally their printing machine was small enough to fit on a kitchen table, but their publications later included T.S. Eliot's Waste Land, fiction by Maxim Gorky, E.M. Forster, and Katherine Mansfield, and the complete twenty-four-volume translation of the works of Sigmund Freud.

"Have you any notion how many books are written about women in the course of one year? Have you any notion how many are written by men? Are you aware that you are, perhaps, the most discussed animal in the universe?"

Virginia Woolf was born in London, as the daughter of Julia Jackson Duckworth, a member of the Duckworth publishing family, and Sir Leslie Stephen, a literary critic, a friend of Meredith, Henry James, Tennyson, Matthew Arnold, and George Eliot, and the founder of the Dictionary of National Biography. Leslie Stephen's first wife had been the daughter of the novelist William Makepeace Thackeray. His daughter Laura from the first marriage was institutionalized because of mental retardation. In a memoir dated 1907 she wrote of her parents, "Beautiful often, even to our eyes, were their gestures, their glances of pure and unutterable delight in each other." Woolf, who was educated at home by her father, grew up at the family home at Hyde Park Gate. In middle age she described this period in a letter to Vita Sackville-West: "Think how I was brought up! No school; mooning about alone among my father's books; never any chance to pick up all that goes on in schools—throwing balls; ragging; slang; vulgarities; scenes; jealousies!" Woolf's youth was shadowed by series of emotional shocks. Gerald Duckworth, her half-brother, sexually abused her. In 'Sketch of the Past' she wrote: "I can remember the feel of his hands going under my clothes; going firmly and steadily lower and lower, I remember how I hoped that he would stop; how I stiffened and wriggled as his hand approached my private parts. But he did not stop." Julia Jackson Duckworth died when Virginia was in her early teens. Stella Duckworth, her half sister, took her mother's place, but died a scant two years later. Leslie Stephen suffered a slow death from cancer. When her brother Thoby died in 1906, she had a prolonged mental breakdown. Vanessa, Virginia's sister, influenced a number of her characters; in childhood they bathed and slept together. Later in FLUSH Woolf parodies her own devotion to Vanessa.

Following the death of her father in 1904, Woolf moved with her sister and two brothers to the house in Bloomsbury. Vanessa, a painter, agreed to marry the critic of art and literature Clive Bell. Virginia's economic situation improved when she inherited £2,500 from an aunt. Their house become central to activities of the Bloomsbury group. "And part of the charm of those Thursday evenings was that they were astonishingly abstract. It was not only that Moore's book [Principia Ethica, 1903] had set us all discussing philosophy, art, religion; it was that the atmosphere-if in spite of Hawtrey I may use that word-was abstract in the extreme. The young men I have named had no 'manners' in the Hyde Park Gate sense. They criticized our arguments as severely as their own. They never seemed to notice how we were dressed or if we were nice looking or not." (from Moments of Being, ed. by Jeanne Schulkind, 1976)

From 1905 Woolf began to write for the Times Literary Supplement. In 1912 she married the political theorist Leonard Woolf, who had returned from serving as an administrator in Ceylon. Leonard Woolf was born in London as the son of a barrister. He studied at Cambridge and in 1904 he went into civil service to Ceylon. From 1923 to 1930 he was a literary editor on the Nation. In 1917 he set up a small hand press at Hogarth House, and worked as its director until his death. Among Leonard Woolf's works are novels, non-fiction, and his five volume memoirs Sowing, Growing, Beginning Again, Downhill All the Way, and The Journey Not the Arrival Matters.

The voyage out was virginia woolf's first book. In 1919 appeared night and day, a realistic novel about the lifes of two friends, katherine and mary. Jacob's room was based upon the life and death of her brother toby.

With to the lighthouse and the waves woolf established herself as one of the leading writers of modernism. On the publication of To the Lighthouse, Lytton Strachey wrote: "It is really most unfortunate that she rules out copulation-not the ghost of it visible-so that her presentation of things becomes little more... than an arabesque-an exquisite arabesque, of course." The Waves is perhaps Woolf's most difficult novel. It follows in soliloquies the lives of six persons from childhood to old age. Louis Kronenberger noted in The New York Times that Woolf was not really concerned with people, but "the poetic symbols, of life—the changing seasons, day and night, bread and wine, fire and cold, time and space, birth and death and change."

In these works Woolf developed innovative literary techniques in order to reveal women's experience and find an alternative to the male-dominated views of reality. In her essay 'Mr. Bennett and Mrs. Brown' Woolf argued that John Galsworthy, H.G. Wells and other realistic English novelist dealt in surfaces but to get underneath these surfaces one must use less restricted presentation of life, and such devices as stream of consciousness and interior monologue and abandon linear narrative. Marital disappointments and frustrations she often dealt ironically. In To the Lighthouse Woolf wrote: "So that is marriage, Lily thought, a man and a woman looking at a girl throwing a ball."

Mrs. Dalloway formed a web of thoughts of several groups of people during the course of a single day. There is little action, but much movement in time from present to past and back again. The central figure, Clarissa Dalloway, married to Richard Dalloway, is a wealthy London hostess. She spends her day in London preparing for her evening party. She recalls her life before World War I, her friendship with the unconventional Sally Seton, and her relationship with Peter Walsh. At her party she never meets the shell-shocked veteran Septimus Smith, one of the first Englishmen to enlist in the war. Sally returns as Lady Rossetter, Peter Walsh is still enamored with Mrs. Dalloway, the prime minister arrives, and Smith commits suicide. To the Lighthouse had a tripartite structure: part 1 presented the Victorian family life, the second part covers a ten-year period, and the third part is a long account of a morning and reconciliation. The central figure, Mrs. Ramsay, was based on Woolf's mother. Also other characters in the book were drawn from Woolf's family memories.

During the inter-war period, Woolf was a central character of the literary scene both in London and at her home in Rodmell, near Lewes, Sussex. She lived in Richmond from 1915 to 1924, in Bloomsbury from 1924 to 1939, and maintained the house in Rodmell from 1919-41. The Bloomsbury group was initially based at the Gordon Square residence of Virginia and her sister Vanessa (Bell). Its other members included among others E.M. Forster, Lytton Strachey, Clive Bell, Duncan Grant, and Leonard Woolf. The consolidation of the group's beliefs in unifying aesthetic concerns occurred under the influence of the philosopher G.E. Moore. By the early 1930s, the group ceased to exist in its original form.

In the event of a Nazi invastion, Woolf and Leonard had made provisions to kill themselves. After the final attack of mental illness, Woolf loaded her pockets full of stones and drowned herself in the River Ouse near her Sussex home on

March 28, 1941. On her note to her husband she wrote: "I have a feeling I shall go mad. I cannot go on longer in these terrible times. I hear voices and cannot concentrate on my work. I have fought against it but cannot fight any longer. I owe all my happiness to you but cannot go on and spoil your life." Woolf's suicide, like Sylvia Plath's, have much colored the interpretation of both of their work.

Virginia woolf's concern with feminist thematics are dominant in a room of one's own. In it she made her famous statement: "A woman must have money and a room of her own if she is to write fiction." The book originated from two expanded and revised lectures the author presented at Cambridge University's Newnham and Girton Colleges in October 1928. Woolf examined the obstacles and prejudices that have hindered women writers. She separated women as objects of representation and women as authors of representation, and argued that a change in the forms of literature was necessary because most literature had been "made by men out of their own needs for their own uses." In the last chapter Woolf touched the possibility of an androgynous mind. Woolf refers to Coleridge who said that a great mind is androgynous and states that when this fusion takes place the mind is fully fertilized and uses all its faculties. "Perhaps a mind that is purely masculine cannot create, any more than a mind that is purely feminine..." THREE GUINEAS urged women to make a claim for their own history and literature.

Orlando, a fantasy novel, traced the career of the androgynous protagonist, Orlando, from a masculine identity within the Elisabethan court to a feminine identity in 1928. Chief model for the character was writer Vita Sackville-West, with whom Woolf had a lesbian relationship. The book was illustrated with pictures of Vita Sackville-West, dressed as Orlando. According to Nigel Nicolson, the initiative to start the affair came as much on Virginia's side as on the more experienced Vita's. Their relationship coincided with a period of great creative productivity in Woolf's career. In 1994 Eileen Atkins dramatized their letters in her play Vita and Virginia, starring Atkins and Vanessa Redgrave. As an essayist Woolf was prolific. She published some 500 essays in periodicals and collections, beginning 1905. Characteristic for Woolf's essays are dialogic nature of style-her reader is often directly addressed, in a conversational tone. A number of her writings are autobiographical. In the essay on the art of Walter Sickert, which was inspired by her visit in his retrospective show, Woolf asked how words can express colour, and answered that all great writers are great colorists: "Each of Shakespeare's plays has its dominant colour. And each writers differs of course as a colourist..." (Walter Sickert: A Conversation, 1934). Woolf rejection of an authoritative voice links her essays to the tradition of Montaigne.

Chapter 3

Chronology

Virginia Woolf was an English novelist and critic during the Modern Period whose writings are highly esteemed by modern Feminist Critics.

Adeline Virginia Stephen was born in London on January 25, 1882. She was one of four children of the prominent Victorian critic, philosopher, biographer, and scholar, Leslie Stephen. In 1904, Virginia's father died. At that time she settled with her sister and two brothers in the Bloomsbury district of London.

During this time, Virginia, her brothers and her sister became affiliated with the intellectual circle known as "The Bloomsbury, Group." The Bloomsbury Group included highly prominent thinkers of the day such as the biographer Lytton Strachey, the economist J.M. Keynes, the art critics Roger Fry and Clive Bell, the writer E.M. Forester, and the journalist and essayist Leonard Woolf.

In 1912, Virginia married Leonard Woolf. Five years later, in 1917, the Woolfs founded the Hogarth Press which in addition to publishing Virginia's writings, also published many of the era's most renowned texts; such the English translations of Freud and manuscripts by T.S. Eliot and Katherine Mansfield.

Virginia Woolf wrote many reviews and critical essays as well as novels. She was greatly concerned with the position of professional women and the constrictions under which they suffered, and in response wrote one of her most famous essays, "A Room of One's Own". Woolf experimented a great deal with her novels. Her early novels are in "traditional form," but later novels are masters of the "stream of consciousness" style. Unfortunately, Virginia suffered bouts of nervous depression her entire adult life. This condition, along with fears that she was going insane and that she would become a burden to her husband, led her to commit suicide on March 28, 1941.

1882 January 25, Adeline Virginia Stephen born at 22 Hyde Park Gate, London, third child and second daughter of Leslie Stephen and Julia Duckworth Stephen. Her sister Vanessa is 2 ½, her brother Thoby is 1 ½, and there are three siblings by her parents' previous marriages: the Duckworths, George, age, 13, Stella, age 12, and Gerald, age 11; and Laura Stephen, age 11. Her parents will have one more child, Adrian, in October.

In November 1882, Leslie Stephen becomes editor of the Dictionary of National Biography, a position he will hold for the next 9 years, editing the articles of the first 26 volumes, writing 378 entries himself.

1895 May 5, Julia Stephen dies, aged 49. Virginia's first breakdown is that summer.

1897 Stella Duckworth marries Jack Hills April 10, dies of peritonitis July 19, aged 28.

1899 Thoby Stephen enters Trinity College, Cambridge, where he becomes friends with Lytton Strachey, Saxon Sydney-Turner, Clive Bell, and Leonard Woolf.

1904 Feb 22 Sir Leslie Stephen dies of cancer. Virginia has her second breakdown that summer, and is ill the rest of the year. Vanessa, Thoby, and Adrian move into 46 Gordon Square.

1905 Thoby starts "Thursday Evenings" for his Cambridge friends and others, and Vanessa organises "Friday Club" for painters. Virginia begins writing book reviews and articles for various journals, including the Anglo-Catholic clerical paper the Guardian, Cornhill Magazine, and most significantly the Times Literary Supplement. Woolf's published works during her lifetime included seven volumes of essays.

1906 Vanessa, Virginia, and Violet Dickinson meet Thoby and Adrian in Greece in September. When they return, Thoby and Vanessa are sick, and Thoby dies of typhoid fever on November 20, aged 26. On November 22 Vanessa agrees to marry Clive Bell.

1907 Feb 7 Vanessa marries Clive Bell; they continue to live in 46 Gordon Square, and in April Virginia and Adrian move into 29 Fitzroy Square.

1911 Virginia moves into shared housing at 38 Brunswick Square, with Adrian, Duncan Grant, Maynard Keynes, and Leonard Woolf.

1912 Leonard proposes to Virginia in January, she is ill in February and March, accepts his proposal May 29, and they marry August 10; she is 30, he is 31. Virginia has a major breakdown in the summer, attempts suicide in September, and is not fully restored to health until 1915.

1914 War declared

1915 Virginia and Leonard move to Hogarth House, Richmond and decide to buy a printing press. The Voyage Out is published in March by Gerald Duckworth's publishing house.

1916 Vanessa and her household move to Charleston, Firle.

1917 April The printing press is delivered to Hogarth House. Their first publication is Two Stories: "A Mark on the Wall" and "Three Jews". Later that year Virginia begins the diary she will keep the rest of her life.

1918 Nov 11 Armistice Day.

1919 September Virginia and Leonard move to Monk's House, Rodmell. Night and Day is published in October by the Hogarth Press, which will publish all of her subsequent books.

1922 Jacob's Room published. Virginia meets Vita Sackville-West in December.

1924 March Virginia and Leonard move to 52 Tavistock Square.

"Mr. Bennett and Mrs. Brown" published. Mrs. Dalloway in progress. Friendship with Vita Sackville-West becomes more important. From 1924 till Woolf's death, the Hogarth Press publishes all of Sackville-West's fiction.

1925 The Common Reader published in April, Mrs. Dalloway in May. Virginia collapses at Charleston in August and is unwell for four months. In December, Woolf spends three nights at Vita's home Long Barn, and Vita wrote her husband Harold Nicolson: "I have gone to bed with her." (This is Woolf's only documented sexual relationship with a woman.) Woolf begins writing To the Lighthouse.

1926 Writing To the Lighthouse. Vita gives the Woolfs a dog, later the model for Flush.

1927 To the Lighthouse completed in January, published in May.

1928 Orlando published in October. Virginia, accompanied by Vita, delivers the two lectures at Cambridge women's colleges that will become A Room of One's Own. Vita begins an affair with Mary Campbell; the relationship with Virginia cools,

1929 "Women and Fiction" published in a journal in March, then much revised as A Room of One's Own, published in October.

1931 The Waves published in October.

1932 Jan 21 Lytton Strachey dies

1933 Flush published in October.

1934 Sept 9 Roger Fry dies.

1936 Virginia finishes The Years and collapses in April, is unwell until May and again from June to October.

1937 The Years published in March. Julian Bell leaves in June to drive an ambulance in the Spanish Civil War; dies on July 18, aged 29.

1938 Three Guineas is published in June.

1939 Britain declares war on Germany. Virginia and Leonard move to their Sussex home permanently (Vanessa moves permanently to Charleston).

1940 Roger Fry published in July. Blitz of London begins in July: in September, Vanessa's studio in Fitzroy

	St. is destroyed by a bomb, and Virginia and Leonard's apartment in Mecklenburgh Square is severely damaged.
1941	Virginia finishes Between the Acts, becomes ill in March with anxiety and depression. Drowns herself in the River Ouse on 28 March. Her body is found three weeks later and cremated 21 April.
1961	7 April Vanessa Bell dies at Charleston.
1969	Leonard Woolf dies
1996	Quentin Bell dies

Chapter 4

Major Works of Virginia Woolf

All but The Voyage Out and Night and Day are from the Hogarth Press in England. After Night and Day, Woolf's U.S. publisher is Harcourt Brace. This list includes primarily works published during Woolf's lifetime. See also the list of biographies and published letters and diaries.

The Voyage Out (26 March 1915, Duckworth; U.S. pub. by Doran, May 1920) Woolf's first novel, begun in 1908 and heavily revised after about 1912. Manuscript editions of the earlier version have been compiled and published by Louise DeSalvo as Melymbrosia, Woolf's working title for the book.

Two Stories: "The Mark on the Wall" by VW and "a story" by Leonard Woolf. The book was published by subscription only, mainly to friends and acquaintances, and was the Hogarth Press's first publication.

Kew Gardens: Ten pages of text by VW, with illustrations by her sister, Vanessa Bell.

Night and Day (20 Oct 1919, Duckworth; U.S. pub. Doran, 1920)

VW considered this her "traditional" novel, in the manner of the nineteenth-century novelists she admired.

Monday or Tuesday (7 April 1921; U.S. pub. Harcourt Brace, Nov. 1921)-stories

Includes "Kew Gardens," "The Mark on the Wall," "An Unwritten Novel" and five previously unpublished sketches.

Jacob's Room (27 Oct 1922; U.S. pub. Harcourt Brace, 1922)

Her first truly experimental novel and the Hogarth Press's first large-scale work, Jacob's Room begins Woolf's reputation as "difficult" or "highbrow." Critics compare her to James

Joyce and Dorothy Richardson. Jacob is based on Woolf's older brother Thoby Stephen, who died of a fever in 1906, when he was in his mid-twenties.

Mr. Bennett and Mrs. Brown: A response to Arnold Bennett's criticism that she "can't create or didn't in Jacob's Room, characters that survive" (Woolf paraphrasing Bennett, Writer's Diary). First version was published in the U.S. and then in England. A later, better-known, version was written as a lecture to the Cambridge Heretics on 18 May 1924, then published in the Criterion under the title "Character in Fiction," and then published by Hogarth Press as Mr. Bennett and Mrs. Brown. Critically, "the essay became a key document, not only in the assessment of Virginia Woolf's work, but in relation to twentieth-century fiction generally".

The Common Reader: The Common Reader was Woolf's title for two series of critical essays she published (the second series was published in 1932), mostly focused on her responses to reading and literature. It includes biographical sketches of many writers and such now-famous essays as "On Not Knowing Greek" and "How it Strikes a Contemporary."

Mrs. Dalloway (14 May 1925; simultaneously in England and U.S.; first time for simultaneous publication in U.S. and England)

A novel that takes place entirely in the space of one day in the life of Clarissa Dalloway, with a parallel plot about a shell-shocked World War I veteran, Septimus Smith. The setting is London.

To the Lighthouse: Woolf's most famous and most autobiographical novel. The novel takes place chiefly at a family summer house based on Woolf's own family's house in Cornwall (though the novel is set in the Hebrides), during two visits, seven years apart, with events in between described abstractly in a middle section called "Time Passes." The "Time Passes" section had been published in French in Dec. 1926.

See also the original holograph draft/transcribed and edited by Susan Dick

(Toronto; Buffalo: University of Toronto Press, 1982).

Orlando: Her most successful novel up to then, in terms

of sales (even though publishing it as a "biography" confused booksellers), Orlando traces the life of an English nobleman, Orlando, from the Renaissance to the very moment of publication. Orlando, based on Woolf's friend Vita Sackville-West, lives 400 years and changes into a woman in the 18th century.

A Room of One's Own: Woolf's first major feminist criticism, originating in two lectures given in October 1928 to students at the two women's colleges of Cambridge University (Newnham and Girton, here fictionalized as "Fernham"). First published as a short essay on "Women and Fiction" in Forum, it was thereafter heavily revised to the present six chapters.

See also a study of extant manuscripts edited by S.P. Rosenbaum, Virginia Woolf/Women & Fiction: The Manuscript Versions of A Room of One's Own.

The Waves: This novel is generally considered Woolf's masterpiece, though it is also her most experimental work.

NOTE: The first book-length criticism of VW appeared in 1932, Winifrid Holtby's biography and Floris Delattre's Le Roman psychologique de Virginia Woolf. Delattre writes on VW's use of time.

The Common Reader: This collection includes both new and revised critical essays, including biographical sketches of Mary Wollstonecraft and Dorothy Wordsworth, and the now-famous essay "How Should One Read a Book?"

Flush: A comic novel written from the point of view of Elizabeth Barrett Browning's cocker spaniel Flush.

The Years (13 March 1937): A bestseller, popular with critics and readers, this novel traces the life of a Victorian family, the Pargiters, from 1880 to the "Present Day." Begun as a sequel to A Room of One's Own, Woolf originally intended to alternate nonfiction essays with the Pargiter's story. Woolf ultimately extracted the nonfiction and changed the working title from "The Pargiters" to The Years.

Mitchell A. Leaska has edited the extracted portions and published them as The Pargiters: The Novel-Essay Portion of The Years, which also includes the earlier version of the 1880 section of the novel.

Three Guineas: These feminist essays function as a sequel to A Room of One's Own, including a critique of patriarchy (illustrated with photographs of public figures) and an argument for pacifism in the face of the growing threat of another world war. The illustrations are not printed in modern editions.

Roger Fry: A biography of Woolf's friend, the art critic and painter, who had introduced post-impressionism to England in the years before World War I.

Between the Acts: Woolf's last novel, published after her death. She had changed her mind about publishing it just days before her death. Like Mrs. Dalloway, the action takes place in a short span of time in June and is focused on a social event, here a community pageant rather than a party. The setting is June 1939 in the English countryside at a house called Pointz Hall, home of the Olivers, and in the nearby village, where Miss LaTrobe is in charge of the pageant. The pageant concerns English history, and parts of it are part of the narrative.

A Writer's Diary: The public's first access to Woolf's diaries came in this heavily edited selection of diary entries concerning writing or particular works Woolf was writing. The selections were prepared by her husband, Leonard Woolf. The more complete 5-volume edition of Woolf's diaries was published 1977-1984, edited by her nephew Quentin Bell's wife, Anne Olivier Bell. Six volumes of Woolf's letters have also been published (ed. Nigel Nicolson and Joanne Trautmann, 1975-1980).

Moments of Being: Woolf often spoke of writing her autobiography, but these unpublished autobiographical writings are as close as we have to formal autobiography. The earliest, "Reminiscences," was written at the birth of her first nephew, Julian Bell, supposedly as a biography of her sister Vanessa. The latest, "A Sketch of the Past," was written near the end of her life, apparently as the beginning of a formal autobiography. The rest are sketches she read to members of the Memoir Club, who met regularly to read such essays.

Chapter 5

Historical Context

World War I

World War I began in 1914, the result of an unresolved and perilous series of Balkan Crises. When Archduke Franz Ferdinand was assassinated, the intense territorial dispute between Austro-Hungary and Serbia intensified, quickly spreading through the rest of Europe.

Great Britain, Russia, and France joined together as the Allied Powers against the Central Power Alliance of Austro-Hun-gary and Germany. After Russia dropped out of the Allied forces, and the Luisitania was sunk, America eventually entered the fray.

The war, known in Europe as the Great War, took place on a scale never before seen in history. It lasted four years, cost $350 billion, and took the lives of 22 million people. In To the Lighthouse Andrew Ramsay becomes one of the victims of the war. World War I revealed a new and horrifying form of warfare that took place in the trenches and the air, both innovations.

It was also the most technologically advanced war, relying on a number of new inventions, such as machine guns, mortar bombs, and barbed wire. Most scarring was innovations in biological weaponry. Death by mustard gas in the bunkers and trenches created a profound sense of shock in the surviving troops and horrible deaths for the fallen. Movingly documented by English War Poets like Siegfried Sassoon and Wilfred Owen, the Great War sent thousands of emotionally and physically shell-shocked men back to their homes.

Modernism

Modernism is a literary, artistic, and philosophical movement that began at the end of the nineteenth century. Modernists feel that earlier forms of art have reached their goals and become uninteresting, and they reject the realism of the nineteenth century.

In response to older forms, the new art and literature was consciously nonrepresentational and experimental, refusing to portray significant action, and emphasizing human reactions and interpretations instead of physical realities. Freudian psychology was often incorporated into the new writing and art, since it overturns previous philosophies and makes the internal life of a person the most important aspect of reality.

The new art exploded into an unwelcome world in 1913, at The Armory Show. This international exhibition of modern art took place at the 69th Regiment Armory in New York City, opening in February and then travelling to Chicago, and Boston. It drew crowds of more than 100,000 people, and brought Postimpressionism and Cubism to international attention. The Armory Show, or Armory Circus, as some preferred to call it, was the first exhibition of modern art in America and the catalyst for many of the major modernist movements. In To the Lighthouse, this new and shocking art is the kind that Lily Briscoe attempts to create.

The Twenties: The Twenties were characterized by what Joseph Wood Krutch called the "Modern Temper." This was the new intellectual and social climate that rejected many of the traditional beliefs in progress, patriotism and art, at the same time as it looked for new forms of politics. Following the Russian Revolution of 1917, Marxism and socialism had gained a new importance in European thought. With Lenin in power and the genocidal legacy of Stalinism still unimaginable, the Soviet Union was taken as a model for many young idealists. relations in Britain reached conditions bordering on class war. The coal miners led the Trade Union Congress in a general strike, paralyzing the country. They demanded, "Not a penny off the pay; not a minute on the day." Changes in social climate fostered new freedoms. In 1918, the Women's Suffrage movement triumphed, and British women over the age of thirty were granted the right to vote. Those between the ages of twenty-one and thirty were allowed to vote starting in 1928.

The Wall Street Crash plunged the World into economic depression in 1929 and exacerbated social divides. In 1927, however, Europe had finally begun to recover from the Great War, and there was a sense of optimism among the privileged "bright young things" of the British social scene. Writers like Nancy Mitford and Evelyn Waugh represented the new kind of young person — dashing, daring, and flippant. The scandalous young women of this social set were the British equivalent of the American "flappers." Like the younger Ramsay daughters, they refuse to take anything too seriously, and wear their hair and skirts short.

Compare and Contrast

1910s: Unrest grows in Tsarist Russia as the oppressive state cracks down on reformers and activists.

1920s: The Bolshevik revolution has taken place, and Lenin is in power. His New Economic Policy is being instituted, which allows greater economic freedom and a measure of controlled capitalism.

Today:Communist Soviet Union has collapsed, and Russia is in ruins following a disastrous attempt to switch to a U.S.-style free market economy.

1910s: After World War I the 1919 Treaty of Versailles establishes an international body that will arbitrate disputes. It also demands that Germany pay reparations for the war.

1920s: The League of Nations has been formed, but its powers are very limited. America refuses to be involved, and has not ratified the Treaty of Versailles. The League is powerless, and fails to prevent the events that lead to World War II.

Today: The United Nations has been in place since 1945, and has learned from the fate of the League of Nations. The UN provides a working arena for international diplomacy, peacekeeping, and aid.

1910s: The British Labour Party is a new creation, struggling to find a support base. Many members of the British intellectual scene are in sympathy with its socialist ideology. After the Russian Revolution, the ruling classes of Britain become obsessed with the possibility of a similar British uprising.

1920s: Britain is brought almost to the brink of class war in a series of major industrial actions that culminate in the great General Strike.

Today: The Labour Party, led by Prime Minister Tony Blair, is the governing party in Great Britain.

1910s: The British Women's Suffrage movement demands the right to vote.

1920s: British women over thirty are granted the right to vote in 1918. American women win their battle in 1919. It is a long struggle that is resisted by many men—Switzerland will not accept women's suffrage in full until 1971.

Today: Generations of legal rights have still not resulted in equality between men and women. In Britain and America, women's pay averages less than 70 percent of men's, and women still make up a tiny proportion of CEOs and politicians.

Chapter 6

Plot Summary

The Window

The action of To the Lighthouse takes place on two days, separated by ten years. The novel begins on a September evening in the Hebrides before World War I, in the middle of a discussion about the possibility of going to the Lighthouse the next day. Mrs. Ramsay, who is sitting in the window with her son, James, thinks the weather will be fair; Mr. Ramsay, who has been walking back and forth on the path with his student Charles Tansley, says that it most definitely will not be. After a prolonged discussion, Mrs. Ramsay reads "The Fisherman and His Wife" to James, and Mr. Ramsay continues his walking.

Meanwhile, Lily Briscoe is painting Mrs. Ramsay and James; she decides to show what she has accomplished to William Bankes, an old friend of Mr. Ramsay. As they are looking at the picture, Cam Ramsay runs past, nearly upsetting the easel. Meanwhile, guests Minta Doyle and Paul Rayley are walking with Andrew and Nancy Ramsay; after the four become separated, Nancy finds Minta and Paul kissing behind a rock. Minta loses her grandmother's brooch in the rocks, and Paul tells her he will search for it the next day, when there is more light.

Minta, Paul, Nancy, and Andrew have not yet returned when everyone sits down to dinner. When they enter, Minta says that she has lost her brooch. Mrs. Ramsay decides that Minta and Paul must have gotten engaged, and Lily uses a salt shaker to remind herself that she will move a tree in her picture the next day. At the end of the meal, another guest, Augustus Carmichael, and Mr. Ramsay recite the poem "Luriana Lurilee" in tribute to Mrs. Ramsay.

After dinner, Mrs. Ramsay finds that Cam and James are still awake. Cam is scared of the boar's head that is hanging on the wall, while James screams when it is touched. Mrs. Ramsay covers the skull with her shawl, so that Cam can't see it, but James will know the skull is still in the room. Mrs. Ramsay assures James that on the next fine day, they will go to the Lighthouse.

With the children asleep, Mr. and Mrs. Ramsay sit quietly together. Mrs. Ramsay tells Mr. Ramsay that Paul and Minta are engaged. Mr. Ramsay wants Mrs. Ramsay to tell him she loves him, but instead she tells him that his weather forecast was accurate and they won't be able to go to the Lighthouse the next day after all. She feels she has triumphed by not telling him she loves him.

Time Passes

Time moves forward and the nights become colder and wilder. During one of those cold, wild nights, Mrs. Ramsay dies. Prue Ramsay marries, then dies in childbirth. Andrew Ramsay dies in France during the war. The abandoned house begins to deteriorate, and the caretaker, Mrs. McNab, decides she can't fight the decay of the house. Ten years after Mrs. Ramsay's death, one of the Ramsay children asks Mrs. McNab to ready the house for guests, expecting it to be the same as it was left. With help, Mrs. McNab restores the condition of the house, and the Ramsays and their guests visit in September.

The Lighthouse

Mr. Ramsay has coerced Cam and James into visiting the Lighthouse. Lily decides to finish the picture she started ten years ago. Before he leaves for the Lighthouse, Mr. Ramsay goes to Lily demanding sympathy, but she praises his boots instead. After the three Ramsays leave, Lily begins to paint, with Carmichael sitting near her. As Lily paints, she begins to think of Mrs. Ramsay, and cries out for her, wanting her to return. Meanwhile, the three Ramsays are sailing to the Lighthouse, and Cam and James are resentful of their father's tyranny. Macalister tells them stories of disasters at sea, and Macalister's boy catches a mackerel.

Lily has a vision of Mrs. Ramsay sitting on the beach with her, and thinks of the disastrous marriage of the Rayleys, which has only been righted by Paul's affair with another woman, and of her cherished friendship with William Bankes. Lily continues to cry out for Mrs. Ramsay. In the boat, Macalister's boy cuts a square out of the mackerel and throws it back into the sea.

After Mr. Ramsay finishes the book he has been reading, they reach the Lighthouse. James and Cam feel reconciled to their father after he praises James's steering, and James is satisfied with the Lighthouse. On shore, Lily thinks they must have reached the Lighthouse, and she realizes that Mrs. Ramsay isn't there, and that she doesn't want her any longer. Lily adds a line in the centre of her painting, completing it at last, and feels that she has had her vision. The novel ends with the Ramsays' successful trip to the Lighthouse and Lily's completion of her painting.

Chapter 7

Characters

Andrew the Just

The oldest son of the Ramsays, Andrew accompanies Paul Rayley and Minta Doyle on their engagement walk to the beach. He is a gifted mathematician, but he dies fighting in World War I.

William Bankes

William Bankes is an old botanist friend of Mr. Ramsay's who has come to stay at the Ramsay home. The years since the two first became friends have changed both men, and Bankes is jealous and resentful of Mr. Ramsay. Mrs. Ramsay senses Bankes's loneliness and wants to pair him off with Lily Briscoe. Bankes is a childless widower, and tries to assuage his envy of the Ramsay household by suggesting that his old friend's philosophical work is secondhand and past its prime. He is, however, drawn to Mrs. Ramsay's beauty and the warm domesticity of the Ramsays' lives. Rejected by little Cam, he hides his loneliness by denigrating marriage and children to Lily. Lily, on the other hand, realizes that he is isolated and that he carries a torch for Mrs. Ramsay.

Bankes is intellectually open, willing to understand and appreciate Lily's abstract painting, which suggests the essentially positive character that is hidden beneath his bitterness. The two become very good friends. He dies during the middle section of the novel, and Lily looks back on her friendship with him and remembers him as a good and profoundly lonely man, whom she will always love.

Lily Briscoe

Lily is an artist who stays with the Ramsay family in the first section of the novel, and returns with them to their Scottish summerhouse in the final section. She is a Post-Impressionist painter, descendant of a poor family, and has spent most of her life taking care of her father. In many ways, Lily is the chorus figure of the book — providing the histories of the characters and commenting on their actions. The beginning and completion of her painting form the frame of To the Lighthouse, and her final line, "I have had my vision," is the final line of the novel, acting as Woolf's own comment on her book.

Lily, a lonely character who never marries, is both consumed by her art as well as in need of love and connection. She is "in love with the Ramsays," seeing them as the embodiment of the affection that is missing from her life, and especially adores Mrs. Ramsay. Just as she is unable to show love, she is phobic about allowing her art to be seen. When William Bankes sees her painting, they form a connection, and talk about the Ramsays. Both of them find things to fault about the family because they are so jealous of them, but both secretly understand each other's feelings. Lily does not like Mr. Ramsay because of the way he treats his wife, and she sees him as emotionless and too logical. She is taken aback when she and Bankes run into Mr. Ramsay spouting poetry on the lawn. Later, she realizes that she has misjudged him and that he is a man of strong emotion who adores his wife.

In the final section of the novel, Lily stands watching the Ramsays sail to the Lighthouse. While she tries to paint, memories and intense emotions surface. The desolation of the Ramsays that has occurred and the years of loss overcome her, and she cries out for Mrs. Ramsay. As Mr. Carmichael joins her, Lily realizes that Mr. Ramsay must have reached the Lighthouse. With this resolution achieved, she puts the final line on her painting and says, "It is finished." She has had her vision.

Cam the Wicked

Cam is the Ramsays' youngest daughter. She is an

energetic and mischievous child, and Mrs. Ramsay laments that she must grow up and suffer. Cam sails with James and Mr. Ramsay to the Lighthouse in the final section of the novel.

Augustus Carmichael

Augustus Carmichael is a charismatic man who stays with the Ramsays when the family is in Scotland. He has had a bad marriage, and has spent time in India. Mrs. Ramsay was there when his wife threw him out, and she thinks that he doesn't like her because he's had bad experiences with women. Initially offering to teach while at the Ramsays, he ends up lounging about on the tennis courts instead, and Mrs. Ramsay thinks of him as a "great cat" with green eyes. Between his two stays with the Ramsays in Scotland, he becomes an important poet. Later, Lily thinks of him as "old pagan god." At the very end of the novel he stands with Lily looking out over the sea and says, "He has landed It is finished," and Lily feels that he has "crowned the occasion."

Minta Doyle

Daughter of the Ramsays' upper-class acquaintances, Minta is a guest at the Ramsays' summer home. Her parents are stuffy and very traditional, the subjects of many jokes between Mr. and Mrs. Ramsay. Minta, however, is very different — an energetic, scruffy young woman whom Mrs. Ramsay calls "a tom-boy." She wonders what Minta's parents make of this modern girl who gads about with holes in her stockings. Minta and Paul Rayley get engaged and celebrate with the Ramsays. Ten years later, when the Ramsays return to Scotland, Lily thinks about Minta and Paul. Their marriage has not been wonderful, for Paul is a bo-hemian man who spends his time in meetings and coffeehouses. Since Paul obtained a mistress, however, he and Minta have settled into a comfortable marriage of friendship, not love.

James the Ruthless

The youngest Ramsay child, James is six years old when the book begins. He adores his mother and is violently resentful of his father. He enjoys cutting images out of magazines and wants desperately to go to the Lighthouse when he is young.

Mrs. Mcnab

Mrs. McNab is the housekeeper of the Ramsays' summer home. She is the only person who is actively in the "Time Passes" section, tending to the house as it gradually fills with dust and the Ramsays meet their fates. She is the only character who takes some of the flowers home with her. The family has simply been sending money to her to clean, and never write or visit. Mrs. McNab often thinks of Mrs. Ramsay, and when she hears that the house may be sold, she locks the house and leaves. After receiving a letter stating that the family may be coming for the summer, she cleans the house from top to bottom.

Prue the Beautiful

Prue is the oldest of the Ramsays' daughters, and her mother expects her to be an exceptional beauty when she grows up. Although Prue marries, she dies during the following summer of an illness related to childbirth.

Andrew Ramsay

Andrew, one of the Ramsay sons, is killed in the trenches of World War I. He is a brilliant young man, with a genius for mathematics and an interest in zoology.

Cam Ramsay

Cam, the little Ramsay daughter, is a "wild and fierce child" at the beginning of the book who refuses to give William Bankes a flower. When the family returns after the death of Mrs. Ramsay, she has conflicting emotions about being at the summer home. Cam is bitter about Mr. Ramsay's "crash blindness and tyranny of which had poisoned her childhood and raised bitter storms, so that even now she woke in the night trembling with rage and remembered some command of his."

Because the Lighthouse holds such harsh memories for them, neither she nor James wish to go to it, but they agree to their father's wish out of duty. As they drift out she looks back at the house and feels love and pride for her father, but cannot help thinking about the past and the people that are now gone. Mr. Ramsay teases her about not knowing the points of the compass, but sees that she is frightened. He wants to make her feel better, and Cam knows this. She remembers the good things about him, the times she felt safe with him, but is still torn by bitterness. She looks at the shore and feels that the people that used to be there are now free. As they reach the Lighthouse, Mr. Ramsay finally praises his son James. Cam knows that this is a point that James has been waiting for his whole life, and with a greater sense of hopefulness they step ashore.

James Ramsay

James Ramsay is the youngest child of Mr. and Mrs. Ramsay. As a little boy he is an extremely sensitive child who idolizes his mother. Wracked by intense emotions, he fantasizes about killing his father in order to have Mrs. Ramsay to himself. His desire to go to the Lighthouse is the focus of the novel's first section. His mother tries to make his wish come true, while his father and Charles Tansley insist that the weather will prevent them. He does not get his wish.

When they return to the summer home ten years later, James is bitter. He feels it is too late to get to the Lighthouse now, and Mr. Ramsay's need to make the trip seems to James to be a fruitless endeavor. He still hates his father for the way he perceived his mother was treated. Though James tells himself he feels nothing for his father, it is clear he desperately wants his approval. As they wait for another breeze to get them to the Lighthouse, James remembers feeling angry with his mother, and then is consumed by rage for his father when he looks at him reading. While he thinks about his mother, the wind picks up, and they move on.

As the group gets closer to the Lighthouse, Mr. Ramsay opens up the lunch, and James finally realizes that his father is lonely, "which was for both of them the truth about things." When they pass over where three men drowned, Cam and James expect Mr. Ramsay to spout bombastic poetry, and when he doesn't they realise that he has changed. James steers the family to shore, bitter that his father will not praise him. As their voyage ends, Mr. Ramsay compliments him on steering them like a born sailor. With his father's approval finally given, James is full of an overwhelming, fierce happiness that is too great to share, and a new hopefulness fills the surviving family members.

Jasper Ramsay

A son of the Ramsays, Jasper likes to shoot birds in his free time.

Mr. Ramsay

Mr. Ramsay is the father of the family. He is the most misunderstood character in the book, a man whose children hate him because they think he is viciously unemotional and cold. They and Lily think of him as stern and sarcastic — a man who "never altered a disagreeable word to suit the pleasure or convenience of any mortal being, least of all his own children." Mrs. Ramsay has a very different picture of him. She knows how insecure he is about his abilities as a philosopher and a provider. He is a man who acknowledges the shortcomings of his own skills, knowing that he will never be able to go beyond "Q" in the "alphabet" of great thinking. He is also possessed of many more emotions than his children give him credit for, and is not the exclusively rational man that Lily Briscoe first sees. Her view of him is turned upside down when she runs into him on the lawn reciting poetry and acting it out. Later at the dinner table, Mr. Ramsay talks to Minta and everyone is able to see the charming, attractive man that he can be.

When the Ramsays return to Scotland in the last section of the book, Mr. Ramsay is broken and alone, though neither Lily nor his children can acknowledge this. His need to go to the Lighthouse with Cam and James is an attempt to reconcile himself with them, to share their loss of Mrs. Ramsay, and to make amends for his past behaviour. When he finally gives James the praise he has always withheld from him, the process of forgiveness is complete.

Mrs. Ramsay

Mrs. Ramsay is the mother of the Ramsay family who dies during the middle section of the novel. A beautiful, caring woman, she means all things to all people, and each character of To the Lighthouse has a different perception of her personality. Lily sees her as a mother, and doesn't think she has ever inspired romantic passion. William Bankes and Charles Tansley adore her, and think she doesn't realise how beautiful she is. The children see her as the "Lighthouse" of their lives — the stable, warm force that protects and guides them. Mr. Ramsay adores and resents her because of her huge capacity for love. Sometimes he feels he would have been a greater thinker if he had no wife or children, but underneath he knows that he is utterly dependent on her.

In her own mind, Mrs. Ramsay is far more complex. She loves her husband, but alternates between pitying and reverencing him, knowing that his intellectual powers are waning and that people will eventually realise that he depends on her too much. She loves to make other people happy and is constantly encouraging love matches, expediting the engagement of Minta and Paul, and trying to match Lily and William Bankes.

At the same time, she becomes jealous when attention is focused on others, feeling resentful and left out when Minta and Paul celebrate their engagement. She is used to being loved and relies on it, but is aware of this, and it is balanced by her generous impulses and love. She is happiest when loving, and wishes that she could "always be holding a baby." Her compassion leads her to worry about the plight of the poor, and she is constantly doing charitable things — knitting stockings for the Lighthouse keeper's sick child and taking food to poor people in the area.

After her death she remains the "Lighthouse" of the

Ramsay family, the most powerful force in the lives of Lily, Cam, James, and Mr. Ramsay. As they begin to accept the loss of her, the surviving Ramsays finally make the trip to the Lighthouse that Mrs. Ramsay had desperately wanted them to be able to make. While Lily breaks down and cries out for her, James, Cam, and Mr. Ramsay make their symbolic voyage to the emotional centre that is Mrs. Ramsay. When they arrive they have finally done what she wanted — ceased fighting and recognized their equal love for her and for each other.

Nancy Ramsay

Nancy is one of Mr. and Mrs. Ramsay's daughters. She witnesses a kiss between Paul Rayley and Minta Doyle.

Prue Ramsay

One of Mr. and Mrs. Ramsay's eight children, Prue dies in childbirth.

Roger Ramsay

Another Ramsay offspring, Roger is referred to as a "wild creature" by his mother.

Rose Ramsay

Rose is a daughter of the Ramsays, who "had a wonderful gift with her hands."

Minta Rayley

A young woman visiting the Ramsays at their summer home, Minta accepts Paul Rayley's marriage proposal.

Paul Rayley

Paul Rayley is a guest of the Ramsays who is courting Minta Doyle. Mrs. Ramsay does not respect his intelligence much, and thinks that he's a "boobie." He and Minta get married, and he is irresponsible, spending his time in meetings and coffeehouses. He begins an affair with a "serious woman, with her hair in a plait" who shares his interests. Because of this, he and Minta develop a comfortable marriage.

The Atheist Tansley

An odious athiest whom none of the Ramsays particularly like, Charles is one of Mr. Ramsay's philosophy pupils. He is insulting and chauvinistic, trying to discourage Lily from painting. He is often concerned with the affairs and status of others and is very self-centered. He finds Mrs. Ramsay quite beautiful and is proud to be seen walking with her.

Charles Tansley

Charles Tansley is a student of Mr. Ramsay, visiting the Lighthouse while he does his dissertation. The product of a lower-middle-class home, he has worked himself up the educational and social scale, and remains uneasy about his status. This makes him overeager to prove himself, and the Ramsay children think of him as a pompous prig. Inclined always to agree with whatever Mr. Ramsay says, it is really Mrs. Ramsay who becomes the focus of Charles's attention. He, like all of the characters, is in love with her. She pities him the poverty of his childhood — he has never even been to a circus — but dislikes him for his thoughtless behaviour to her son James. Tansley's insecurity often leads him to be unnecessarily harsh, and he tells Lily that women have no business being painters.

Major Themes

War

In To the Lighthouse, the Great War takes place during the "Time Passes" section. The structure of the novel reflects the impact of World War I on European society. Part One is set in the golden haze of prewar innocence and love. Mr. Ramsay entertains himself by reciting Lord Tennyson's poem The Charge of the Light Brigade, a poem about death during the Crimean War, which valorizes the heroism of the then-unprecedented loss of a cavalry unit. Tennyson's celebration of patriotism and glorious death would be rejected by the traumatized survivors of the Great War who had witnessed death on a scale unimaginable to the Victorian poet. As Wilfred Owen wrote, World War I ended "that great lie — Dulce et decorum est pro patria mori [it is sweet and proper to die for one's country]." Owen himself would not make it home from the war.

During the middle section of Woolf's novel, the scarifying time period of 1914 to 1918 is represented by the death that comes to many of the characters, including Mrs. Ramsay and Andrew, who is killed in combat by a shell. Part Two is concerned with survivors, with a shell-shocked culture attempting to come to terms with its losses. The war marks an end to many of the old ways of life, a change in social climate and the first rumblings of collapse for the British institutions so important to the older characters, especially the Indian Empire. Britain would not grant control to India until 1947, but as Woolf's novel shows, the younger, postwar generation was already beginning to question the culture of empire building.

Philosophy

Debates about philosophy, particularly theories about visual reality, figure prominently in To the Lighthouse. In the first section of the novel, "The Window," Mr. Ramsay, an Oxford philosopher, does his work on the three main philosophers of British empiricism, John Locke, George Berkeley, and David Hume. The basic argument of Empiricism is that human concepts and beliefs apply to a world outside oneself, and that it is by way of the senses that this world acts upon the individual. The question that is debated is just how much the mind itself contributes to the task of processing its sensory input. One of the points that Mr. Ramsay's philosophy debates is whether or not a person can be empirically certain that objects have a distinct and continued existence apart from our perceptions of them. Andrew Ramsay sums this philosophy up to Lily in mundane, domestic terms, saying "Think of a kitchen table then when you're not there."

Throughout the novel, the characters reflect on objects and people that are "not there," especially Mrs. Ramsay. Mrs. Ramsay's effect on everyone and everything is like the imaginary "kitchen table" of Andrew's explanation. Her continuing impact even after death is contrasted with the cold logic of Mr. Ramsay's philosophy, which denies these kinds of connections between reality, mind and personality. Lily's painting style shows a different kind of reality in which objects and perception can be different for every person. As she explains to William Bankes, her view of Mrs. Ramsay does not look like its subject because it is abstract. However, it is still "like" Mrs. Ramsay because she is trying to paint the emotional and spatial impact of the woman. Like Woolf's stream of consciousness narrative style, Mrs. Ramsay's reality changes depending on how she is feeling — making William Bankes either a tyrant or a pitiful person according to her emotions at the time. While Mr. Ramsay blindly wrestles with skepticism on masculine philosophical grounds, Mrs. Ramsay and Lily show maternal and painterly domestic eyes at work, creating a distinctly female "epistemology" — or theory about the nature and limits of human knowledge.

Freudian Psychology

The character of James Ramsay is central to the narrative impetus of To the Lighthouse. His desire to go on the trip, and the conflicting reactions of parents form the structure and title of the novel, and are drawn in patterns established by Freudian theories. As a child, James is very hostile to his father and adores his mother. His mother promises that the day will be pleasant enough for them to sail, while his father promises that it will rain and make sailing impossible. James wishes for an "axe, or a poker, any weapon that would have gashed a hole in his father's breast and killed him, there and then." Every time that his father distracts Mrs. Ramsay's attention from him, James feels similar homicidal urges.

This desire to kill his father to keep his mother's attention corresponds to Freud's Oedipal complex. This famous theory is based on the Greek myth of Oedipus, who accidentally murdered his father and wed his mother. Freud said that all males go through an Oedipal stage in which they want to kill their fathers and marry their mothers. In order to grow to emotional maturity, they must get over this impulse and embrace their fathers, as James eventually does.

Perception and Consciousness

In To the Lighthouse Woolf uses a "decorated process of thought" in which the physical world around a character takes on their form of thought. As a result, the world that surrounds the characters has a symbolic status with different and specific meanings for each character. Throughout the novel, the personality and consciousness of each person expresses itself in the way that the world seems when they stand in it. The most important symbol of the book is the Lighthouse itself. Just as it dominates the bay, the Lighthouse dominates Woolf's novel, both physically and symbolically. The characters each see it differently, depending on their emotions and needs.

For Mrs. Ramsay, the Lighthouse represents her isolation as well as warmth and comfort, an integral part of the rhythm of her days that allows her to nurture and be nurtured. The Lighthouse is not just a building, it is "something immune which shines out." For Lily Briscoe, the true "lighthouse" of the novel is Mrs. Ramsay herself — a beacon that casts an organizing light on the whole family and continues to illuminate and connect them even after her death. Mr. Ramsay's presence makes the Lighthouse a "stark tower on a bare rock," which symbolizes his unemotional logic. For James, the Lighthouse is a shifting symbol that seems to represent his mother, even as it is representative of the stark rationalism of his father. His analysis of the situations sums up the thematic point: "So that was the Lighthouse, was it? No the other was also the Lighthouse. For nothing was simply one thing."

Chapter 8

Style

Stream of Consciousness

The narrative technique that Woolf uses for most of To the Lighthouse is normally called stream of consciousness. This technique was a product of Modernism, a literary movement characterized by introspection, self-awareness and an openness to the unconscious. Associated primarily with Woolf and James Joyce, this technique was a way of representing the whole mind of an individual, not just conscious thought. It is based on the psychological theory that human minds are made up of many layers of awareness, from highly articulated rational thought, to emotional responsiveness, all the way to the animal pre-speech level of need and instinct. The basis of the technique is the notion that all of these layers are present in the mind of a human at any given moment — a "stream of consciousness" composed of the flow of sensations, thoughts, memories, associations, and reflections. If the exact pattern of the mind is to be described, then these varied, disjointed, and illogical elements must find expression in a flow of words, images and ideas similar to the unorganized flow of the mind. In To the Lighthouse Woolf describes the technique while talking about Lily Briscoe:

> To follow her thought was like following a voice which speaks too quickly to be taken down by one's pencil, and the voice was her own voice saying with out prompting undeniable, everlasting, contradictory things

Woolf's characteristic version of the stream of consciousness puts a new spin on the technique. Instead of being an attempt to capture the complexities of one individual mind, her novel is an attempt to capture the minds of a large group of people as they interact over time. This is achieved by the constant shifting of point of view and narrative chronology — often within the same paragraph or line.

Free Association

Part of the stream of consciousness style of Woolf's novel, free association is a term that describes the connections, or associations, that a person's mind makes between seemingly random things. A major part of the Freudian method of analysis is to ask people to say the first thing that comes to mind when they are given a word or object. By looking at the kinds of associations that occur, the analyst can find patterns in the randomness that reveal much about the character of the patient.

In To the Lighthouse, Woolf uses this free association style to reveal her characters. Charles Tansley, for example, sees Mrs. Ramsay next to a picture of Queen Victoria and realizes that she is beautiful. From that he thinks of flowers, bouquets and Mrs. Ramsay "stepping through fields of flowers with the stars in her eyes and the wind in her hair" gathering "fallen lambs" to her breast. The patterns of his thoughts reveal his character in ways that an analyst would be able to see. Mrs. Ramsay is the "queen" of his life, because he thinks of her after seeing a real queen. He associates her with flowers because his studies shut him off from the natural world, and she brings him out of his studious mind-set. He imagines her gathering "lost lambs" because he feels orphaned, and sees her as a Christ-like parental figure.

Psychology

The theories of the new Freudian psychology are used throughout the novel. The narrative structure is a literary version of the emphasis that psychology places on the subjective reality of emotions and desires. Freudian psychology suggests that emotions, needs, and instincts are more important in understanding personality than rational thoughts. In keeping with this theory, rational thought is shown to be useless to describe characters throughout To the Lighthouse. When, for example, William Tansley tells himself that he doesn't like Mrs. Ramsay because she is "fifty at least," his "freely-associated" emotions tell the real story. Also part of Freudian theory is the emphasis placed on childhood experiences and emotions in the formation of adult personality. Mrs. Ramsay sums this up when she says, "Children never forget."

Chapter 9

Criticism

Jane Elizabeth Dougherty

Dougherty is a doctoral candidate at Tufts University. In the following essay, she examines the characterization of Lily Briscoe in To the Lighthouse.

In an essay, Virginia Woolf wrote, "xamine for a moment an ordinary mind on an ordinary day. The mind receives a myriad of impressions-trivial, fantastic, evanescent, or engraved with the sharpness of steel." Woolf's character Lily Briscoe struggles with the myriad and momentary nature of reality throughout Woolf's fifth novel, To the Lighthouse. As Suzanne Raitt notes in Virginia Woolf's To the Lighthouse, Lily shares "the novel's strange obsession with solutions." Lily tries to find a shape within the chaotic nature of existence and achieve an artistic vision that will give her a sense of the meaning of life. In the course of her struggle, many of the novel's themes are illuminated: the nature of reality, the search for completion, the role of women, and the relationship of art and life.

As an artist, Lily struggles to express herself creatively. Her creativity is hampered by the continued interruptions of the outside world, which occur both within her physical space and within her mind:

She would not have considered it honest to tamper with the bright violet and the staring white, since she saw them like that, fashionable though it was, since Mr. Paunceforte's visit, to see everything pale, elegant, semi-transparent. Then beneath the colour there was the shape. She could see it all so clearly, so commandingly, when she looked: it was when she took her brush in hand that the whole thing changed. It was in that moment's flight between the picture and her canvas that the demons set on her who often brought her to the verge of tears and made this passage from conception to work as dreadful as any down a dark passage for a child. Such she often felt herself — struggling against terrific odds to maintain her courage; to say: "But this is what I see; this is what I see," and so to clasp some miserable remnant of her vision to her breast, which a thousand forces did their best to pluck from her.

Among the "thousand forces" which try to "pluck" Lily's vision from her is the conflict between the experience of living and the theory of existence, which is represented by the Ramsays. Mrs. Ramsay is a character who seems comfortable with the ebb and flow of daily life; as Thomas A. Vogler comments in his introduction to Twentieth Century Interpretations of To the Lighthouse, "the 'life' character lives or represents the human reality of the story." By contrast, Mr. Ramsay tries to come to "objective" truths about the nature of reality. As A. D. Moody writes in the same volume, Lily's "abstract aesthetic problem becomes an analogy for her main concern, and the novel's, which is to bring Mr. and Mrs. Ramsay, and the worlds they represent, into a harmonious relation." As an artist, Lily tries to find larger truths about human existence, as does Mr. Ramsay, but as a woman, she is confronted with the subjective and personalized nature of existence, as is Mrs. Ramsay. Appropriately, Lily feels that when she stays with the Ramsays, she struggles to find harmony between opposites:

For at any rate, she said to herself, catching sight of the salt cellar on the pattern, she need not marry, thank Heaven: she need not undergo that dilution. She would move the tree rather more to the middle.

Such was the complexity of things. For what happened to her, especially staying with the Ramsays, was to be made to feel violently two opposite things at the same time; that's what you feel, was one; that's what I feel, was the other, and then they fought together in her mind, as now. It is so beautiful, so exciting, this love, that I tremble on the verge of it, and offer, quite out of my own habit, to look for a brooch on the beach; also it is the stupidest, the most barbaric of human passions, and turns a nice young man with a profile like a gem's into a bully with a crowbar (he was swaggering, he was insolent) in the Mile End Road. Yet, she said to herself, from the dawn of time odes have been sung to love; wreathes heaped and roses; and if you asked nine people out of ten they would say they wanted nothing but this – love; while the women, judging from her own experience, would all the time be feeling, This is not what we want, there is nothing more tedious, puerile, and inhumane than this; yet it is also beautiful and necessary.

Lily's own thoughts and perceptions are interrupted by, and in conflict with, the expectations of her society. In particular, she feels inadequate both as a woman and as an artist, because it is not expected that she can be both. She knows that as a woman she is supposed to be fulfilled by love and marriage, yet in her experience that is never the case. She appreciates Mrs. Ramsay's ability to be nurturing, but does not feel that she can fulfill Mrs. Ramsay's role. As Raitt states, Lily "experiences her conflicts over femininity primarily in the context of her relationship to Mrs. Ramsay." Yet she also feels inadequate as a painter, because men like Charles Tansley tell her that "women can't paint. Women can't write." Lily struggles to define herself as a creative woman in a culture that does not acknowledge that women can be creative.

As a female artist, Lily longs to bring together seemingly opposed forces and to find a "solution" to the problem of life's incoherence. For example, she asks how is it possible to analyse all the conflicting information that one gets about another person and decide that one likes or dislikes that person. As Thomas Matro explains in PMLA, "Lily's ambivalence, suspension and subsequent 'explosion' stem from her felt inability to know another person and from the necessity she yet feels to form a clear, consistent opinion." After dinner, for example, she felt rather inclined just for a moment to stand still after all that chatter, and pick out one particular thing; the thing that mattered; to detach it; separate it off; clean it of all the emotions and odds and ends of things, and so hold it before her, and bring it to the tribunal where, ranged about in conclave, sat the judges she had set up to decide these things. Is it good, is it bad, is it right or wrong? Where are we all going to? And so on. So she righted herself after the shock of the event, and quite unconsciously and incongruously, used the branches of the elm trees outside to help her stabilize her position. Her world was changing: they were still. The event had given her a sense of movement. All must be in order. She must get that right and that right, she thought, insensibly approving of the dignity of the trees' stillness, and now again of the superb upward rise (like the beak of a ship up a wave) of the elm branches as the wind raised them.

Lily longs to see things without emotion, objectively. She is able to reorient herself by situating herself in relation to the trees outside, which she sees as objective because they are unchanging. In the passage, she progresses from thinking abstractly about "the thing that mattered," which she cannot identify and about which she asks, "is it right or wrong?" to righting herself by focusing on the unchanging nature of the trees, to deciding she must get them right in her painting. By using the word "right," the narrator shifts Lily, and the reader, from abstract conceptions of rightness to natural, eternal rightness to an aesthetic rightness in which rightness is defined as the ability to see clearly.

But that is not the final step on Lily's artistic quest; though she says that she must get what she sees on canvas, the narrator shows how, through her use of the word "right," Lily is still clinging to a kind of aesthetics based on objectivity, an unchanging and universal "truth." Lily thinks the natural world is unchanging, but in the second section of the novel, "Time Passes," the narrator shows us how the natural world slowly encroaches on, and nearly destroys, the house. Lily thinks that she must get what she sees "right," but in the third section, "The Lighthouse," she discov-ers that what she sees is her own particular vision, not a universal truth. In the section called "The Lighthouse," Lily decides to finish the picture she had started ten years earlier, but is interrupted by Mr. Ramsay: Yes, it must have been precisely here that she had stood ten years ago. There was the wall, the hedge, the tree. The question was of some relation between those masses. She had borne it in her mind all these years. It seemed as if the solution had come to her: she knew now what she wanted to do. But with Mr. Ramsay bearing down on her, she could do nothing. Every time he approached — he was walking up and down the terrace — ruin approached, chaos approached. She could not paint.

Lily associates chaos with being unable to paint, unable to hold things in their proper places. Mr. Ramsay makes her unable to paint because, with his insatiable demands for sympathy, he makes it impossible for Lily to listen to her own feelings. She is once again confronted with the "dilution" of other people, with the attempt to hold together two opposing forces: her own feelings and those of another person. It is only when Mr. Ramsay leaves that she can return to her painting.

As she paints, Lily falls into a kind of trance in which she imagines Mrs. Ramsay, for whom she has been crying out, is sitting beside her. She remembers how Mrs. Ramsay united her with her "opposite," Charles Tansley:

The great revelation had never come. The great revelation perhaps never did come. Instead there were little daily miracles, illuminations, matches struck unexpectedly in the dark; here was one. This, that, and the other; herself and Charles Tansley and the breaking wave; Mrs. Ramsay bringing them together; Mrs. Ramsay saying, 'Life stand still here'; Mrs. Ramsay making of the moment something permanent (as in another sphere Lily herself tried to make of the moment something permanent) — this was of the nature of a revelation. In the midst of chaos there was shape; this eternal passing and flowing (she looked at the clouds going and the leaves shaking) was struck into stability. Life stand still here, Mrs. Ramsay said. 'Mrs. Ramsay! Mrs. Ramsay!' she repeated. She owed it all to her. Whereas earlier Lily had thought that her artistry depended on "getting it right," and that the natural world was unchanging, she now sees, with Mrs. Ramsay's help, that the job of the artist is to make a moment permanent by capturing it in art. In coming to this realization, Lily is able to see her resemblance to Mrs. Ramsay, to see that she really is a woman, as Mrs. Ramsay was, but a woman whose female identity is expressed in art rather than in relationships. Lily is at last able to mourn for Mrs. Ramsay, realizing that the "solution" to the problem of "wanting and not having" is to understand that all of life is momentary and that the best that humans can do is to say "life stand still here" and capture a moment in memory or in art. At the end of the novel, Lily feels that she is able to unify opposing forces, achieve completion, express her own personal truths, and to be both a woman and an artist. Through Lily, Woolf shows that in creative self-expression, humans may achieve a sense of completion and unify the disparate elements of life.

Critical Overview

To the Lighthouse was a critical success as soon as it was published, and won Woolf the Prix Femina in 1928. Initial reviews and criticism focused on the novel's stylistic innovations, praising Woolf's artistic refinement of the stream of consciousness narrative. Louis Kronenberger, for example, announced in The New York Times, "here is prose of an extraordinary distinction in our time: here is poetry." Woolf's death in 1941 prompted a flood of books and articles that celebrated her mastery of prose style. Eric Auerbach's important 1946 study of art and literature Mimesis: The Representation of Reality in Western Literature elevated Woolf's novel to the status of great literature and gave her the tag "Brown Stocking" (a play on the phrase "bluestockings" which was used to describe a group of intellectual women authors in the eighteenth century). Putting To the Lighthouse at the top of the modern literary canon, he praised the achievements of its narrative style over the works of her contemporaries, calling it the "creation of something new and elemental."

In the 1950s and 1960s, critical focus centered on symbolism, looking at myth, philosophy, and history as the unifying strategies of the novel. In The Glass Roof: Virginia Woolf as Novelist, James Halfley suggested that both Mrs. Ramsay and the Lighthouse were, "cosmic symbols" that represented a "vital synthesis of time and eternity." Along the same lines, Joseph L. Blotner's essay, "Mythic Patterns in To the Lighthouse," argued that Mrs. Ramsay should be understood as a "primordial goddess" composed of "the major female characters of pagan myth." He also made a case for the importance of Freudian thought in the novel.

The 1970s and 1980s marked a revolution in Woolf studies — a move away from quasi-Jungian analysis based on her symbolism, and a new focus on the role of gender and art in To the Lighthouse instead. Where the older critics found unity in the work, these new voices found disharmony and con-flict. Emphasis was placed on the roles of gender and class, reflecting the general critical trends of the late 1970s and 1980s. Irene Dash, Deena Kushner, and Deborah Moore looked at the novel from a sociological stance, examining the challenges women face between "being mothers and being artists," from the perspectives of a mother, daughter, and artist, in "How Light a Lighthouse for Today's Women?" Jane Lilienfeld, in "'The Deceptiveness of Beauty': Mother Love and Mother Hate in To the Lighthouse" performed a biographical reading, suggesting that the relationship between Lily Briscoe and Mrs. Ramsay is an outlet for Woolf's feelings about her relationship with her mother, Julia Stephen.

Another critic, Elaine Showalter, caused controversy by arguing that the novel reveals Woolf's abandonment of feminism for a retreat into mysticism, in A Literature of Their Own: British Women Novelists from Bronte to Lessing. Claiming that Showalter's analysis revealed her tendency to "traditional humanism," Toril Moi's hugely influential 1985 book Sexual/Textual Politics: Feminist Literary Theory countered this by suggesting that Woolf's novel, "rejects the metaphysical essentialism underlying patriarchal ideology, which hails God, the father or the phallus, as its

Transcendental signified," both in its shifting-consciousness narrative style and in the rejection of Mr. Ramsay's logic. Rachel Bowlby's important study, Virginia Woolf: Feminist Destinations, used Freudian and Lacanian psychoanalytic theories to read the novel, suggesting that, "To the Lighthouse makes evident the mapping of human subjectivity in terms of figurations inseparable from sexual difference."

Reflecting the general shifts in academia, the 1990s has seen a stronger emphasis on post-colonial and historically contextual readings of To the Lighthouse. These approaches stress the novel's relationship to the major historical contexts of its setting — World War I, the General Strike, and the British Empire. Characteristic of this approach is "'Something Out Of Harmony': To the Lighthouse and the Subject of Empire" by Janet Winston. Picking up on the scene in which Charles Tansley compares Mrs. Ramsay to Queen Victoria, Winston suggested that the novel, "invites us to read not only with attention to codes of imperialist representation but to Mrs. Ramsay's role as Queen in a text of imperial allegory." The images of "sinking" that appear throughout the novel become — in this argument — evidence for authorial anxiety about the imminent collapse — "sinking" — of the British Empire.

Chapter 10

Complete Text of To the Lighthouse

THE WINDOW

- "Yes, of course, if it's fine tomorrow," said Mrs Ramsay. "But you'llhave to be up with the lark," she added.

To her son these words conveyed an extraordinary joy, as if it weresettled, the expedition were bound to take place, and tne wonder to whichhe had looked forward, for years and years it seemed, was, after a night'sdarkness and a day's sail, within touch. Since he belonged, even at theage of six, to that great clan which cannot keep this feeling separatefrom that, but must let future prospects, with their joys and sorrows,cloud what is actually at hand, since to such people even in earliestchildhood any turn in the wheel of sensation has the power to crystalliseand transfix the moment upon which its gloom or radiance rests, JamesRamsay, sitting on the floor cutting out pictures from the illustratedcatalogue of the Army and Navy stores, endowed the picture of arefrigerator, as his mother spoke, with heavenly bliss.

It was fringedwith joy. The wheelbarrow, the lawnmower, the sound of poplar trees,leaves whitening before rain, rooks cawing, brooms knocking, dressesrustling—all these were so coloured and distinguished in his mind that hehad already his private code, his secret language, though he appeared theimage of stark and uncompromising severity, with his high forehead and hisfierce blue eyes, impeccably candid and pure, frowning slightly at thesight of human frailty, so that his mother, watching him guide hisscissors neatly round the refrigerator, imagined him all red and ermine onthe Bench or directing a stern and momentous enterprise in some crisis ofpublic affairs.

"But," said his father, stopping in front of the drawing-room window, "itwon't be fine."Had there been an axe handy, a poker, or any weapon that would have gasheda hole in his father's breast and killed him, there and then, James wouldhave seized it. Such were the extremes of emotion that Mr Ramsay excitedin his children's breasts by his mere presence; standing, as now, lean asa knife, narrow as the blade of one, grinning sarcastically, not only withthe pleasure of disillusioning his son and casting ridicule upon his wife,who was ten thousand times better in every way than he was, but also with some secret conceit at his own accuracy ofjudgement. What he said was true.

It was always true. He was incapableof untruth; never tampered with a fact; never altered a disagreeable wordto suit the pleasure or convenience of any mortal being, least of all ofhis own children, who, sprung from his loins, should be aware fromchildhood that life is difficult; facts uncompromising; and the passage tothat fabled land where our brightest hopes are extinguished, our frailbarks founder in darkness (here Mr Ramsay would straighten his back andnarrow his little blue eyes upon the horizon), one that needs, above all,courage, truth, and the power to endure.

"But it may be fine—I expect it will be fine," said Mrs Ramsay, makingsome little twist of the reddish brown stocking she was knitting,impatiently. If she finished it tonight, if they did go to the Lighthouseafter all, it was to be given to the Lighthouse keeper for his little boy,who was threatened with a tuberculous hip; together with a pile of oldmagazines, and some tobacco, indeed, whatever she could find lying about,not really wanted, but only littering the room, to give those poorfellows, who must be bored to death sitting all day with nothing to do butpolish the lamp and trim the wick and rake about on their scrap of garden,something to amuse them. For how would you like to be shut up for a wholemonth at a time, and possibly more in stormy weather, upon a rock the sizeof a tennis lawn? she would ask; and to have no letters or newspapers, andto see nobody; if you were married, not to see your wife, not to know howyour children were,—if they were ill, if they had fallen down and brokentheir legs or arms; to see the same dreary waves breaking week after week,and then a dreadful storm coming, and the windows covered with spray, andbirds dashed against the lamp, and the whole place rocking, and not beable to put your nose out of doors for fear of being swept into the sea?How would you like that? she asked, addressing herself particularly to herdaughters. So she added, rather differently, one must take them whatever-comforts one can.

"It's due west," said the atheist Tansley, holding his bony fingers spreadso that the wind blew through them, for he was sharing Mr Ramsay'sevening walk up and down, up and down the terrace. That is to say, thewind blew from the worst possible direction for landing at the Lighthouse.Yes, he did say disagreeable things, Mrs Ramsay admitted; it was odiousof him to rub this in, and make James still more disappointed; but at thesame time, she would not let them laugh at him. "The atheist," theycalled him; "the little atheist." Rose mocked him; Prue mocked him;Andrew, Jasper, Roger mocked him; even old Badger without a tooth in hishead had bit him, for being the hundred and tenth youngman to chase them all the way up to the Hebrides when it was ever so muchnicer to be alone.

"Nonsense," said Mrs Ramsay, with great severity. Apart from the habitof exaggeration which they had from her, and from the implication that she asked too many people to stay, and had to lodge some inthe town, she could not bear incivility to her guests, to young men inparticular, who were poor as churchmice, "exceptionally able," her husbandsaid, his great admirers, and come there for a holiday. Indeed, she hadthe whole of the other sex under her protection; for reasons she could notexplain, for their chivalry and valour, for the fact that they negotiatedtreaties, ruled India, controlled finance; finally for an attitude towardsherself which no woman could fail to feel or to find agreeable, somethingtrustful, childlike, reverential; which an old woman could take from ayoung man without loss of dignity, and woe betide the girl—pray Heaven itwas none of her daughters!—who did not feel the worth of it, and allthat it implied, to the marrow of her bones!She turned with severity upon Nancy. He had not chased them, she said.He had been asked.

They must find a way out of it all. There might be some simpler way, someless laborious way, she sighed. When she looked in the glass and saw herhair grey, her cheek sunk, at fifty, she thought, possibly she might havemanaged things better—her husband; money; his books. But for her ownpart she would never for a single second regret her decision, evadedifficulties, or slur over duties. She was now formidable to behold, andit was only in silence, looking up from their plates, after she had spokenso severely about Charles Tansley, that her daughters, Prue, Nancy,Rose—could sport with infidel ideas which they had brewed for themselvesof a life different from hers; in Paris, perhaps; a wilder life; notalways taking care of some man or other; for there was in all their mindsa mute questioning of deference and chivalry, of the Bank of England andthe Indian Empire, of ringed fingers and lace, though to them all therewas something in this of the essence of beauty, which called out themanliness in their girlish hearts, and made them, as they sat at tablebeneath their mother's eyes, honour her strange severity, her extremecourtesy, like a queen's raising from the mud to wash a beggar's dirtyfoot, when she admonished them so very severely about that wretchedatheist who had chased them—or, speaking accurately, been invited tostay with them—in the Isle of Skye.

"There'll be no landing at the Lighthouse tomorrow," said Charles Tansley,clapping his hands together as he stood at the window with her husband.Surely, he had said enough. She wished they would both leave her andJames alone and go on talking. She looked at him. He was such amiserable specimen, the children said, all humps and hollows. He couldn'tplay cricket; he poked; he shuffled. He was a sarcastic brute, Andrewsaid. They knew what he liked best—to be for ever walking up and down,up and down, with Mr Ramsay, and saying who had won this, who had wonthat, who was a "first rate man" at Latin verses, who was "brilliant but Ithink fundamentally unsound," who was undoubtedly the "ablest fellow inBalliol," who had buried his light temporarily at Bristol or Bedford, butwas bound to be heard of later when his Prolegomena, of which Mr Tansleyhad the first pages in proof with him if Mr Ramsay would like to seethem, to some branch of mathematics or philosophy saw the light of day.That was what they talked about.She could not help laughing herself sometimes. She said, the other day,something about "waves mountains high." Yes, said Charles Tansley, itwas a little rough. "Aren't you drenched to the skin?" she had said."Damp, not wet through," said Mr Tansley, pinching his sleeve, feelinghis socks.

But it was not that they minded, the children said. It was not his face;it was not his manners. It was him—his point of view. When they talkedabout something interesting, people, music, history, anything, even saidit was a fine evening so why not sit out of doors, then what theycomplained of about Charles Tansley was that until he had turned the wholething round and made it somehow reflect himself and disparage them—he wasnot satisfied. And he would go to picture galleries they said, and hewould ask one, did one like his tie? God knows, said Rose, one did not.

Disappearing as stealthily as stags from the dinner-table directly themeal was over, the eight sons and daughters of Mr and Mrs Ramsay soughttheir bedrooms, their fastness in a house where there was no other privacyto debate anything, everything; Tansley's tie; the passing of the ReformBill; sea birds and butterflies; people; while the sun poured into thoseattics, which a plank alone separated from each other so that everyfootstep could be plainly heard and the Swiss girl sobbing for her fatherwho was dying of cancer in a valley of the Grisons, and lit up bats,flannels, straw hats, ink-pots, paint-pots, beetles, and the skulls ofsmall birds, while it drew from the long frilled strips of seaweed pinnedto the wall a smell of salt and weeds, which was in the towels too,gritty with sand from bathing.

Strife, divisions, difference of opinion, prejudices twisted into the veryfibre of being, oh, that they should begin so early, Mrs Ramsay deplored.They were so critical, her children. They talked such nonsense. She wentfrom the dining-room, holding James by the hand, since he would not gowith the others. It seemed to her such nonsense—inventing differences,when people, heaven knows, were different enough without that. The realdifferences, she thought, standing by the drawing-room window, are enough,quite enough. She had in mind at the moment, rich and poor, high and low;the great in birth receiving from her, half grudging, some respect, forhad she not in her veins the blood of that very noble, if slightlymythical, Italian house, whose daughters, scattered about Englishdrawing-rooms in the nineteenth century, had lisped so charmingly, hadstormed so wildly, and all her wit and her bearing and her temper camefrom them, and not from the sluggish English, or the cold Scotch; but moreprofoundly, she ruminated the other problem, of rich and poor, and thethings she saw with her own eyes, weekly, daily, here or in London, whenshe visited this widow, or that struggling wife in person with a bag onher arm, and a note-book and pencil with which she wrote down in columnscarefully ruled for the purpose wages and spendings, employment andunemployment, in the hope that thus she would cease to be a private womanwhose charity was half a sop to her own indignation, half a relief to herown curiosity, and become what with her untrained mind she greatlyadmired, an investigator, elucidating the social problem.

Insoluble questions they were, it seemed to her, standing there, holdingJames by the hand. He had followed her into the drawing-room, that youngman they laughed at; he was standing by the table, fidgeting withsomething, awkwardly, feeling himself out of things, as she knew withoutlooking round. They had all gone—the children; Minta Doyle and PaulRayley; Augustus Carmichael; her husband—they had all gone. So sheturned with a sigh and said, "Would it bore you to come with me,Mr Tansley?"

She had a dull errand in the town; she had a letter or two

to write; shewould be ten minutes perhaps; she would put on her hat. And, with herbasket and her parasol, there she was again, ten minutes later, giving outa sense of being ready, of being equipped for a jaunt, which, however, shemust interrupt for a moment, as they passed the tennis lawn, to askMr Carmichael, who was basking with his yellow cat's eyes ajar, so thatlike a cat's they seemed to reflect the branches moving or the cloudspassing, but to give no inkling of any inner thoughts or emotionwhatsoever, if he wanted anything.

For they were making the great expedition, she said, laughing. They weregoing to the town. "Stamps, writing-paper, tobacco?" she suggested,stopping by his side. But no, he wanted nothing. His hands claspedthemselves over his capacious paunch, his eyes blinked, as if he wouldhave liked to reply kindly to these blandishments (she was seductive but alittle nervous) but could not, sunk as he was in a grey-green somnolencewhich embraced them all, without need of words, in a vast and benevolentlethargy of well-wishing; all the house; all the world; all the people init, for he had slipped into his glass at lunch a few drops of something,which accounted, the children thought, for the vivid streak ofcanary-yellow in moustache and beard that were otherwise milk white. No,nothing, he murmured.

He should have been a great philosopher, said Mrs Ramsay, as they wentdown the road to the fishing village, but he had made an unfortunatemarriage. Holding her black parasol very erect, and moving with anindescribable air of expectation, as if she were going to meet some oneround the corner, she told the story; an affair at Oxford with some girl;an early marriage; poverty; going to India; translating a little poetry"very beautifully, I believe," being willing to teach the boys Persian orHindustanee, but what really was the use of that?—and then lying, as theysaw him, on the lawn.

It flattered him; snubbed as he had been, it soothed him that Mrs Ramsayshould tell him this. Charles Tansley revived. Insinuating, too, as shedid the greatness of man's intellect, even in its decay, the subjection ofall wives—not that she blamed the girl, and the marriage had been happyenough, she believed—to their husband's labours, she made him feel betterpleased with himself than he had done yet, and he would have liked, hadthey taken a cab, for example, to have paid the fare. As for her littlebag, might he not carry that? No, no, she said, she always carried THATherself. She did too. Yes, he felt that in her. He felt many things,something in particular that excited him and disturbed him for reasonswhich he could not give. He would like her to see him, gowned and hooded,walking in a procession. A fellowship, a professorship, he felt capableof anything and saw himself—but what was she looking at? At a manpasting a bill. The vast flapping sheet flattened itself out, and eachshove of the brush revealed fresh legs, hoops, horses, glistening reds andblues, beautifully smooth, until half the wall was covered with theadvertisement of a circus; a hundred horsemen, twenty performing seals, lions, tigers... Craning forwards, for she was short-sighted, she read itout... "will visit this town," she read. It was terribly dangerous workfor a one-armed man, she exclaimed, to stand on top of a ladder likethat—his left arm had been cut off in a reaping machine two years ago.

"Let us all go!" she cried, moving on, as if all those riders and horseshad filled her with childlike exultation and made her forget her pity.

"Let's go," he said, repeating her words, clicking them out, however, witha self-consciousness that made her wince. "Let us all go to the circus."No. He could not say it right. He could not feel it right. But why not?she wondered. What was wrong with him then? She liked him warmly, at themoment. Had they not been taken, she asked, to circuses when they werechildren? Never, he answered, as if she asked the very thing he wanted;had been longing all these days to say, how they did not go to circuses.It was a large family, nine brothers and sisters, and his father was aworking man. "My father is a chemist, Mrs Ramsay. He keeps a shop." Hehimself had paid his own way since he was thirteen. Often he went withouta greatcoat in winter. He could never "return hospitality" (those werehis parched stiff words) at college. He had to make things last twice thetime other people did; he smoked the cheapest tobacco; shag; the same theold men did in the quays. He worked hard—seven hours a day; his subjectwas now the influence of something upon somebody—they were walking on andMrs Ramsay did not quite catch the meaning, only the words, here andthere... dissertation... fellowship... readership... lectureship. Shecould not follow the ugly academic jargon, that rattled itself off soglibly, but said to herself that she saw now why going to the circus hadknocked him off his perch, poor little man, and why he came out,instantly, with all that about his father and mother and brothers andsisters, and she would see to it that they didn't laugh at him any more;she would tell Prue about it. What he would have liked, she supposed,would have been to say how he had gone not to the circus but to Ibsen withthe Ramsays. He was an awful prig—oh yes, an insufferable bore. For,though they had reached the town now and were in the main street, withcarts grinding past on the cobbles, still he went on talking, aboutsettlements, and teaching, and working men, and helping our own class,and lectures, till she gathered that he had got back entireself-confidence, had recovered from the circus, and was about (and nowagain she liked him warmly) to tell her—but here, the houses fallingaway on both sides, they came out on the quay, and the whole bayspread before them and Mrs Ramsay could not help exclaiming, "Oh,how beautiful!" For the great plateful of blue water was before her;the hoary Lighthouse, distant, austere, in the midst; and on the right,as far as the eye could see, fading and falling, in soft low pleats,the green sand dunes with the wild flowing grasses on them, which alwaysseemed to be running away into some moon country, uninhabited of men.That was the view, she said, stopping, growing greyer-eyed, that herhusband loved.

She paused a moment. But now, she said, artists had come here. Thereindeed, only a few paces off, stood one of them, in Panama hat and yellowboots, seriously, softly, absorbedly, for all that he was watched by tenlittle boys, with an air of profound contentment on his round red facegazing, and then, when he had gazed, dipping; imbuing the tip of hisbrush in some soft mound of green or pink. Since Mr Paunceforte had beenthere, three years before, all the pictures were like that, she said,green and grey, with lemon-coloured sailing-boats, and pink women on thebeach.

But her grandmother's friends, she said, glancing discreetly as theypassed, took the greatest pains; first they mixed their own colours, andthen they ground them, and then they put damp cloths to keep them moist.

So Mr Tansley supposed she meant him to see that that man's picture wasskimpy, was that what one said? The colours weren't solid? Was that whatone said? Under the influence of that extraordinary emotion which had beengrowing all the walk, had begun in the garden when he had wanted to takeher bag, had increased in the town when he had wanted to tell hereverything about himself, he was coming to see himself, and everything hehad ever known gone crooked a little. It was awfully strange.

There he stood in the parlour of the poky little house where she had takenhim, waiting for her, while she went upstairs a moment to see a woman. Heheard her quick step above; heard her voice cheerful, then low; looked atthe mats, tea-caddies, glass shades; waited quite impatiently; lookedforward eagerly to the walk home; determined to carry her bag; then heardher come out; shut a door; say they must keep the windows open and thedoors shut, ask at the house for anything they wanted when, suddenly, in she came, stood for a moment silent (as ifshe had been pretending up there, and for a moment let herself be now),stood quite motionless for a moment against a picture of Queen Victoriawearing the blue ribbon of the Garter; when all at once he realised thatit was this: it was this:—she was the most beautiful person he had everseen.

With stars in her eyes and veils in her hair, with cyclamen and wildviolets—what nonsense was he thinking? She was fifty at least; she hadeight children. Stepping through fields of flowers and taking to herbreast buds that had broken and lambs that had fallen; with the stars inher eyes and the wind in her hair—He had hold of her bag.

"Good-bye, Elsie," she said, and they walked up the street,

she holdingher parasol erect and walking as if she expected to meet some one roundthe corner, while for the first time in his life Charles Tansley felt anextraordinary pride; a man digging in a dràin stopped digging and lookedat her, let his arm fall down and looked at her; for the first time in hislife Charles Tansley felt an extraordinary pride; felt the wind and thecyclamen and the violets for he was walking with a beautiful woman. Hehad hold of her bag.

- "No going to the Lighthouse, James," he said, as trying in deference to Mrs Ramsay to soften his voice into some semblance of geniality at least. Odious little man, thought Mrs Ramsay, why go on saying that?
- "Perhaps you will wake up and find the sun shining and the birds singing," she said compassionately, smoothing the little boy's hair, for her husband, with his caustic saying that it would not be fine, had dashed his spirits she could see. This going to the Lighthouse was a passion of his, she saw, and then, as if her husband had not said enough, with his caustic saying that it would not be fine tomorrow, this odious little man went and rubbed it in all over again.

"Perhaps it will be fine tomorrow," she said, smoothing his hair.

All she could do now was to admire the refrigerator, and turn the pages ofthe Stores list in the hope that she might come upon something like arake, or a mowing-machine, which, with its prongs and its handles, wouldneed the greatest skill and care in cutting out. All these young menparodied her husband, she reflected; he said it would rain; they said itwould be a positive tornado.But here, as she turned the page, suddenly her search for the picture of arake or a mowing-machine was interrupted. The gruff murmur, irregularlybroken by the taking out of pipes and the putting in of pipes which hadkept on assuring her, though she could not hear what was said (as she satin the window which opened on the terrace), that the men were happilytalking; this sound, which had lasted now half an hour and had taken itsplace soothingly in the scale of sounds pressing on top of her, such asthe tap of balls upon bats, the sharp, sudden bark now and then,"How's that? How's that?" of the children playing cricket, had ceased;so that the monotonous fall of the waves on the beach, which for the mostpart beat a measured and soothing tattoo to her thoughts and seemedconsolingly to repeat over and over again as she sat with the childrenthe words of some old cradle song, murmured by nature, "I am guardingyou—I am your support," but at other times suddenly and unexpectedly, especially when her mind raised itself slightly from the task actually inhand, had no such kindly meaning, but like a ghostly roll of drumsremorselessly beat the measure of life, made one think of the destructionof the island and its engulfment in the sea, and warned her whose day hadslipped past in one quick doing after another that it was all ephermal asa rainbow—this sound which had been obscured and concealed under theother sounds suddenly thundered hollow in her ears and made her look upwith an impulse of terror.

They had ceased to talk; that was the explanation. Falling in one secondfrom the tension which had gripped her to the other extreme which, as ifto recoup her for her unnecessary expense of emotion, was cool, amused,and even faintly malicious, she concluded that poor Charles Tansley hadbeen shed. That was of little account to her. If her husband requiredsacrifices she cheerfully offered up to him Charles Tansley, who had snubbed her little boy.

One moment more, with her head raised, she listened, as if she waited forsome habitual sound, some regular mechanical sound; and then, hearingsomething rhythmical, half said, half chanted, beginning in the garden, asher husband beat up and down the terrace, something between a croak and asong, she was soothed once more, assured again that all was well, andlooking down at the book on her knee found the picture of a pocket knifewith six blades which could only be cut out if James was very careful.

Suddenly a loud cry, as of a sleep-walker, half roused, something about Stormed at with shot and shell sung out with the utmost intensity in her ear, made her turn apprehensively to see if anyone had heard him. Only Lily Briscoe, she was glad to find; and that did not matter. But the sight of the girl standing on the edge of the lawn painting reminded her; she was supposed to be keeping her head as much in the same position as possible for Lily's picture. Lily's picture! Mrs Ramsay smiled. With her little Chinese eyes and her puckered-up face, she would never marry; one could not take her painting very seriously; she was an independent little creature, and Mrs Ramsay liked her for it; so, remembering her promise, she bent her head.

- Indeed, he almost knocked her easel over, coming down upon her with his hands waving shouting out, "Boldly we rode and well," but, mercifully, he turned sharp, and rode off, to die gloriously she supposed upon the heights of Balaclava. Never was anybody at once so ridiculous and so alarming. But so long as he kept like that, waving, shouting, she was safe; he would not stand still and look at her picture. And that was what Lily Briscoe could not have endured. Even while she looked at the mass, at the line, at the colour, at Mrs Ramsay sitting in the window with James, she kept a feeler on her surroundings lest some one should creep up, and suddenly she should find her picture looked at. But now, with all her senses quickened as they were, looking, straining, till the colour of the wall and the jacmanna beyond burnt into her eyes, she was aware of someone coming out of the house, coming toward her; but somehow divined, from the footfall, William Bankes, so that though her brush quivered, she did not, as she would have done had it been Mr Tansley, Paul Rayley, Minta Doyle, or practically anybody else, turn her canvas upon the grass, but let it stand. William Bankes stood beside her.

They had rooms in the village, and so, walking in, walking out, partinglate on door-mats, had said little things about the soup, about thechildren, about one thing and another which made them allies; so that whenhe stood beside her now in his judicial way (he was old enough to be herfather too, a botanist, a widower, smelling of soap, very scrupulous andclean) she just stood there. He just stood there. Her shoes wereexcellent, he observed. They allowed the toes their natural expansion.Lodging in the same house with her, he had noticed too, how orderly shewas, up before breakfast and off to paint, he believed, alone: poor,presumably, and without the complexion or the allurement of Miss Doylecertainly, but with a good sense which made her in his eyes superior tothat young lady. Now, for instance, when Ramsay bore down on them,shouting, gesticulating, Miss Briscoe, he felt certain, understood.

Some one had blundered: Mr Ramsay glared at them. He glared at them without seeming to see them.That did make them both vaguely uncomfortable. Together they had seen athing they had not been meant to see. They had encroached upon a privacy.So, Lily thought, it was probably an excuse of his for moving, for gettingout of earshot, that made Mr Bankes almost immediately say somethingabout its being chilly and suggested taking a stroll. She would come,yes. But it was with difficulty that she took her eyes off her picture.

The jacmanna was bright violet; the wall staring white. She would nothave considered it honest to tamper with the bright violet and the staringwhite, since she saw them like that, fashionable though it was, sinceMr Paunceforte's visit, to see everything pale, elegant, semitransparent.Then beneath the colour there was the shape. She could see it all soclearly, so commandingly, when she looked: it was when she took her brushin hand that the whole thing changed. It was in that moment's flightbetween the picture and her canvas that the demons set on her who oftenbrought her to the verge of tears and made this passage from conception towork as dreadful as any down a dark passage for a child. Such she oftenfelt herself—struggling against terrific odds to maintain her courage; tosay: "But this is what I see; this is what I see," and so to clasp somemiserable remnant of her vision to her breast, which a thousand forces didtheir best to pluck from her. And it was then too, in that chill andwindy way, as she began to paint, that there forced themselves upon herother things, her own inadequacy, her insignificance, keeping house forher father off the Brompton Road, and had much ado to control her impulseto fling herself (thank Heaven she had always resisted so far) atMrs Ramsay's knee and say to her—but what could one say to her? "I'm inlove with you?" No, that was not true. "I'm in love with this all,"waving her hand at the hedge, at the house, at the children. It wasabsurd, it was impossible. So now she laid her brushes neatly in the box,side by side, and said to William Bankes:

"It suddenly gets cold. The sun seems to give less heat," she said,looking about her, for it was bright enough, the grass still a soft deepgreen, the house starred in its greenery with purple passion flowers, androoks dropping cool cries from the high blue. But something moved,flashed, turned a silver wing in the air. It was September after all,the middle of September, and past six in the evening. So off theystrolled down the garden in the usual direction, past the tennis lawn,past the pampas grass, to that break in the thick hedge, guarded by redhot pokers like brasiers of clear burning coal, between which the bluewaters of the bay looked bluer than ever.

They came there regularly every evening drawn by some need. It was as ifthe water floated off and set sailing thoughts which had grown stagnant ondry land, and gave to their bodies even some sort of physical relief.First, the pulse of colour flooded the bay with blue, and the heartexpanded with it and the body swam, only the next instant to be checkedand chilled by the prickly blackness on the ruffled waves. Then, upbehind the great black rock, almost every evening spurted irregularly, sothat one had to watch for it and it was a delight when it came, a fountainof white water; and then, while one waited for that, one watched, on thepale semicircular beach, wave after wave shedding again and againsmoothly, a film of mother of pearl.They both smiled, standing there. They both felt a common hilarity,excited by the moving waves; and then by the swift cutting race of asailing boat, which, having sliced a curve in the bay, stopped; shivered;let its sails drop down; and then, with a natural instinct to complete thepicture, after this swift movement, both of them looked at the dunesfar away, and instead of merriment felt come over them somesadness—because the thing was completed partly, and partly becausedistant views seem to outlast by a million years the gazerand to be communing already with a sky which beholds an earth entirelyat rest.

Looking at the far sand hills, William Bankes thought of Ramsay: thoughtof a road in Westmorland, thought of Ramsay striding along a road byhimself hung round with that solitude which seemed to be his natural air.But this was suddenly interrupted, William Bankes remembered (and thismust refer to some actual incident), by a hen, straddling her wings out inprotection of a covey of little chicks, upon which Ramsay, stopping,pointed his stick and said "Pretty—pretty," an odd illumination in tohis heart, Bankes had thought it, which showed his simplicity, hissympathy with humble things; but it seemed to him as if their friendshiphad ceased, there, on that stretch of road. After that, Ramsay hadmarried. After that, what with one thing and another, the pulp had goneout of their friendship. Whose fault it was he could not say, only, aftera time, repetition had taken the place of newness. It was to repeat thatthey met. But in this dumb colloquy with the sand dunes he maintainedthat his affection for Ramsay had in no way diminished; but there, likethe body of a young man laid up in peat for a century, with the red freshon his lips, was his friendship, in its acuteness and reality, laid upacross the bay among the sandhills.

He was anxious for the sake of this friendship and perhaps too in order toclear himself in his own mind from the imputation of having dried andshrunk—for Ramsay lived in a welter of children, whereas Bankes waschildless and a widower—he was anxious that Lily Briscoe should notdisparage Ramsay yet should understand howthings stood between them. Begun long years ago, their friendship hadpetered out on a Westmorland road, where the hen spread her wings beforeher chicks; after which Ramsay had married, and their paths lyingdifferent ways, there had been, certainly for no one's fault, sometendency, when they met, to repeat.

Yes. That was it. He finished. He turned from the view. And, turningto walk back the other way, up the drive, Mr Bankes was alive to thingswhich would not have struck him had not those sandhills revealed to himthe body of his friendship lying with the red on its lips laid up inpeat—for instance, Cam, the little girl, Ramsay's youngest daughter. Shewas picking Sweet Alice on the bank. She was wild and fierce. She wouldnot "give a flower to the gentleman" as the nursemaid told her.No! no! no! she would not! She clenched her fist. She stamped. AndMr Bankes felt aged and saddened and somehow put into the wrong by herabout his friendship.

He must have dried and shrunk: The Ramsays were not rich, and it was a wonder how they managed tocontrive it all. Eight children! To feed eight children on philosophy!Here was another of them, Jasper this time, strolling past, to have a shotat a bird, he said, nonchalantly, swinging Lily's hand like a pump-handleas he passed, which caused Mr Bankes to say, bitterly, how SHE was afavourite. There was education now to be considered (true, Mrs Ramsayhad something of her own perhaps) let alone the daily wear and tear ofshoes and stockings which those "great fellows," all well grown, angular,ruthless youngsters, must require. As for being sure which was which, orin what order they came, that was beyond him.

He called them privatelyafter the Kings and Queens of England; Cam the Wicked, James the Ruthless,Andrew the Just, Prue the Fair—for Prue would have beauty, he thought,how could she help it?—and Andrew brains. While he walked up the driveand Lily Briscoe said yes and no and capped his comments (for she was inlove with them all, in love with this world) he weighed Ramsay's case,commiserated him, envied him, as if he had seen him divest himself of allthose glories of isolation and austerity which crowned him in youth tocumber himself definitely with fluttering wings and cluckingdomesticities. They gave him something—William Bankes acknowledged that;it would have been pleasant if Cam had stuck a flower in his coat orclambered over his shoulder, as over her father's, to look at a pictureof Vesuviusin eruption;

but they had also, his old friends could not butfeel, destroyed something. What would a stranger think now? What didthis Lily Briscoe think? Could one help noticing that habits grew on him?eccentricities, weaknesses perhaps? It was astonishing that a man of hisintellect could stoop so low as he did—but that was too harsh aphrase—could depend so much as he did upon people's praise.

"Oh, but," said Lily, "think of his work!": Whenever she "thought of his work" she always saw clearly before her alarge kitchen table. It was Andrew's doing. She asked him what hisfather's books were about. "Subject and object and the nature ofreality," Andrew had said. And when she said Heavens, she had no notionwhat that meant. "Think of a kitchen table then," he told her, "whenyou're not there."

So now she always saw, when she thought of Mr Ramsay's work, a scrubbedkitchen table. It lodged now in the fork of a pear trec, for they hadreached thc orchard. And with a painful effort of concentration, shefocused her mind, not upon the silver bossed bark of the tree, or upon itsfish-shaped leaves, but upon a phantom kitchen table, one of thosescrubbed board tables, grained and knotted, whose virtue seems to havebeen laid bare by years of muscular integrity, which stuck there, its fourlegs in air. Naturally, if one's days were passed in this seeing ofangular essences, this reducing of lovely evenings, with all theirflamingo clouds and blue and silver to a white deal four-legged table(and it was a mark of the finest minds to do so), naturally one could notbe judged like an ordinary person.

Mr Bankes liked her for bidding him "think of his work." He had thoughtof it, often and often. Times without number, he had said, "Ramsay is oneof those men who do their best work before they are forty." He had made adefinite contribution to philosophy in one little book when he was onlyfive and twenty; what came after was more or less amplification,repetition. But the number of men who make a definite contribution toanything whatsoever is very small, he said, pausing by the pear tree, wellbrushed, scrupulously exact, exquisitel; judicial. Suddenly, as if themovement of his hand had released it, the load of her accumulatedimpressions of him tilted up, and down poured in a ponderous avalanche allshe felt about him. That was one sensation. Then up rose in a fume theessence of his being. That was another. She felt herself transfixedby the intensity of her perception; it was his severity; his goodness. Irespect you (she addressed silently him in person) in every atom; you arenot vain; you are entirely impersonal; you are finer than Mr Ramsay; youare the finest human being that I know; you have neither wife nor child(without any sexual feeling, she longed to cherish that loneliness), youlive for science (involuntarily, sections of potatoes rose before hereyes); praise would be an insult to you; generous, pure-hearted, heroicman! But simultaneously, she remembered how he had brought a valet allthe way up here; objected to dogs on chairs; would prose for hours (untilMr Ramsay slammed out of the room) about salt in vegetables and theiniquity of English cooks.

How then did it work out, all this? How did one judge people, think ofthem? How did one add up this and that and conclude that it was likingone felt or disliking? And to those words, what meaning attached, afterall? Standing now, apparently transfixed, by the pear tree, impressionspoured in upon her of those two men, and to follow her thought was likefollowing a voice which speaks too quickly to be taken down by one'spencil, and the voice was her own voice saying without promptingundeniable, everlasting, contradictory things, so that even thefissures and humps on the bark of the pear tree were irrevocablyfixed there for eternity. You have greatness, she continued, butMr Ramsay has none of it. He is petty, selfish, vain, egotistical; he isspoilt; he is a tyrant; he wears Mrs Ramsay to death; but he has what you have not; a fiery unworldliness; he knowsnothing about trifles; he loves dogs and his children. He has eight.Mr Bankes has none. Did he not come down in two coats the other nightand let Mrs Ramsay trim his hair into a pudding basin? All of thisdanced up and down, like a company of gnats, each separate but allmarvellously controlled in an invisible elastic net—danced up and down inLily's mind, in and about the branches of the pear tree, where still hungin effigy the scrubbed kitchen table, symbol of her profound respect forMr Ramsay's mind, until her thought which had spun quicker and quickerexploded of its own intensity; she felt released; a shot went off close athand, and there came, flying from its fragments, frightened, effusive,tumultuous, a flock of starlings.

"Jasper!" said Mr Bankes. They turned the way the starlings flew, overthe terrace. Following the scatter of swift-flying birds in the sky theystepped through the gap in the high hedge straight into Mr Ramsay, whoboomed tragically at them, "Some one had blundered!" His eyes, glazed with emotion, defiant with tragic intensity, met theirsfor a second, and trembled on the verge of recognition; but then, raisinghis hand, half-way to his face as if to avert, to brush off, in an agonyof peevish shame, their normal gaze, as if he begged them to withhold fora moment what he knew to be inevitable, as if he impressed upon them hisown child-like resentment of interruption, yet even in the moment ofdiscovery was not to be routed utterly, but was determined to hold fast tosomething of this delicious emotion, this impure rhapsody of which he wasashamed, but in which he revelled—he turned abruptly, slammed his privatedoor on them; and, Lily Briscoe and Mr Bankes, looking uneasily up intothe sky, observed that the flock of starlings which Jasper had routed withhis gun had settled on the tops of the elm trees.

- "And even if it isn't fine tomorrow," said Mrs Ramsay, raising her eyesto glance at William Bankes and Lily Briscoe as they passed, "it will beanother day. And now," she said, thinking that Lily's charm was herChinese eyes, aslant in her white, puckered little face, but it would takea clever man to see it, "and now stand up, and let me measure your leg,"for they might go to the Lighthouse after all, and she must see if thestocking did not need to be an inch or two longer in the leg.

Smiling, for it was an admirable idea, that had flashed upon her this verysecond—William and Lily should marry—she took the heather-mixturestocking, with its criss-cross of steel needles at the mouth of it, andmeasured it against James's leg."My dear, stand still," she said, for in his jealousy, not liking to serveas measuring block for the Lighthouse keeper's little boy, James fidgetedpurposely; and if he did that, how could she see, was it too long, was it too short? she asked.

She looked up—what demon possessed him, her youngest, her cherished?—andsaw the room, saw the chairs, thought them fearfully shabby. Theirentrails, as Andrew said the other day, were all over the floor; but thenwhat was the point, she asked, of buying good chairs to let them spoil uphere all through the winter when the house, with only one old woman to seeto it, positively dripped with wet? Never mind, the rent was preciselytwopence half-penny; the children loved it; it did her husband good to bethree thousand, or if she must be accurate, three hundred miles from hislibraries and his lectures and his disciples; and there was room forvisitors. Mats, camp beds, crazy ghosts of chairs and tables whose Londonlife of service was done—they did well enough here; and a photograph ortwo, and books.

Books, she thought, grew of themselves. She never hadtime to read them. Alas! even the books that had been given her andinscribed by the hand of the poet himself: "For her whose wishes must beobeyed"... "The happier Helen of our days"... disgraceful to say, shehad never read them. And Croom on the Mind and Bates on the SavageCustoms of Polynesia ("My dear, stand still," she said)—neither of thosecould one send to the Lighthouse. At a certain moment, she supposed, thehouse would become so shabby that something must be done. If they couldbe taught to wipe their feet and not bring the beach in with them—thatwould be something. Crabs, she had to allow, if Andrew really wished todissect them, or if Jasper believed that one could make soup from seaweed,one could not prevent it; or Rose's objects—shells, reeds, stones; forthey were gifted, her children, but all in quite different ways. And theresult of it was, she sighed, taking in the whole room from floor toceiling, as she held the stocking against James's leg, that things gotshabbier and got shabbier summer after summer. The mat was fading; thewallpaper was flapping. You couldn't tell any more that those were roseson it. Still, if every door in a house is left perpetually open, and nolockmaker in the whole of Scotland can mend a bolt, things must spoil.What was the use of flinging a green Cashemere shawl over the edge ofa picture frame? In two weeks it would be the colour of pea soup.But it was the doors that annoyed her; every door was left open.She listened.

The drawing-room door was open; the hall door was open;it sounded as if the bedroom doors were open; and certainly the windowon the landing was open, for that she had opened herself. That windowsshould be open, and doors shut—simple as it was, could none of themremember it? She would go into the maids' bedrooms at night and findthem sealed like ovens, except for Marie's, the Swiss girl, whowould rather go without a bath than without fresh air, but thenat home, she had said, "the mountains are so beautiful." She had saidthat last night looking out of the window with tears in her eyes."The mountains are so beautiful."

Her father was dying there,Mrs Ramsay knew. He was leaving them fatherless. Scolding anddemonstrating (how to make a bed, how to open a window, with hands thatshut and spread like a Frenchwoman's) all had folded itself quietly abouther, when the girl spoke, as, after a flight through the sunshine thewings of a bird fold themselves quietly and the blue of its plumagechanges from bright steel to soft purple. She had stood there silent forthere was nothing to be said. He had cancer of the throat. At therecolection—how she had stood there, how the girl had said, "At home themountains are so beautiful," and there was no hope, no hope whatever, shehad a spasm of irritation, and speaking sharply, said to James:

"Stand still. Don't be tiresome," so that he knew instantly that herseverity was real, and straightened his leg and she measured it.The stocking was too short by half an inch at least, making allowance forthe fact that Sorley's little boy would be less well grown than James.

"It's too short," she said, "ever so much too short."

Never did anybody look so sad. Bitter and black, half-way down, in thedarkness, in the shaft which ran from the sunlight to the depths, perhapsa tear formed; a tear fell; the waters swayed this way and that, receivedit, and were at rest. Never did anybody look so sad.

But was it nothing but looks, people said? What was there behind it—herbeauty and splendour? Had he blown his brains out, they asked, had hedied the week before they were married—some other, earlier lover, of whomrumours reached one? Or was there nothing? nothing but anincomparablebeauty which she lived behind, and could do nothing to disturb? Foreasily though she might have said at some moment of intimacy when storiesof great passion, of love foiled, of ambition thwarted came her way howshe too had known or felt or been through it herself, she never spoke.She was silent always. She knew then—she knew without having learnt.Her simplicity fathomed what clever people falsified. Her singleness ofmind made her drop plumb like a stone, alight exact as a bird, gave her,naturally, this swoop and fall of the spirit upon truth which delighted,eased, sustained—falsely perhaps. ("Nature has but little clay," said Mr Bankes once, much moved by hervoice on the telephone, though she was only telling him a fact about atrain, "like that of which she moulded you." He saw her at the end of theline, Greek, blue-eyed, straight-nosed. How incongruous it seemed to betelephoning to a woman like that. The Graces assembling seemed to havejoined hands in meadows of asphodel to compose that face. Yes, he wouldcatch the 10:30 at Euston.

"But she's no more aware of her beauty than a child," said Mr Bankes,replacing the receiver and crossing the room to see what progress theworkmen were making with an hotel which they were building at the back ofhis house. And he thought of Mrs Ramsay as he looked at that stir amongthe unfinished walls. For always, he thought, there was some thing incongruous to be worked into the harmony of her face. She clapped adeer-stalker's hat on her head; she ran across the lawn in galoshes tosnatch a child from mischief. So that if it was her beauty merely thatone thought of, one must remember the quivering thing, the living thing(they were carrying bricks up a little plank as he watched them), and workit into the picture;

or if one thought of her simply as a woman, one mustendow her with some freak of idiosyncrasy—she did not like admiration—orsuppose some latent desire to doff her royalty of form as if her beautybored her and all that men say of beauty, and she wanted only to be likeother people, insignificant. He did not know. He did not know. He mustgo to his work.)Knitting her reddish-brown hairy stocking, with her head outlined absurdlyby the gilt frame, the green shawl which she had tossed over the edge ofthe frame, and the authenticated masterpiece by Michael Angelo,Mrs Ramsay smoothed out what had been harsh in her manner a momentbefore, raised his head, and kissed her little boy on the forehead."Let us find another picture to cut out," she said.

But what had happened?

Some one had blundered.

Starting from her musing she gave meaning to words which she had held meaningless in her mind for a long stretch of time. "Some one hadblundered"—Fixing her short-sighted eyes upon her husband, who was nowbearing down upon her, she gazed steadily until his closeness revealed toher (the jingle mated itself in her head) that something had happened,some one had blundered. But she could not for the life of her think what.

He shivered; he quivered. All his vanity, all his satisfaction in his ownsplendour, riding fell as a thunderbolt, fierce as a hawk at the head ofhis men through the valley of death, had been shattered, destroyed.Stormed at by shot and shell, boldly we rode and well, flashed through thevalley of death, volleyed and thundered—straight into Lily Briscoe andWilliam Bankes. He quivered; he shivered.

Not for the world would she have spoken to him, realising, from thefamiliar signs, his eyes averted, and some curious gathering togetherof his person, as if he wrapped himself about and needed privacy intowhich to regain his equilibrium, that he was outraged and anguished. Shestroked James's head; she transferred to him what she felt for herhusband, and, as she watched him chalk yellow the white dress shirt of agentleman in the Army and Navy Stores catalogue, thought what a delight itwould be to her should he turn out a great artist; and why should he not?He had a splendid forehead. Then, looking up, as her husband passed heronce more, she was relieved to find that the ruin was veiled; domesticitytriumphed; custom crooned its soothing rhythm, so that when stoppingdeliberately, as his turn came round again, at the window he bentquizzically and whimsically to tickle James's bare calf with a sprig ofsomething, she twitted him for having dispatched "that poor young man,"Charles Tansley. Tansley had had to go in and write his dissertation,he said.

"James will have to write HIS dissertation one of these days," he added ironically, flicking his sprig.

Hating his father, James brushed away the tickling spray with which in a manner peculiar to him, compound of severity and humour, he teased his youngest son's bare leg.

She was trying to get these tiresome stockings finished to send to Sorley's little boy tomorrow, said Mrs Ramsay.

There wasn't the slightest possible chance that they could go to the Lighthouse tomorrow, Mr Ramsay snapped out irascibly.

How did he know? she asked. The wind often changed.

The extraordinary irrationality of her remark, the folly of women's minds enraged him. He had ridden through the valley of death, been shattered and shivered; and now, she flew in the face of facts, made his children hope what was utterly out of the question, in effect, told lies. He stamped his foot on the stone step. "Damn you," he said. But what had she said? Simply that it might be fine tomorrow. So it might.

Not with the barometer falling and the wind due west.

To pursue truth with such astonishing lack of consideration for other people's feelings, to rendthe thin veils of civilization so wantonly, so brutally, was to her so horrible an outrage of human decency that, without replying, dazed and blinded, she bent her head as if to let the pelt of jagged hail, the drench of dirty water, bespatter her unrebuked. There was nothing to be said.

He stood by her in silence. Very humbly, at length, he

said that he would step over and ask the Coastguards if she liked. There was nobody whom she reverenced as she reverenced him. She was quite ready to take his word for it, she said. Only then they need not cut sandwiches—that was all. They came to her, naturally, since she was a woman, all day long with this and that; one wanting this, another that; the children were growing up; she often felt she was nothing but a sponge sopped full of human emotions. Then he said, Damn you. He said, It must rain. He said, It won't rain; and instantly a Heaven of security opened before her. There was nobody she reverenced more. She was not good enough to tie his shoe strings, she felt.

Already ashamed of that petulance, of that gesticulation of the hands when

charging at the head of his troops, Mr Ramsay rather sheepishly proddedhis son's bare legs once more, and then, as if he had her leave for it,with a movement which oddly reminded his wife of the great sea lion at theZoo tumbling backwards after swallowing his fish and walloping off so thatthe water in the tank washes from side to side, he dived into the eveningair which, already thinner, was taking the substance from leaves andhedges but, as if in return, restoring to roses and pinks a lustre whichthey had not had by day.

"Some one had blundered," he said again, striding off, up and down the terrace.

But how extraordinarily his note had changed! It was like the cuckoo;"in June he gets out of tune"; as if he were trying over, tentativelyseeking, some phrase for a new mood, and having only this at hand, usedit, cracked though it was. But it sounded ridiculous—"Some one hadblundered"—said like that, almost as a question, without any conviction,melodiously. Mrs Ramsay could not help smiling, and soon, sure enough,walking up and down, he hummed it, dropped it, fell silent.

He was safe, he was restored to his privacy. He stopped to light hispipe, looked once at his wife and son in the window, and as one raisesone's eyes from a page in an express train and sees a farm, a tree, acluster of cottages as an illustration, a confirmation of something on theprinted page to which one returns, fortified, and satisfied, so withouthis distinguishing either his son or his wife, the sight of them fortifiedhim and satisfied him and consecrated his effort to arrive at a perfectlyclear understanding of the problem which now engaged the energies of hissplendid mind.

It was a splendid mind. For if thought is like the keyboard of a piano,divided into so many notes, or like the alphabet is ranged in twenty-sixletters all in order, then his splendid mind had no sort of difficultyin running over those letters one by one, firmly and accurately, untilit had reached, say, the letter Q. He reached Q. Very few people inthe whole of England ever reach Q. Here, stopping for one momentby the stone urn which held the geraniums, he saw, but now far, faraway, like children picking up shells, divinely innocent and occupied withlittle trifles at their feet and somehow entirely defenceless against adoom which he perceived, his wife and son, together, in the window. Theyneeded his protection; he gave it them. But after Q? What comes next?After Q there are a number of letters the last of which is scarcelyvisible to mortal eyes, but glimmers red in the distance. Z is onlyreached once by one man in a generation. Still, if he could reach R itwould be something. Here at least was Q. He dug his heels in at Q. Q hewas sure of. Q he could demonstrate. If Q then is Q—R—. Here heknocked his pipe out, with two or three resonant taps on the handle of theurn, and proceeded. "Then R..." He braced himself. He clenchedhimself.

Qualities that would have saved a ship's company exposed on a broilingsea with six biscuits and a flask of water—endurance and justice,foresight, devotion, skill, came to his help. R is then—what is R?A shutter, like the leathern eyelid of a lizard, flickered over theintensity of his gaze and obscured the letter R. In that flash ofdarkness he heard people saying—he was a failure—that R was beyond him.He would never reach R. On to R, once more. R—Qualities that in a desolate expedition across the icy solitudes of thePolar region would have made him the leader, the guide, the counsellor,whose temper, neither sanguine nor despondent, surveys with equanimitywhat is to be and faces it, came to his help again. R...

The lizard's eye flickered once more. The veins on his forehead bulged.The geranium in the urn became startlingly visible and, displayed amongits leaves, he could see, without wishing it, that old, that obviousdistinction between the two classes of men; on the one hand the steadygoers of superhuman strength who, plodding and persevering, repeat thewhole alphabet in order, twenty-six letters in all, from start to finish;on the other the gifted, the inspired who, miraculously, lump all theletters together in one flash—the way of genius. He had not genius; helaid no claim to that: but he had, or might have had, the power to repeatevery letter of the alphabet from A to Z accurately in order. Meanwhile,he stuck at Q. On, then, on to R.

Feelings that would not have disgraced a leader who, now that the snow hasbegun to fall and the mountain top is covered in mist, knows that he mustlay himself down and die before morning comes, stole upon him, paling thecolour of his eyes, giving him, even in the two minutes of his turn onthe terrace, the bleached look of withered old age. Yet he would not dielying down; he would find some crag of rock, and there, his eyes fixedon the storm, trying to the end to pierce the darkness, he would diestanding. He would never reach R.

He stood stock-still, by the urn, with the geranium flowing over it. Howmany men in a thousand million, he asked himself, reach Z after all?Surely the leader of a forlorn hope may ask himself that, and answer,without treachery to the expedition behind him, "One perhaps." One in ageneration. Is he to be blamed then if he is not that one? provided hehas toiled honestly, given to the best of his power, and till he has nomore left to give? And his fame lasts how long? It is permissible evenfor a dying hero to think before he dies how men will speak of himhereafter. His fame lasts perhaps two thousand years. And what are twothousand years? (asked Mr Ramsay ironically, staring at the hedge).What, indeed, if you look from a mountain top down the long wastes of theages? The very stone one kicks with one's boot will outlast

Shakespeare.His own little light would shine, not very brightly, for a year or two,and would then be merged in some bigger light, and that in a bigger still.(He looked into the hedge, into the intricacy of the twigs.) Who thencould blame the leader of that forlorn party which after all has climbedhigh enough to see the waste of the years and the perishing of the stars,if before death stiffens his limbs beyond the power of movement he does alittle consciously raise his numbed fingers to his brow, and square hisshoulders, so that when the search party comes they will find him dead athis post, the fine figure of a soldier? Mr Ramsay squared his shouldersand stood very upright by the urn.

Who shall blame him, if, so standing for a moment he dwells upon fame,upon search parties, upon cairns raised by grateful followers over hisbones? Finally, who shall blame the leader of the doomed expedition, if,having adventured to the uttermost, and used his strength wholly to thelast ounce and fallen asleep not much caring if he wakes or not, he nowperceives by some pricking in his toes that he lives, and does not on thewhole object to live, but requires sympathy, and whisky, and some one totell the story of his suffering to at once? Who shall blame him? Whowill not secretly rejoice when the hero puts his armour off, and halts bythe window and gazes at his wife and son, who, very distant at first,gradually come closer and closer, till lips and book and head are clearlybefore him, though still lovely and unfamiliar from the intensity of hisisolation and the waste of ages and the perishing of the stars, andfinally putting his pipe in his pocket and bending his magnificent headbefore her—who will blame him if he does homage to the beauty of theworld?

- But his son hated him. He hated him for coming up to them, for stopping and looking down on them; he hated him for interrupting them; he hated him for the exaltation and sublimity of his gestures; for the magnificence of his head; for his exactingness and egotism (for there he stood, commanding them to attend to him) but most of all he hated the twang and twitter of his father's emotion which, vibrating round them, disturbed the perfect simplicity and good sense of his relations with his mother. By looking fixedly at the page, he hoped to make him move on; by pointing his finger at a word, he hoped to recall his mother's attention, which, he knew angrily, wavered instantly his father stopped. But, no. Nothing would make Mr Ramsay move on. There he stood, demanding sympathy.

Mrs Ramsay, who had been sitting loosely, folding her son in her arm,braced herself, and, half turning, seemed to raise herself with an effort,and at once to pour erect into the air a rain of energy, a column ofspray, looking at the same time animated and alive as if all her energieswere being fused into force, burning and illuminating (quietly though shesat, taking up her stocking again), and into this delicious fecundity,this fountain and spray of life, the fatal sterility of the male plungeditself, like a beak of brass, barren and bare. He wanted sympathy. Hewas a failure, he said. Mrs Ramsay flashed her needles. Mr Ramsayrepeated, never taking his eyes from her face, that he was a failure.She blew the words back at him. "Charles Tansley..." she said. But hemust have more than that. It was sympathy he wanted, to be assured of hisgenius, first of all, and then to be taken within the circle of life,warmed and soothed, to have his senses restored to him, his barrennessmade furtile, and all the rooms of the house made full of life—thedrawing-room; behind the drawing-room the kitchen; above the kitchen thebedrooms; and beyond them the nurseries; they must be furnished, they mustbe filled with life.

Charles Tansley thought him the greatest metaphysician of the time, shesaid. But he must have more than that. He must have sympathy. He mustbe assured that he too lived in the heart of life; was needed; not onlyhere, but all over the world. Flashing her needles, confident, upright,she created drawing-room and kitchen, set them all aglow; bade him takehis ease there, go in and out, enjoy himself. She laughed, she knitted.Standing between her knees, very stiff, James felt all her strengthflaring up to be drunk and quenched by the beak of brass, the aridscimitar of the male, which smote mercilessly, again and again,demanding sympathy. He was a failure, he repeated. Well, look then, feel then. Flashing herneedles, glancing round about her, out of the window, into the room, atJames himself, she assured him, beyond a shadow of a doubt, by her laugh,her poise, her competence (as a nurse carrying a light across a dark roomassures a fractious child), that it was real; the house was full; thegarden blowing. If he put implicit faith in her, nothing should hurt him;however deep he buried himself or climed high, not for a second should hefind himself without her. So boasting of her capacity to surround andprotect, there was scarcely a shell of herself left for her to knowherself by; all was so lavished and spent; and James, as he stood stiffbetween her knees, felt her rise in a rosy-flowered fruit tree laid withleaves and dancing boughs into which the beak of brass, the arid scimitarof his father, the egotistical man, plunged and smote, demanding sympathy.

Filled with her words, like a child who drops off satisfied, he said, atlast, looking at her with humble gratitude, restored, renewed, that hewould take a turn; he would watch the children playing cricket. He went.

Immediately, Mrs Ramsey seemed to fold herself together, one petal closedin another, and the whole fabric fell in exhaustion upon itself, so thatshe had only strength enough to move her finger, in exquisite abandonmentto exhaustion, across the page of Grimm's fairy story, while therethrobbed through her, like a pulse in a spring which has expanded to itsfull width and now gently ceases to beat, the rapture of successfulcreation.

Every throb of this pulse seemed, as he walked away, to enclose her andher husband, and to give to each that solace which two different notes,one high, one low, struck together, seem to give each other as theycombine. Yet as the resonance died, and she turned to the Fairy Taleagain, Mrs Ramsey felt not only exhausted in body (afterwards, not at thetime, she always felt this) but also there tinged her physical fatiguesome faintly disagreeable sensation with another origin. Not that, asshe read aloud the story of the Fisherman's Wife, she knew precisely whatit came from; nor did she let herself put into words her dissatisfactionwhen she realized, at the turn of the page when she stopped and hearddully, ominously, a wave fall, how it came from this: she did not like,even for a second, to feel finer than her husband; and further, could notbear not being entirely sure, when she spoke to him, of the truth of whatshe said. Universities and people wanting him, lectures and books andtheir being of the highest importance—all that she did not doubt for amoment; but it was their relation, and his coming to her like that,openly, so that any one could see, that discomposed her; for then peoplesaid he depended on her, when they must know that of the two he wasinfinitely the more important, and what she gave the world, in comparisonwith what he gave, negligable. But then again, it was the other thingtoo—not being able to tell him the truth, being afraid, for instance,about the greenhouse roof and the expense it would be, fifty poundsperhaps to mend it; and then about his books, to be afraid that he mightguess, what she a little suspected, that his last book was not quite hisbest book (she gathered that from William Bankes); and then to hide smalldaily things, and the children seeing it, and the burden it laid onthem—all this diminished the entire joy, the pure joy, of the two notessounding together, and let the sound die on her ear now with a dismalflatness.

A shadow was on the page; she looked up. It was Augustus Carmichaelshuffling past, precisely now, at the very moment when it was painful tobe reminded of the inadequacy of human relationships, that the mostperfect was flawed, and could not bear the examination which, loving herhusband, with her instinct for truth, she turned upon it; when it waspainful to feel herself convicted of unworthiness, and impeded in herproper function by these lies, these exaggerations,—it was at thismoment when she was fretted thus ignobly in the wake of her exaltation,that Mr Carmichael shuffled past, in his yellow slippers, and some demonin her made it necessary for her to call out, as he passed,

"Going indoors Mr Carmichael?"

• He said nothing. He took opium. The children said he had stained hisbeard yellow with it. Perhaps.

What was obvious to her was that the poorman was unhappy, came to them every year as an escape; and yet every yearshe felt the same thing; he did not trust her. She said, "I am going tothe town. Shall I get you stamps, paper, tobacco?" and she felt himwince. He did not trust her. It was his wife's doing. She rememberedthat iniquity of his wife's towards him, which had made her turn to steeland adamant there, in the horrible little room in St John's Wood, whenwith her own eyes she had seen that odious woman turn him out of thehouse. He was unkempt; he dropped things on his coat; he had thetiresomeness of an old man with nothing in the world to do; and she turnedhim out of the room. She said, in her odious way, "Now, Mrs Ramsay and Iwant to have a little talk together," and Mrs Ramsay could see, as ifbefore her eyes, the innumerable miseries of his life. Had he moneyenough to buy tobacco? Did he have to ask her for it? half a crown?eighteenpence? Oh, she could not bear to think of the little indignitiesshe made him suffer. And always now (why, she could not guess, exceptthat it came probably from that woman somehow) he shrank from her. Henever told her anything. But what more could she have done? There was asunny room given up to him. The children were good to him. Never did sheshow a sign of not wanting him. She went out of her way indeed to befriendly. Do you want stamps, do you want tobacco? Here's a book youmight like and so on. And after all—after all (here insensibly she drewherself together, physically, the sense of her own beauty becoming, as itdid so seldom, present to her) after all, she had not generally anydifficulty in making people like her; for instance, George Manning; MrWallace; famous as they were, they would come to her of an evening,quietly, and talk alone over her fire. She bore about with her, she couldnot help knowing it, the torch of her beauty; she carried it erect intoany room that she entered; and after all, veil it as she might, and shrinkfrom the monotony of bearing that it imposed on her, her beauty wasapparent. She had been admired. She had been loved. She had enteredrooms where mourners sat. Tears had flown in her presence. Men, andwomen too, letting go to the multiplicity of things, had allowedthemselves with her the relief of simplicity. It injured her that heshould shrink. It hurt her. And yet not cleanly, not rightly. That waswhat she minded, coming as it did on top of her discontent with herhusband; the sense she had now when Mr Carmichael shuffled past, justnodding to her question, with a book beneath his arm, in his yellowslippers, that she was suspected; and that all this desire of hers togive, to help, was vanity. For her own self-satisfaction was it that shewished so instinctively to help, to give, that people might say of her,"O Mrs Ramsay! dear Mrs Ramsay... Mrs Ramsay, of course!" and need herand send for her and admire her? Was it not secretly this that shewanted, and therefore when Mr Carmichael shrank away from her, as he didat this moment, making off to some corner where he did acrosticsendlessly, she did not feel merely snubbed back in her instinct, but madeaware of the pettiness of some part of her, and of human relations, howflawed they are, how despicable, how self-seeking, at their best. Shabbyand worn out, and not presumably (her cheeks were hollow, her hair waswhite) any longer a sight that filled the eyes with joy, she had betterdevote her mind to the story of the Fisherman and his Wife and so pacifythat bundle of sensitiveness (none of her children was as sensitive as hewas), her son James."The man's heart grew heavy," she read aloud, "and he would not go. Hesaid to himself, 'It is not right,' and yet he went. And when he came tothe sea the water was quite purple and dark blue, and grey and thick, andno longer so green and yellow, but it was still quiet. And he stood thereand said—"

Mrs Ramsay could have wished that her husband had not chosen that momentto stop. Why had he not gone as he said to watch the children playingcricket? But he did not speak; he looked; he nodded; he approved; he wenton.

He slipped, seeing before him that hedge which had over and overagain rounded some pause, signified some conclusion, seeing his wife andchild, seeing again the urns with the trailing of red geraniums which hadso often decorated processes of thought, and bore, written up among theirleaves, as if they were scraps of paper on which one scribbles notes inthe rush of reading—he slipped, seeing all this, smoothly intospeculation suggested by an article in THE TIMES about the number ofAmericans who visit Shakespeare's house every year. If Shakespearehad never existed, he asked, would the world have differed much from whatit is today? Does the progress of civilization depend upon great men? Isthe lot of the average human being better now than in the time of thePharaohs? Is the lot of the average human being, however, he askedhimself, the criterion by which we judge the measure of civilization?Possibly not. Possibly the greatest good requires the existence of aslave class. The liftman in the Tube is an eternal necessity.

Thethought was distasteful to him. He tossed his head. To avoid it, hewould find some way of snubbing the predominance of the arts. He wouldargue that the world exists for the average human being; that the arts aremerely a decoration imposed on the top of human life; they do not expressit. Nor is Shakespeare necessary to it. Not knowing precisely why it wasthat he wanted to disparage Shakespeare and come to the rescue of the manwho stands eternally in the door of the lift, he picked a leaf sharplyfrom the hedge. All this would have to be dished up for the young men atCardiff next month, he thought; here, on his terrace, he was merelyforaging and picnicking (he threw away the leaf that he had picked sopeevishly) like a man who reaches from his horse to pick a bunch of roses,or stuffs his pockets with nuts as he ambles at his ease through the lanesand fields of a country known to him from boyhood. It was all familiar;this turning, that stile, that cut across the fields. Hours he wouldspend thus, with his pipe, of an evening, thinking up and down and in andout of the old familiar lanes and commons, which were all stuck about withthe history of that campaign there, the life of this statesman here, withpoems and with anecdotes, with figures too, this thinker, that soldier;all very brisk and clear; but at length the lane, the field, the common,the fruitful nut-tree and the flowering hedge led him on to that furtherturn of the road where he dismounted always, tied his horse to a tree,and proceeded on foot alone. He reached the edge of the lawn and lookedout on the bay beneath.

It was his fate, his peculiarity, whether he wished it or not, to come outthus on a spit of land which the sea is slowly eating away, and there tostand, like a desolate sea-bird, alone. It was his power, his gift,suddenly to shed all superfluities, to shrink and diminish so that helooked barer and felt sparer, even physically, yet lost none of hisintensity of mind, and so to stand on his little ledge facing the dark ofhuman ignorance, how we know nothing and the sea eats away the ground westand on—that was his fate, his gift.

But having thrown away, when hedismounted, all gestures and fripperies, all trophies of nuts and roses,and shrunk so that not only fame but even his own name was forgottenby him, kept even in that desolation a vigilance which spared nophantom and luxuriated in no vision, and it was in this guise thathe inspired in William Bankes and in Charles Tansleyand in his wife now, when she looked up and saw himstanding at the edge of the lawn, profoundly, reverence, and pity, andgratitude too, as a stake driven into the bed of a channel upon which thegulls perch and the waves beat inspires in merry boat-loads a feeling ofgratitude for the duty it is taking upon itself of marking the channel outthere in the floods alone.

"But the father of eight children has no choice." Muttering half aloud,so he broke off, turned, sighed, raised his eyes, sought the figure of hiswife reading stories to his little boy, filled his pipe. He turned fromthe sight of human ignorance and human fate and the sea eating the groundwe stand on, which, had he been able to contemplate it fixedly might haveled to something; and found consolation in trifles so slight compared withthe august theme just now before him that he was disposed to slur thatcomfort over, to deprecate it, as if to be caught happy in a world ofmisery was for an honest man the most despicable of crimes.

It was true;he was for the most part happy; he had his wife; he had his children; hehad promised in six weeks' time to talk "some nonsense" to the young menof Cardiff about Locke, Hume, Berkeley, and the causes of the French Revolution. But this and his pleasure in it, his glory in the phrases hemade, in the ardour of youth, in his wife's beauty, in the tributes thatreached him from Swansea, Cardiff, Exeter, Southampton, Kidderminster, Oxford, Cambridge—all had to be deprecated and concealed under the phrase"talking nonsense," because, in effect, he had not done the thing he mighthave done. It was a disguise; it was the refuge of a man afraid to ownhis own feelings, who could not say, This is what I like—this is what Iam; and rather pitiable and distasteful to William Bankes and Lily Briscoe,who wondered why such concealments should be necessary; why he neededalways praise; why so brave a man in thought should be so timid in life;how strangely he was venerable and laughable at one and the same time.

Teaching and preaching is beyond human power, Lily suspected. If you are exalted you must somehow come acropper. Mrs Ramsay gave him what he asked too easily. Then the changemust be so upsetting, Lily said. He comes in from his books and finds usall playing games and talking nonsense. Imagine what a change from thethings he thinks about, she said.He was bearing down upon them. Now he stopped dead and stood looking insilence at the sea. Now he had turned away again.

- Yes, Mr Bankes said, watching him go. It was a thousand pities. (Lilyhad said something about his frightening her—he changed from one mood toanother so suddenly.) Yes, said Mr Bankes, it was a thousand pities thatRamsay could not behave a little more like other people. (For he likedLily Briscoe; he could discuss Ramsay with her quite openly.) It was forthat reason, he said, that the young don't read Carlyle. A crusty oldgrumbler who lost his temper if the porridge was cold, why should hepreach to us? was what Mr Bankes understood that young people saidnowadays.

It was a thousand pities if you thought, as he did, thatCarlyle was one of the great teachers of mankind. Lily was ashamed to saythat she had not read Carlyle since she was at school. But in her opiniononе liked Mr Ramsay all the better for thinking that if his little fingerached the whole world must come to an end. It was not THAT she minded.For who could be deceived by him? He asked you quite openly to flatterhim, to admire him, his little dodges deceived nobody. What she dislikedwas his narrowness, his blindness, she said, looking after him."A bit of a hypocrite?" Mr Bankes suggested, looking too at Mr Ramsay'sback, for was he not thinking of his fricndship, and of Cam refusing togive him a flower, and of all those boys and girls, and his own house,full of comfort, but, since his wife's death, quiet rather? Of course,he had his work... All the same, he rather wished Lily to agree thatRamsay was, as he said, "a bit of a hypocrite."

Lily Briscoe went on putting away her brushes, looking up, looking down.Looking up, there he was—Mr Ramsay—advancing towards them, swinging,careless, oblivious, remote. A bit of a hypocrite? she repeated. Oh,no—the most sincere of men, the truest, the best; but,looking down, she thought, he is absorbed in himself, he is tyrannical,he is unjust; and kept looking down, purposely, for only so could she keepsteady, staying with the Ramsays. Directly one looked up and saw them,what she called "being in love" flooded them. They became part of thatunreal but penetrating and exciting universe which is the world seenthrough the eyes of love. The sky stuck to them; the birds sang throughthem.

And, what was even more exciting, she felt, too, as she saw MrRamsay bearing down and retreating, and Mrs Ramsay sitting with James inthe window and the cloud moving and the tree bending, how life, from beingmade up of little separate incidents which one lived one by one, becamecurled and whole like a wave which bore one up and threw one down withit, there, with a dash on the beach. Mr Bankes expected her to answer. And she was about to say something criticizing Mrs Ramsay, how she was alarming, too, in her way, high-handed, or words to that effect, when Mr Bankes made it entirely unnecessary for her to speak by his rapture.

For such it was considering his age, turned sixty, and his cleanliness and his impersonality, and the white scientific coat which seemed to clothe him. For him to gaze as Lily saw him gazing at Mrs Ramsay was a rapture, equivalent, Lily felt, to the loves of dozens of young men (and perhaps Mrs Ramsay had never excited the loves of dozens of young men). It was love, she thought, pretending to move her canvas, distilled and filtered; love that never attempted to clutch its object; but, like the love which mathematicians bear their symbols, or poets their phrases, was meant to be spread over the world and become part of the human gain.

So it was indeed. The world by all means should have shared it, could Mr Bankes have said why that woman pleased him so; why the sight of her reading a fairy tale to her boy had upon him precisely the same effect as the solution of a scientific problem, so that he rested in contemplation of it, and felt, as he felt when he had proved something absolute about the digestive system of plants, that barbarity was tamed, the reign of chaos subdued.

Such a rapture—for by what other name could one call it?—made LilyBriscoe forget entirely what she had been about to say. It was nothing ofimportance; something about Mrs Ramsay. It paled beside this "rapture,"this silent stare, for which she felt intense gratitude; for nothing sosolaced her, eased her of the perplexity of life, and miraculously raisedits burdens, as this sublime power, this heavenly gift, and one would nomore disturb it, while it lasted, than break up the shaft of sunlight,lying level across the floor.

That people should love like this, that Mr Bankes should feel this forMrs Ramsey was helpful, was exalting. Shewiped one brush after another upon a piece of old rag, menially, onpurpose. She took shelter from the reverence which covered all women; shefelt herself praised. Let him gaze; she would steal a look at herpicture.

She could have wept. It was bad, it was bad, it was infinitely bad! Shecould have done it differently of course; the colour could have beenthinned and faded; the shapes etherealised; that was how Paunceforte wouldhave seen it. But then she did not see it like that. She saw the colourburning on a framework of steel; the light of a butterfly's wing lyingupon the arches of a cathedral. Of all that only a few random marksscrawled upon the canvas remained. And it would never be seen; never behung even, and there was Mr Tansley whispering in her ear, "Women can'tpaint, women can't write..." She now remembered what she had been going to say about Mrs Ramsay. Shedid not know how she would have put it; but it would have been somethingcritical.

She had been annoyed the other night by some highhandedness.Looking along the level of Mr Bankes's glance at her, she thought that nowoman could worship another woman in the way he worshipped; they couldonly seek shelter under the shade which Mr Bankes extended over them both.Looking along his beam she added to it her different ray, thinking thatshe was unquestionably the loveliest of people; thebest perhaps; but also, different too from the perfect shape which one sawthere. But why different, and how different? she asked herself, scrapingher palette of all those mounds of blue and green which seemed to her likeclods with no life in them now, yet she vowed, she would inspire them,force them to move, flow, do her bidding tomorrow. How did she differ?What was the spirit in her, the essential thing, by which, had you found acrumpled glove in the corner of a sofa, you would have known it, from itstwisted finger, hers indisputably? She was like a bird for speed, anarrow for directness. She was willful; she was commanding (of course,Lily reminded herself, I am thinking of her relations with women, and I ammuch younger, an insignificant person, living off the Brompton Road).

Sheopened bedroom windows. She shut doors. (So she tried to start the tuneof Mrs Ramsay in her head.) Arriving late at night, with a light tap onone's bedroom door, wrapped in an old fur coat (for the setting of herbeauty was always that—hasty, but apt), she would enact again whatever itmight be—Charles Tansley losing his umbrella; Mr Carmichael snuffling andsniffing; Mr Bankes saying, "The vegetable salts are lost." All this shewould adroitly shape; even maliciously twist; and, moving over to thewindow, in pretence that she must go,—it was dawn, she could see the sunrising,—half turn back, more intimately, but still always laughing,insist that she must, Minta must, they all must marry, since in the wholeworld whatever laurels might be tossed to her (but Mrs Ramsay cared not afig for her painting), or triumphs won by her (probably Mrs Ramsay hadhad her share of those), and here she saddened, darkened, and came back toher chair, there could be no disputing this: an unmarried woman (shelightly took her hand for a moment), an unmarried woman has missed thebest of life. The house seemed full of children sleeping and Mrs Ramsaylistening; shaded lights and regular breathing.

Oh, but, Lily would say, there was her father; her home; even, had shedared to say it, her painting. But all this seemed so little, sovirginal, against the other. Yet, as the night wore on, and white lightsparted the curtains, and even now and then some bird chirped in thegarden, gathering a desperate courage she would urge her own exemptionfrom the universal law; plead for it; she liked to be alone; she liked tobe herself; she was not made for that; and so have to meet a serious starefrom eyes of unparalleled depth, and confront Mrs Ramsay's simplecertainty that her dear Lily, her littleBrisk, was a fool. Then, she remembered, she had laid her head on MrsRamsay's lap and laughed and laughed and laughed, laughed almosthysterically at the thought of Mrs Ramsay presiding with immutable calmover destinies which she completely failed to understand. There she sat,simple, serious. She had recovered her sense of her now—this was theglove's twisted finger. But into what sanctuary had one penetrated?Lily Briscoe had looked up at last, and there was Mrs Ramsay, unwittingentirely what had caused her laughter, still presiding, but now with everytrace of wilfulness abolished, and in its stead, something clear as thespace which the clouds at last uncover—the little space of sky whichsleeps beside the moon. Was it wisdom?

Was it knowledge? Was it, once more, the deceptiveness ofbeauty, so that all one's perceptions, half way to truth, were tangled ina golden mesh? or did she lock up within her some secret which certainlyLily Briscoe believed people must have for the world to go on at all?Every one could not be as helter skelter, hand to mouth as she was. Butif they knew, could they tell one what they knew? Sitting on the floorwith her arms round Mrs Ramsay's knees, close as she could get, smilingto think that Mrs Ramsay would never know the reason of that pressure, sheimagined how in the chambers of the mind and heart of the woman who was,physically, touching her, were stood, like the treasures in the tombs ofkings, tablets bearing sacred inscriptions, which if one could spell themout, would teach one everything, but they would never be offered openly,never made public. What art was there, known to love or cunning, by whichone pressed through into those secret chambers? What device for becoming,like waters poured into one jar, inextricably the same, one with theobject one adored? Could the body achieve, or the mind, subtly minglingin the intricate passages of the brain? or the heart? Could loving,as people called it, make her and Mrs Ramsay one? for it was not knowledgebut unity that she desired, not inscriptions on tablets, nothing thatcould be written in any language known to men, but intimacy itself, whichis knowledge, she had thought, leaning her head on Mrs Ramsay's knee.

Nothing happened. Nothing! Nothing! as she leant her head againstMrs Ramsay's knee. And yet, she knew knowledge and wisdom were stored upin Mrs Ramsay's heart. How, then, she had asked herself, did one know onething or another thing about people, sealed as they were? Only like abee, drawn by some sweetness or sharpness in the air intangible to touchor taste, one haunted the dome-shaped hive, ranged the wastes of the airover the countries of the world alone, and then haunted the hives withtheir murmurs and their stirrings; the hives, which were people.Mrs Ramsay rose. Lily rose. Mrs Ramsay went. For days there hung abouther, as after a dream some subtle change is felt in the person one hasdreamt of, more vividly than anything she said, the sound of murmuringand, as she sat in the wicker arm-chair in the drawing-room window shewore, to Lily's eyes, an august shape; the shape of a dome.

This ray passed level with Mr Bankes's ray straight to Mrs Ramsay sittingreading there with James at her knee. But now while she still looked,Mr Bankes had done. He had put on his spectacles. He had stepped back.He had raised his hand. He had slightly narrowed his clear blue eyes,when Lily, rousing herself, saw what he was at, and winced like a dog whosees a hand raised to strike it. She would have snatched her picture offthe easel, but she said to herself, One must. She braced herself to standthe awful trial of some one looking at her picture. One must, she said,one must. And if it must be seen, Mr Bankes was less alarming thananother. But that any other eyes should see the residue of herthirty-three years, the deposit of each day's living mixed with somethingmore secret than she had ever spoken or shown in the course of all thosedays was an agony. At the same time it was immensely exciting.Nothing could be cooler and quieter.

Taking out a pen-knife, Mr Bankestapped the canvas with the bone handle. What did she wish to indicate bythe triangular purple shape, "just there"? he asked.It was Mrs Ramsay reading to James, she said. She knew his objection—that no one could tell it for a human shape. But she had made no attemptat likeness, she said. For what reason had she introduced them then? heasked. Why indeed?—except that if there, in that corner, it was bright,here, in this, she felt the need of darkness. Simple, obvious,commonplace, as it was, Mr Bankes was interested. Mother and childthen—objects of universal veneration, and in this case the mother wasfamous for her beauty—might be reduced, he pondered, to a purple shadowwithout irreverence.

But the picture was not of them, she said. Or, not in his sense. Therewere other senses too in which one might reverence them. By a shadow hereand a light there, for instance. Her tribute took that form if, as shevaguely supposed, a picture must be a tribute. A mother and child mightbe reduced to a shadow without irreverence. A light here required ashadow there. He considered. He was interested. He took itscientifically in complete good faith. The truth was that all hisprejudices were on the other side, he explained. The largest picture inhis drawing-room, which painters had praised, and valued at a higher pricethan he had given for it, was of the cherry trees in blossom on the banksof the Kennet. He had spent his honeymoon on the banks of the Kennet, hesaid.

Lily must come and see that picture, he said. But now—he turned,with his glasses raised to the scientific examination of her canvas. Thequestion being one of the relations of masses, of lights and shadows,which, to be honest, he had never considered before, he would like to haveit explained—what then did she wish to make of it? And he indicated thescene before them. She looked. She could not show him what she wished tomake of it, could not see it even herself, without a brush in her hand.She took up once more her old painting position with the dim eyes and theabsent-minded manner, subduing all her impressions as a woman to somethingmuch more general; becoming once more under the power of that vision whichshe had seen clearly once and must now grope for among hedges and housesand mothers and children—her picture. It was a question, she remembered,how to connect this mass on the right hand with that on the left.

Shemight do it by bringing the line of the branch across so; or break thevacancy in the foreground by an object so. But the dangerwas that by doing that the unity of the whole might be broken. Shestopped; she did not want to bore him; she took the canvas lightly off theeasel. But it had been seen; it had been taken from her. This man had sharedwith her something profoundly intimate. And, thanking Mr Ramsay for itand Mrs Ramsay for it and the hour and the place, crediting the world witha power which she had not suspected—that one could walk away down thatlong gallery not alone any more but arm in arm with somebody—thestrangest feeling in the world, and the most exhilarating—she nickedthe catch of her paint-box to, more firmly than was necessary, and thenick seemed to surround in a circle forever the paint-box, the lawn,Mr Bankes, and that wild villain, Cam, dashing past.

- For Cam grazed the easel by an inch; she would not stop for Mr Bankesand Lily Briscoe; though Mr Bankes, who would have liked a daughter ofhis own, held out his hand; she would not stop for her father, whom shegrazed also by an inch; nor for her mother, who called "Cam! I wantyou a moment!" as she dashed past. She was off like a bird, bullet, orarrow, impelled by what desire, shot by whom, at what directed, whocould say? What, what? Mrs Ramsay pondered, watching her. It mightbe a vision—of a shell, of a wheelbarrow, of a fairy kingdom on thefar side of the hedge; or it might be the glory of speed; no one knew.But when Mrs Ramsay called "Cam!" a second time, the projectile droppedin mid career, and Cam came lagging back, pulling a leaf by the way, toher mother.

What was she dreaming about, Mrs Ramsay wondered, seeing her engrossed,as she stood there, with some thought of her own, so that she had torepeat the message twice—ask Mildred if Andrew, Miss Doyle, and MrRayley have come back?—The words seemed to be dropped into a well,where, if the waters were clear, they were also so extraordin arilydistorting that, even as they descended, one saw them twisting about tomake Heaven knows what pattern on the floor of the child's mind. Whatmessage would Cam give the cook? Mrs Ramsay wondered. And indeed itwas only by waiting patiently, and hearing that there was an old woman inthe kitchen with very red cheeks, drinking soup out of a basin, thatMrs Ramsay at last prompted that parrot-like instinct which had picked upMildred's words quite accurately and could now produce them, if onewaited, in a colourless singsong. Shifting from foot to foot, Camrepeated the words, "No, they haven't, and I've told Ellen to clear awaytea."

Minta Doyle and Paul Rayley had not come back then. That could onlymean, Mrs Ramsay thought, one thing. She must accept him, or she mustrefuse him. This going off after luncheon for a walk, even thoughAndrew was with them—what could it mean? except that she had decided,rightly, Mrs Ramsay thought (and she was very, very fond of Minta), toaccept that good fellow, who might not be brilliant, but then, thoughtMrs Ramsay, realising that James was tugging at her, to make her go onreading aloud the Fisherman and his Wife, she did in her own heartinfinitely prefer boobies to clever men who wrote dissertations;Charles Tansley, for instance. Anyhow it must have happened, one wayor the other, by now.

But she read, "Next morning the wife awoke first, and it was justdaybreak, and from her bed she saw the beautiful country lying beforeher. Her husband was still stretching himself..." But how could Minta say now that she would not have him? Not if sheagreed to spend whole afternoons trapesing about the country alone—forAndrew would be off after his crabs—but possibly Nancy was with them.She tried to recall the sight of them standing at the hall door afterlunch. There they stood, looking at the sky, wondering about theweather, and she had said, thinking partly to cover their shyness,partly to encourage them to be off (for her sympathies were with Paul),"There isn't a cloud anywhere within miles," at which she could feellittle Charles Tansley, who had followed them out, snigger. But shedid it on purpose.

Whether Nancy was there or not, she could not becertain, looking from one to the other in her mind's eye.She read on: "Ah, wife," said the man, "why should we be King? I donot want to be King." "Well," said the wife, "if you won't be King, Iwill; go to the Flounder, for I will be King.""Come in or go out, Cam," she said, knowing that Cam was attracted onlyby the word "Flounder" and that in a moment she would fidget and fightwith James as usual. Cam shot off. Mrs Ramsay went on reading,relieved, for she and James shared the same tastes and were comfortabletogether.

"And when he came to the sea, it was quite dark grey, and the water heavedup from below, and smelt putrid. Then he *went and stood by it and said,*

'Flounder, flounder, in the sea,
Come, I pray thee, here to me;
For my wife, good Ilsabil,
Wills not as I'd have her will.

'Well, what does she want then?' said the Flounder." And where werethey now? Mrs Ramsay wondered, reading and thinking, quite easily,both at the same time; for the story of the Fisherman and his Wife waslike the bass gently accompanying a tune, which now and then ran upunexpectedly into the melody. And when should she be told? If nothinghappened, she would have to speak seriously to Minta. For she couldnot go trapesing about all over the country, even if Nancy were withthem (she tried again, unsuccessfully, to visualize their backs goingdown the path, and to count them). She was responsible to Minta'sparents—the Owl and the Poker.

Her nicknames for them shot into hermind as she read. The Owl and the Poker—yes, they would be annoyed ifthey heard—and they were certain to hear—that Minta, staying with theRamsays, had been seen etcetera, etcetera, etcetera. "He wore a wig inthe House of Commons and she ably assisted him at the head of thestairs," she repeated, fishing them up out of her mind by a phrasewhich, coming back from some party, she had made to amuse her husband.Dear, dear, Mrs Ramsay said to herself, how did they produce thisincongruous daughter? this tomboy Minta, with a hole in her stocking?How did she exist in that portentous atmosphere where the maid wasalways removing in a dust-pan the sand that the parrot had scattered,and conversation was almost entirely reduced to the exploits—interestingperhaps, but limited after all—of that bird? Naturally, one had askedher to lunch, tea, dinner, finally to stay with them up at Finlay, whichhad resulted in some friction with the Owl, her mother, and more calling,and more conversation, and more sand, and really at the end of it, she hadtold enough lies about parrots to last her a lifetime (so she had saidto her husband that night, coming back from the party). However,Minta came...Yes, she came, Mrs Ramsay thought, suspecting some thornin the tangle of this thought; and disengaging it found it to be this: awoman had once accused her of "robbing her of her daughter's affections"; something Mrs Doyle had said made her remember that charge again. Wishingto dominate, wishing to interfere, making people do what she wished—thatwas the charge against her, and she thought it most unjust.

How couldshe help being "like that" to look at? No one could accuse her oftaking pains to impress. She was often ashamed of her own shabbiness.Nor was she domineering, nor was she tyrannical. It was more trueabout hospitals and drains and the dairy. About things like that shedid feel passionately, and would, if she had the chance, have liked totake people by the scruff of their necks and make them see. Nohospital on the whole island. It was a disgrace. Milk delivered atyour door in London positively brown with dirt. It should be madeillegal. A model dairy and a hospital up here—those two things shewould have liked to do, herself. But how? With all these children?When they were older, then perhaps she would have time; when they wereall at school.

Oh, but she never wanted James to grow a day older! or Cam either.These two she would have liked to keep for ever just as they were,demons of wickedness, angels of delight, never to see them grow up intolong-legged monsters. Nothing made up up for the loss. When she readjust now to James, "and there were numbers of soldiers with kettledrumsand trumpets," and his eyes darkened, she thought, why should they growup and lose all that? He was the most gifted, the most sensitive ofher children. But all, she thought, were full of promise. Prue, aperfect angel with the others, and sometimes now, at night especially,she took one's breath away with her beauty. Andrew—even her husbandadmitted that his gift for mathematics was extraordinary. And Nancyand Roger, they were both wild creatures now, scampering about over thecountry all day long. As for Rose, her mouth was too big, but she hada wonderful gift with her hands. If they had charades, Rose made thedresses; made everything; liked best arranging tables, flowers,anything.

She did not like it that Jasper should shoot birds; but itwas only a stage; they all went through stages. Why, she asked,pressing her chin on James's head, should they grow up so fast? Whyshould they go to school? She would have liked always to have had ababy. She was happiest carrying one in her arms. Then people mightsay she was tyrannical, domineering, masterful, if they chose; she didnot mind. And, touching his hair with her lips, she thought, he willnever be so happy again, but stopped herself, remembering how itangered her husband that she should say that. Still, it was true. Theywere happier now than they would ever be again. A tenpenny tea setmade Cam happy for days. She heard them stamping and crowing on thefloor above her head the moment they awoke. They came bustling alongthe passage.

Then the door sprang open and in they came, fresh asroses, staring, wide awake, as if this coming into the dining-roomafter breakfast, which they did every day of their lives, was apositive event to them, and so on, with one thing after another, allday long, until she went up to say good-night to them, and found themnetted in their cots like birds among cherries and raspberries, stillmaking up stories about some little bit of rubbish—something they hadheard, something they had picked up in the garden. They all had theirlittle treasures... And so she went down and said to her husband, Whymust they grow up and lose it all? Never will they be so happy again.And he was angry. Why take such a gloomy view of life? he said. Itis not sensible. For it was odd; and she believed it to be true; thatwith all his gloom and desperation he was happier, more hopeful on thewhole, than she was. Less exposed to human worries—perhaps that wasit. He had always his work to fall back on. Not that she herself was"pessimistic," as he accused her of being. Only she thought life—anda little strip of time presented itself to her eyes—her fiftyyears. There it was before her—life. Life, she thought—but she didnot finish her thought. She took a look at life, for she had a clearsense of it there, something real, something private, which she sharedneither with her children nor with her husband. A sort of transactionwent on between them, in which she was on one side, and life was onanother, and she was always trying to get the better of it, as it wasof her; and sometimes they parleyed; there were,she remembered, great reconciliation scenes; but for the most part,oddly enough, she must admit that she felt this thing that she calledlife terrible, hostile, and quick to pounce on you if you gave it achance.

There were eternal problems: suffering; death; the poor. Therewas always a woman dying of cancer even here. And yet she had said toall these children, You shall go through it all. To eight people shehad said relentlessly that (and the bill for the greenhouse would befifty pounds). For that reason, knowing what was before them—love andambition and being wretched alone in dreary places—she had often thefeeling, Why must they grow up and lose it all? And then she said toherself, brandishing her sword at life, Nonsense. They will beperfectly happy. And here she was, she reflected, feeling life rathersinister again, making Minta marry Paul Rayley; because whatever shemight feel about her own transaction, she had had experiences whichneed not happen to every one (she did not name them to herself); shewas driven on, too quickly she knew, almost as if it were an escape forher too, to say that people must marry; people must have children.Was she wrong in this, she asked herself, reviewing her conduct for thepast week or two, and wondering if she had indeed put any pressure uponMinta, who was only twenty-four, to make up her mind. She was uneasy.Had she not laughed about it? Was she not forgetting again howstrongly she influenced people?

Marriage needed—oh, all sorts ofqualities (the bill for the greenhouse would be fifty pounds); one—sheneed not name it—that was essential; the thing she had with herhusband. Had they that? "Then he put on his trousers and ran away like a madman," she read."But outside a great storm was raging and blowing so hard that he couldscarcely keep his feet; houses and trees toppled over, the mountainstrembled, rocks rolled into the sea, the sky was pitch black, and itthundered and lightened, and the sea came in with black waves as highas church towers and mountains, and all with white foam at the top."

She turned the page; there were only a few lines more, so that shewould finish the story, though it was past bed-time. It was gettinglate. The light in the garden told her that; and the whitening of theflowers and something grey in the leaves conspired together, to rousein her a feeling of anxiety. What it was about she could not think atfirst. Then she remembered; Paul and Minta and Andrew had not comeback. She summoned before her again the little group on the terrace infront of the hall door, standing looking up into the sky. Andrew hadhis net and basket. That meant he was going to catch crabs and things.That meant he would climb out on to a rock; he would be cut off.

Orcoming back single file on one of those little paths above the cliffone of them might slip. He would roll and then crash. It was growingquite dark.But she did not let her voice change in the least as she finished thestory, and added, shutting the book, and speaking the last words as ifshe had made them up herself, looking into James's eyes: "And therethey are living still at this very time."

"And that's the end," she said, and she saw in his eyes, as theinterest of the story died away in them, something else take its place;something wondering, pale, like the reflection of a light, which atonce made him gaze and marvel. Turning, she looked across the bay, andthere, sure enough, coming regularly across the waves first two quickstrokes and then one long steady stroke, was the light of theLighthouse. It had been lit.In a moment he would ask her, "Are we going to the Lighthouse?" Andshe would have to say, "No: not tomorrow; your father says not."Happily, Mildred came in to fetch them, and the bustle distracted them.But he kept looking back over his shoulder as Mildred carried him out,and she was certain that he was thinking, we are not going to theLighthouse tomorrow; and she thought, he will remember that all hislife:

- No, she thought, putting together some of the pictures he had cut out—a refrigerator, a mowing machine, a gentleman in evening dress—children never forget. For this reason, it was so important what onesaid, and what one did, and it was a relief when they went to bed. Fornow she need not think about anybody. She could be herself, byherself. And that was what now she often felt the need of—to think;well, not even to think. To be silent; to be alone. All the being andthe doing, expansive, glittering, vocal, evaporated; and one shrunk,with a sense of solemnity, to being oneself, a wedge-shaped core ofdarkness, something invisible to others. Although she continued toknit, and sat upright, it was thus that she felt herself; and this selfhaving shed its attachments was free for the strangest adventures. Whenlife sank down for a moment, the range of experience seemed limitless.And to everybody there was always this sense of unlimited resources,she supposed; one after another, she, Lily, Augustus Carmichael, mustfeel, our apparitions, the things you know us by, are simply childish.Beneath it is all dark, it is all spreading, it is unfathomably deep;but now and again we rise to the surface and that is what you see usby. Her horizon seemed to her limitless. There were all the placesshe had not seen; the Indian plains; she felt herself pushing aside thethick leather curtain of a church in Rome. This core of darkness couldgo anywhere, for no one saw it. They could not stop it, she thought,exulting. There was freedom, there was peace, there was, mostwelcome of all, a summoning together, a resting on a platformof stability. Not as oneself did one find rest ever, in her experience(she accomplished here something dexterous with her needles) but as awedge of darkness. Losing personality, one lost the fret, the hurry,the stir; and there rose to her lips always some exclamation of triumphover life when things came together in this peace, this rest, thiseternity; and pausing there she looked out to meet that stroke of theLighthouse, the long steady stroke, the last of the three, which washer stroke, for watching them in this mood always at this hour onecould not help attaching oneself to one thing especially of the thingsone saw; and this thing, the long steady stroke, was her stroke. Oftenshe found herself sitting and looking, sitting and looking, with herwork in her hands until she became the thing she looked at—that light,for example. And it would lift up on it some little phrase or otherwhich had been lying in her mind like that—"Children don't forget,children don't forget"—which she would repeat and begin adding to it,It will end, it will end, she said. It will come, it will come, whensuddenly she added, We are in the hands of the Lord.

But instantly she was annoyed with herself for saying that. Who hadsaid it? Not she; she had been trapped into saying something she didnot mean. She looked up over her knitting and met the third stroke andit seemed to her like her own eyes meeting her own eyes, searching asshe alone could search into her mind and her heart, purifying out ofexistence that lie, any lie. She praised herself in praising thelight, without vanity, for she was stern, she was searching, she wasbeautiful like that light. It was odd, she thought, how if one wasalone, one leant to inanimate things; trees, streams, flowers; feltthey expressed one; felt they became one; felt they knew one, in asense were one; felt an irrational tenderness thus (she looked at thatlong steady light) as for oneself. There rose, and she looked andlooked with her needles suspended, there curled up off the floor of themind, rose from the lake of one's being, a mist, a bride to meet herlover.

What brought her to say that: "We are in the hands of the Lord?" shewondered. The insincerity slipping in among the truths roused her,annoyed her. She returned to her knitting again. How could any Lordhave made this world? she asked. With her mind she had always seizedthe fact that there is no reason, order, justice: but suffering, death,the poor. There was no treachery too base for the world to commit; sheknew that. No happiness lasted; she knew that.

She knitted with firmcomposure, slightly pursing her lips and, without being aware of it, sostiffened and composed the lines of her face in a habit of sternnessthat when her husband passed, though he was chuckling at the thoughtthat Hume, the philosopher, grown enormously fat, had stuck in a bog,he could not help noting, as he passed, the sternness at the heart ofher beauty. It saddened him, and her remoteness pained him, and hefelt, as he passed, that he could not protect her, and, when he reachedthe hedge, he was sad. He could do nothing to help her. He must standby and watch her. Indeed, the infernal truth was, he made things worsefor her. He was irritable—he was touchy. He had lost his temper overthe Lighthouse. He looked into the hedge, into its intricacy, itsdarkness. Always, Mrs Ramsay felt, one helped oneself out of solitude reluctantlyby laying hold of some little odd or end, some sound, some sight. Shelistened, but it was all very still; cricket was over; the childrenwere in their baths; there was only the sound of the sea. She stoppedknitting; she held the long reddish-brown stocking dangling in herhands a moment. She saw the light again.

With some irony in herinterrogation, for when one woke at all, one's relations changed, shelooked at the steady light, the pitiless, the remorseless, which was somuch her, yet so little her, which had her at its beck and call (shewoke in the night and saw it bent across their bed, stroking thefloor), but for all that she thought, watching it with fascination,hypnotised, as if it were stroking with its silver fingers some sealedvessel in her brain whose bursting would flood her with delight, shehad known happiness, exquisite happiness, intense happiness, and itsilvered the rough waves a little more brightly, as daylight faded, andthe blue went out of the sea and it rolled in waves of pure lemon whichcurved and swelled and broke upon the beach and the ecstasy burst inher eyes and waves of pure delight raced over the floor of her mind andshe felt, It is enough! It is enough!

He turned and saw her. Ah! She was lovely, lovelier now than ever hethought. But he could not speak to her. He could not interrupt her.He wanted urgently to speak to her now that James was gone and she wasalone at last. But he resolved, no; he would not interrupt her. Shewas aloof from him now in her beauty, in her sadness. He would let herbe, and he passed her without a word, though it hurt him that sheshould look so distant, and he could not reach her, he could do nothingto help her. And again he would have passed her without a word had shenot, at that very moment, given him of her own free will what she knewhe would never ask, and called to him and taken the green shawl off thepicture frame, and gone to him. For he wished, she knew, to protecther.

- She folded the green shawl about her shoulders. She took his arm. Hisbeauty was so great, she said, beginning to speak of Kennedy thegardener, at once he was so awfully handsome, that she couldn't dismisshim. There was a ladder against the greenhouse, and little lumps ofputty stuck about, for they were beginning to mend the greenhouse.Yes, but as she strolled along with her husband, she felt that thatparticular source of worry had been placed. She had it on the tip ofher tongue to say, as they strolled, "It'll cost fifty pounds," butinstead, for her heart failed her about money, she talked about Jaspershooting birds, and he said, at once, soothing her instantly, that itwas natural in a boy, and he trusted he would find better ways ofamusing himself before long. Her husband was so sensible, so just.And so she said, "Yes; all children go through stages," and beganconsidering the dahlias in the big bed, and wondering what about nextyear's flowers, and had he heard the children's nickname for CharlesTansley, she asked. The atheist, they called him, the little atheist."He's not a polished specimen," said Mr Ramsay. "Far from it," saidMrs Ramsay.

She supposed it was all right leaving him to his own devices, MrsRamsay said, wondering whether it was any use sending down bulbs; didthey plant them? "Oh, he has his dissertation to write," said MrRamsay. She knew all about THAT, said Mrs Ramsay. He talked ofnothing else. It was about the influence of somebody upon something."Well, it's all he has to count on," said Mr Ramsay. "Pray Heaven hewon't fall in love with Prue," said Mrs Ramsay. He'd disinherit her ifshe married him, said Mr Ramsay. He did not look at the flowers,which his wife was considering, but at a spot about a foot orso above them. There was no harm in him, he added, and was justabout to say that anyhow he was the only young man in England whoadmired his—when he choked it back. He would not bother her againabout his books. These flowers seemed creditable, Mr Ramsay said,lowering his gaze and noticing something red, something brown.

Yes, butthen these she had put in with her own hands, said Mrs Ramsay. Thequestion was, what happened if she sent bulbs down; did Kennedy plantthem? It was his incurable laziness; she added, moving on. If shestood over him all day long with a spade in her hand, he did sometimesdo a stroke of work. So they strolled along, towards the red-hotpokers. "You're teaching your daughters to exaggerate," said MrRamsay, reproving her. Her Aunt Camilla was far worse than she was, MrsRamsay remarked. "Nobody ever held up your Aunt Camilla as a model ofvirtue that I'm aware of," said Mr Ramsay. "She was the most beautifulwoman I ever saw," said Mrs Ramsay. "Somebody else was that," said MrRamsay. Prue was going to be far more beautiful than she was, said MrsRamsay. He saw no trace of it, said Mr Ramsay. "Well, then, looktonight," said Mrs Ramsay.

They paused. He wished Andrew could beinduced to work harder. He would lose every chance of a scholarship ifhe didn't. "Oh, scholarships!" she said. Mr Ramsay thought her foolishfor saying that, about a serious thing, like a scholarship. He shouldbe very proud of Andrew if he got a scholarship, he said. She would bejust as proud of him if he didn't, she answered. They disagreed alwaysabout this, but it did not matter. She liked him to believe inscholarships, and he liked her to be proud of Andrew whatever he did.Suddenly she remembered those little paths on the edge of the cliffs.

Wasn't it late? she asked. They hadn't come home yet. He flicked hiswatch carelessly open. But it was only just past seven. He held hiswatch open for a moment, deciding that he would tell her what he hadfelt on the terrace. To begin with, it was not reasonable to be sonervous. Andrew could look after himself. Then, he wanted to tell herthat when he was walking on the terrace just now—here he becameuncomfortable, as if he were breaking into that solitude, thataloofness, that remoteness of hers. But she pressed him. What hadhe wanted to tell her, she asked, thinking it was about going to theLighthouse; that he was sorry he had said "Damn you." But no. He didnot like to see her look so sad, he said. Only wool gathering, sheprotested, flushing a little. They both felt uncomfortable, as if theydid not know whether to go on or go back. She had been reading fairytales to James, she said. No, they could not share that; they couldnot say that.

They had reached the gap between the two clumps of red-hot pokers, andthere was the Lighthouse again, but she would not let herself look atit. Had she known that he was looking at her, she thought, she wouldnot have let herself sit there, thinking. She disliked anything thatreminded her that she had been seen sitting thinking. So she lookedover her shoulder, at the town. The lights were rippling and runningas if they were drops of silver water held firm in a wind. And all thepoverty, all the suffering had turned to that, Mrs Ramsay thought. Thelights of the town and of the harbour and of the boats seemed like aphantom net floating there to mark something which had sunk. Well, ifhe could not share her thoughts, Mr Ramsay said to himself, he would beoff, then, on his own.

He wanted to go on thinking, telling himself thestory how Hume was stuck in a bog; he wanted to laugh. But first itwas nonsense to be anxious about Andrew. When he was Andrew's age heused to walk about the country all day long, with nothing but a biscuitin his pocket and nobody bothered about him, or thought that he hadfallen over a cliff. He said aloud he thought he would be off for aday's walk if the weather held. He had had about enough of Bankes andof Carmichael. He would like a little solitude. Yes, she said. Itannoyed him that she did not protest. She knew that he would never doit. He was too old now to walk all day long with a biscuit in hispocket. She worried about the boys, but not about him. Years ago,before he had married, he thought, looking across the bay, as theystood between the clumps of red-hot pokers, he had walked all day.

Hehad made a meal off bread and cheese in a public house. He had workedten hours at a stretch; an old woman just popped her head in now andagain and saw to the fire. That was the country he liked best, overthere; those sandhills dwindling away into darkness. One could walkall day without meeting a soul. There was not a house scarcely, not asingle village for miles on end. One could worry things out alone.There were little sandy beaches where no one had been since thebeginning of time. The seals sat up and looked at you. It sometimesseemed to him that in a little house out there, alone—he broke ott,sighing. He had no right. The father of eight children—he remindedhimself. And he would have been a beast and a cur to wish a singlething altered. Andrew would be a better man than he had been. Pruewould be a beauty, her mother said. They would stem the flood a bit.That was a good bit of work on the whole—his eight children. Theyshowed he did not damn the poor little universe entirely, for on anevening like this, he thought, looking at the land dwindling away, thelittle island seemed pathetically small, half swallowed up in the sea. "Poor little place," he murmured with a sigh.

She heard him. He said the most melancholy things, but she noticedthat directly he had said them he always seemed more cheerful thanusual. All this phrase-making was a game, she thought, for if she hadsaid half what he said, she would have blown her brains out by now.

It annoyed her, this phrase-making, and she said to him, in a matter-of-fact way, that it was a perfectly lovely evening. And what was hegroaning about, she asked, half laughing, half complaining, for sheguessed what he was thinking—he would have written better books if hehad not married. He was not complaining, he said. She knew that he did not complain.She knew that he had nothing whatever to complain of. And he seizedher hand and raised it to his lips and kissed it with an intensity thatbrought the tears to her eyes, and quickly he dropped it.

They turned away from the view and began to walk up the path where thesilver-green spear-like plants grew, arm in arm. His arm was almostlike a young man's arm, Mrs Ramsay thought, thin and hard, and shethought with delight how strong he still was, though he was over sixty,and how untamed and optimistic, and how strange it was that beingconvinced, as he was, of all sorts of horrors, seemed not to depresshim, but to cheer him. Was it not odd, she reflected? Indeed heseemed to her sometimes made differently from other people, born blind,deaf, and dumb, to the ordinary things, but to the extraordinarythings, with an eye like an eagle's. His understanding oftenastonished her. But did he notice the flowers? No. Did he notice theview? No. Did he even notice his own daughter's beauty, or whetherthere was pudding on his plate or roast beef? He would sit at tablewith them like a person in a dream. And his habit of talking aloud, orsaying poetry aloud, was growing on him, she was afraid; for sometimesit was awkward— Best and brightest come away!

poor Miss Giddings, when he shouted that at her, almost jumped out ofher skin. But then, Mrs Ramsay, though instantly taking his sideagainst all the silly Giddingses in the world, then, she thought,intimating by a little pressure on his arm that he walked up hill toofast for her, and she must stop for a moment to see whether those werefresh molehills on the bank, then, she thought, stooping down to look,a great mind like his must be different in every way from ours. Allthe great men she had ever known, she thought, deciding that a rabbitmust have got in, were like that, and it was good for young men (thoughthe atmosphere of lecture-rooms was stuffy and depressing to her beyondendurance almost) simply to hear him, simply to look at him. Butwithout shooting rabbits, how was one to keep them down? she wondered.It might be a rabbit; it might be a mole. Some creature anyhow wasruining her Evening Primroses. And looking up, she saw above the thintrees the first pulse of the full-throbbing star, and wanted to makeher husband look at it; for the sight gave her such keen pleasure. Butshe stopped herself. He never looked at things. If he did, all hewould say would be, Poor little world, with one of his sighs.

At that moment, he said, "Very fine," to please her, and pretended toadmire the flowers. But she knew quite well that he did not admirethem, or even realise that they were there. It was only to pleaseher. Ah, but was that not Lily Briscoe strolling along with WilliamBankes? She focussed her short-sighted eyes upon the backs of aretreating couple. Yes, indeed it was. Did that not mean that theywould marry? Yes, it must! What an admirable idea! They must marry!

- He had been to Amsterdam, Mr Bankes was saying as he strolled acrossthe lawn with Lily Briscoe. He had seen the Rembrandts. He had been toMadrid. Unfortunately, it was Good Friday and the Prado was shut. Hehad been to Rome. Had Miss Briscoe never been to Rome? Oh, sheshould—It would be a wonderful experience for her—the SistineChapel; Michael Angelo; and Padua, with its Giottos. His wife had beenin bad health for many years, so that their sight-seeing had been on amodest scale.

She had been to Brussels; she had been to Paris but only for a flyingvisit to see an aunt who was ill. She had been to Dresden; there weremasses of pictures she had not seen; however, Lily Briscoe reflected,perhaps it was better not to see pictures: they only made onehopelessly discontented with one's own work. Mr Bankes thought onecould carry that point of view too far. We can't all be Titians and wecan't all be Darwins, he said; at the same time he doubted whether youcould have your Darwin and your Titian if it weren't for humble peoplelike ourselves. Lily would have liked to pay him a compliment; you'renot humble, Mr Bankes, she would have liked to have said. But he didnot want compliments, and she was a littleashamed of her impulse and said nothing while he remarked that perhapswhat he was saying did not apply to pictures. Anyhow, said Lily,tossing off her little insincerity, she would always go on painting,because it interested her. Yes, said Mr Bankes, he was sure she would,and, as they reached the end of the lawn he was asking her whether shehad difficulty in finding subjects in London when they turned and sawthe Ramsays.

So that is marriage, Lily thought, a man and a womanlooking at a girl throwing a ball. That is what Mrs Ramsay tried totell me the other night, she thought. For she was wearing a greenshawl, and they were standing close together watching Prue andJasper throwing catches. And suddenly the meaning which, for noreason at all, as perhaps they are stepping out of the Tube orringing a doorbell, descends on people, making them symbolical,making them representative, came upon them, and made them in the duskstanding, looking, the symbols of marriage, husband and wife. Then,after an instant, the symbolical outline which transcended the realfigures sank down again, and they became, as they met them, Mr and MrsRamsay watching the children throwing catches.

But still for a moment,though Mrs Ramsay greeted them with her usual smile (oh, she's thinkingwe're going to get married, Lily thought) and said, "I have triumphedtonight," meaning that for once Mr Bankes had agreed to dine with themand not run off to his own lodging where his man cooked vegetablesproperly; still, for one moment, there was a sense of things havingbeen blown apart, of space, of irresponsibility as the ball soaredhigh, and they followed it and lost it and saw the one star and thedraped branches. In the failing light they all looked sharp-edged andethereal and divided by great distances. Then, darting backwards overthe vast space (for it seemed as if solidity had vanished altogether),Prue ran full tilt into them and caught the ball brilliantly high up inher left hand, and her mother said, "Haven't they come back yet?"whereupon the spell was broken.

Mr Ramsay felt free now to laugh outloud at the thought that Hume had stuck in a bog and an old womanrescued him on condition he said the Lord's Prayer, and chuckling tohimself he strolled off to his study. Mrs Ramsay, bringing Prue backinto throwing catches again, from which she had escaped, asked, "Did Nancy go with them?"

- (Certainly, Nancy had gone with them, since Minta Doyle had asked itwith her dumb look, holding out her hand, as Nancy made off, afterlunch, to her attic, to escape the horror of family life. Shesupposed she must go then. She did not want to go. She did not want tobe drawn into it all. For as they walked along the road to the cliffMinta kept on taking her hand. Then she would let it go. Then shewould take it again. What was it she wanted? Nancy asked herself.There was something, of course, that people wanted; for when Minta tookher hand and held it, Nancy, reluctantly, saw the whole world spreadout beneath her, as if it were Constantinople seen through a mist, andthen, however heavy-eyed one might be, one must needs ask, "Is thatSanta Sofia?"

  "Is that the Golden Horn?" So Nancy asked, when Mintatook her hand. "What is it that she wants? Is it that?" And what wasthat? Here and there emerged from the mist (as Nancy looked down uponlife spread beneath her) a pinnacle, a dome; prominent things, withoutnames. But when Minta dropped her hand, as she did when they ran downthe hillside, all that, the dome, the pinnacle, whatever it was thathad protruded through the mist, sank down into it and disappeared.Minta, Andrew observed, was rather a good walker. She wore moresensible clothes that most women. She wore very short skirts and blackknickerbockers. She would jump straight into a stream and flounderacross. He liked her rashness, but he saw that it would not do—shewould kill herself in some idiotic way one of these days. She seemedto be afraid of nothing—except bulls. At the mere sight of a bull ina field she would throw up her arms and fly screaming, which was thevery thing to enrage a bull of course. But she did not mind owning upto it in the least; one must admit that. She knew she was an awfulcoward about bulls, she said. She thought she must have been tossed inher perambulator when she was a baby. She didn't seem to mind what shesaid or did. Suddenly now she pitched down on the edge of the cliffand began to sing some song about

Damn your eyes, damn your eyes: They all had to join in and sing the chorus, and shout out together: Damn your eyes, damn your eyes,but it would be fatal to let the tide come in and cover up all the goodhunting-grounds before they got on to the beach."Fatal," Paul agreed, springing up, and as they went slithering down,he kept quoting the guide-book about "these islands being justlycelebrated for their park-like prospects and the extent and variety oftheir marine curiosities." But it would not do altogether, thisshouting and damning your eyes, Andrew felt, picking his way down thecliff, this clapping him on the back, and calling him "old fellow" andall that; it would not altogether do. It was the worst of taking womenon walks.

Once on the beach they separated, he going out on to thePope's Nose, taking his shoes off, and rolling his socks in them andletting that couple look after themselves; Nancy waded out to her ownrocks and searched her own pools and let that couple look afterthemselves. She crouched low down and touched the smooth rubber-likesea anemones, who were stuck like lumps of jelly to the side of therock. Brooding, she changed the pool into the sea, and made the minnowsinto sharks and whales, and cast vast clouds over this tiny world byholding her hand against the sun, and so brought darkness anddesolation, like God himself, to millions of ignorant and innocentcreatures, and then took her hand away suddenly and let the sun streamdown.

Out on the pale criss-crossed sand, high-stepping, fringed,gauntleted, stalked some fantastic leviathan, and slipped into the vast fissures of the mountain side.And then, letting her eyes slide imperceptibly above the pool and reston that wavering line of sea and sky, on the tree trunks which thesmoke of steamers made waver on the horizon, she became with all thatpower sweeping savagely in and inevitably withdrawing, hypnotised, andthe two senses of that vastness and this tininess flowering within it made her feel that she was boundhand and foot and unable to move by the intensity of feelings whichreduced her own body, her own life, and the lives of all the people inthe world, for ever, to nothingness. So listening to the waves,crouching over the pool, she brooded.

And Andrew shouted that the sea was coming in, so she leapt splashingthrough the shallow waves on to the shore and ran up the beach and wascarried by her own impetuosity and her desire for rapid movement rightbehind a rock and there—oh, heavens! in each other's arms, were Pauland Minta kissing probably. She was outraged, indignant. She andAndrew put on their shoes and stockings in dead silence without sayinga thing about it. Indeed they were rather sharp with each other. Shemight have called him when she saw the crayfish or whatever it was,Andrew grumbled. However, they both felt, it's not our fault.

Theyhad not wanted this horrid nuisance to happen. All the same itirritated Andrew that Nancy should be a woman, and Nancy that Andrewshould be a man, and they tied their shoes very neatly and drew thebows rather tight. It was not until they had climbed right up on to the top of the cliffagain that Minta cried out that she had lost her grandmother's brooch—her grandmother's brooch, the sole ornament she possessed—a weepingwillow, it was set in pearls. They must haveseen it, she said, with the tears running down her cheeks, thebrooch which her grandmother had fastened her cap with till thelast day of her life.

Now she had lost it. She would rather havelost anything than that! She would go back and look for it. They allwent back. They poked and peered and looked. They kept their headsvery low, and said things shortly and gruffly. Paul Rayley searchedlike a madman all about the rock where they had been sitting. All thispother about a brooch really didn't do at all, Andrew thought, as Paultold him to make a "thorough search between this point and that." Thetide was coming in fast. The sea would cover the place where they hadsat in a minute. There was not a ghost of a chance of their finding itnow. "We shall be cut off!" Minta shrieked, suddenly terrified. As ifthere were any danger of that! It was the same as the bulls all overagain—she had no control over her emotions, Andrew thought. Womenhadn't. The wretched Paul had to pacify her. The men (Andrew and Paulat once became manly, and different from usual) took counsel brieflyand decided that they would plant Rayley's stick where they had sat andcome back at low tide again.

There was nothing more that could be donenow. If the brooch was there, it would still be there in the morning,they assured her, but Minta still sobbed, all the way up to the top ofthe cliff. It was her grandmother's brooch; she would rather have lostanything but that, and yet Nancy felt, it might be true that she mindedlosing her brooch, but she wasn't crying only for that. She was cryingfor something else. We might all sit down and cry, she felt. But shedid not know what for.

They drew ahead together, Paul and Minta, and he comforted her, andsaid how famous he was for finding things. Once when he was a littleboy he had found a gold watch. He would get up at daybreak and he waspositive he would find it. It seemed to him that it would bealmost dark, and he would be alone on the beach, and somehow it wouldbe rather dangerous. He began telling her, however, that he wouldcertainly find it, and she said that she would not hear of his gettingup at dawn: it was lost: she knew that: she had had a presentiment whenshe put it on that afternoon. And secretly he resolved that he wouldnot tell her, but he would slip out of the house at dawn when they wereall asleep and if he could not find it he would go to Edinburgh and buyher another, just like it but more beautiful.

He would prove what hecould do. And as they came out on the hill and saw the lights of thetown beneath them, the lights coming out suddenly one by one seemedlike things that were going to happen to him—his marriage, hischildren, his house; and again he thought, as they came out on to thehigh road, which was shaded with high bushes, how they would retreatinto solitude together, and walk on and on, he always leading her, andshe pressing close to his side. As they turned by thecross roads he thought what an appalling experience he had beenthrough, and he must tell some one—Mrs Ramsay of course, for it tookhis breath away to think what he had been and done. It had been farand away the worst moment of his life when he asked Minta to marry him.He would go straight to Mrs Ramsay, because he felt somehow that shewas the person who had made him do it.

She had made him think he coulddo anything. Nobody else took him seriously. But she made him believethat he could do whatever he wanted. He had felt her eyes on him allday today, following him about as if shewere saying, "Yes, you can do it. I believe in you. I expect it ofyou." She had made him feel all that, and directly they got back (helooked for the lights of the house above the bay) he would go to herand say, "I've done it, Mrs Ramsay; thanks to you." And so turning intothe lane that led to the house he could see lights moving about in theupper windows. They must be awfully late then. People were gettingready for dinner. The house was all lit up, and the lights after thedarkness made his eyes feel full, and he said to himself, childishly,as he walked up the drive, Lights, lights, lights, and repeated in adazed way, Lights, lights, lights, as they came into the house staringabout him with his face quite stiff. But, good heavens, he said tohimself, putting his hand to his tie, I must not make a fool ofmyself.)

- "Yes," said Prue, in her considering way, answering her mother's question, "I think Nancy did go with them."
- Well then, Nancy had gone with them, Mrs Ramsay supposed, wondering, asshe put down a brush, took up a comb, and said "Come in" to a tap atthe door, whether the fact that Nancy waswith them made it less likely or more likely that anything wouldhappen; it made it less likely, somehow, Mrs Ramsay felt, veryirrationally, except that after all holocaust on such a scale was notprobable. They could not all be

drowned. And again she felt alone inthe presence of her old antagonist, life.

Jasper and Rose said that Mildred wanted to know whether she should wait dinner. "Not for the Queen of England," said Mrs Ramsay emphatically.

"Not for the Empress of Mexico," she added, laughing at Jasper; for he shared his mother's vice: he, too, exaggerated.

And if Rose liked, she said, while Jasper took the message, she might choose which jewels she was to wear. When there are fifteen peoplesitting down to dinner, one cannot keep things waiting for ever. Shewas now beginning to feel annoyed with them for being so late; it wasinconsiderate of them, and it annoyed her on top of her anxiety aboutthem, that they should choose this very night to be out late, when, infact, she wished the dinner to be particularly nice, since WilliamBankes had at last consented to dine with them; and they were havingMildred's masterpiece—BOEUF EN DAUBE. Everything depended upon thingsbeing served up to the precise moment they were ready. The beef, thebayleaf, and the wine—all must be done to a turn. To keep it waitingwas out of the question. Yet of course tonight, of all nights, outthey went, and they came in late, and things had to be sent out,things had to be kept hot; the BOEUF EN DAUBE would be entirely spoilt.

Jasper offered her an opal necklace; Rose a gold necklace. Whichlooked best against her black dress? Which did indeed, said Mrs Ramsayabsent-mindedly, looking at her neck and shoulders in the glass. And then, while the children rummaged among herthings, she looked out of the window at a sight which always amusedher—the rooks trying to decide which tree to settle on. Every time,they seemed to change their minds and rose up into the air again,because, she thought, the old rook, the father rook, old Joseph was hername for him, was a bird of a very trying and difficult disposition.He was a disreputable old bird, with half his wing feathers missing.He was like some seedy old gentleman in a top hat she had seen playingthe horn in front of a public house.

"Look!" she said, laughing. They were actually fighting.

Joseph andMary were fighting. Anyhow they all went up again, and the air wasshoved aside by their black wings and cut into exquisite scimitar shapes.The movements of the wings beating out, out, out—she could neverdescribe it accurately enough to please herself—was one of theloveliest of all to her. Look at that, she said to Rose, hopingthat Rose would see it more clearly than she could. For one's childrenso often gave one's own perceptions a little thrust forwards.

But which was it to be? They had all the trays of her jewel-caseopen. The gold necklace, which was Italian, or the opal necklace,which Uncle James had brought her from India; or should she wear heramethysts?"Choose, dearests, choose," she said, hoping that they would makehaste.

But she let them take their time to choose: she let Rose, particularly,take up this and then that, and hold her jewels against the blackdress, for this little ceremony of choosing jewels, which was gonethrough every night, was what Rose liked best, she knew. She had somehidden reason of her own for attaching great importance to thischoosing what her mother was to wear. What was the reason, Mrs Ramsaywondered, standing still to let her clasp the necklace she had chosen,divining, through her own past, some deep, some buried, some quitespeechless feeling that one had for one's mother at Rose's age. Likeall feelings felt for oneself, Mrs Ramsay thought, it made one sad.

Itwas so inadequate, what one could give in return; and what Rose feltwas quite out of proportion to anything she actually was. And Rosewould grow up; and Rose would suffer, she supposed, with these deepfeelings, and she said she was ready now, and they would go down, andJasper, because he was the gentleman, should give her his arm, andRose, as she was the lady, should carry her handkerchief, and what else? oh, yes, it might be cold: a shawl.Choose me a shawl, she said, for that would please Rose, who was boundto suffer so. "There," she said, stopping by the window on thelanding, "there they are again." Joseph had settled on another tree-top. "Don't you think they mind," she said to Jasper, "having theirwings broken?" Why did he want to shoot poor old Joseph and Mary? Heshuffled a little on the stairs, and felt rebuked, but not seriously,for she did not understand the fun of shooting birds; and they did notfeel; and being his mother she lived away in another division of theworld, but he rather liked her stories about Mary and Joseph. She madehim laugh. But how did she know that those were Mary and Joseph? Didshe think the same birds came to the same trees every night? he asked.But here, suddenly, like all grown-up people, she ceased to pay him theleast attention. She was listening to a clatter in the hall.

"They've come back!" she exclaimed, and at once she felt much moreannoyed with them than relieved. Then she wondered, had it happened?She would go down and they would tell her—but no. They could not tellher anything, with all these people about. So she must go down andbegin dinner and wait. And, like some queen who, finding her peoplegathered in the hall, looks down upon them, and descends among them,and acknowledges their tributes silently, and accepts their devotionand their prostration before her (Paul did not move a muscle but lookedstraight before him as she passed) she went down, and crossed the halland bowed her head very slightly, as if she accepted what they couldnot say: their tribute to her beauty.But she stopped.

There was a smell of burning. Could they have let theboeuf en daube overboil? she wondered, pray heaven not! when thegreat clangour of the gong announced solemnly, authoritatively, thatall those scattered about, in attics, in bedrooms, on little perches oftheir own, reading, writing, putting the last smooth to their hair, orfastening dresses, must leave all that, and the little odds and ends ontheir washing-tables and dressing tables, and the novels on the bed-tables, and the diaries which were so private, and assemble in thedining-room for dinner.

- But what have I done with my life? thought Mrs Ramsay, taking herplace at the head of the table, and looking at all the plates makingwhite circles on it. "William, sit by me," she said. "Lily," shesaid, wearily, "over there." They had that—Paul Rayley and MintaDoyle—she, only this—an infinitely long table and plates and knives.At the far end was her husband, sitting down, all in a heap, frowning.

What at? She did not know. She did not mind. She could notunderstand how she had ever felt any emotion or affection for him. Shehad a sense of being past everything, through everything, out ofeverything, as she helped the soup, as if there was an eddy—there—and one could be in it, or one could be out of it, and she was out ofit. It's all come to an end, she thought, while they came in one afteranother, Charles Tansley—"Sit there, please," she said—AugustusCarmichael—and sat down. And meanwhile she waited, passively, forsome one to answer her, for something to happen. But this is not athing, she thought, ladling out soup, that one says.Raising her eyebrows at the discrepancy—that was what she wasthinking, this was what she was doing—ladling out soup—she felt, moreand more strongly, outside that eddy; or as if a shade had fallen, and,robbed of colour, she saw things truly. The room was very shabby.

There was no beauty anywhere. She forebore to look atMr Tansley. Nothing seemed to have merged. They all sat separate.And the whole of the effort of merging and flowing and creating restedon her. Again she felt, as a fact without hostility, the sterility ofmen, for if she did not do it nobody would do it, and so, givingherself a little shake that one gives a watch that has stopped, the oldfamiliar pulse began beating, as the watch begins ticking—one, two,three, one, two, three. And so on and so on, she repeated, listeningto it, sheltering and fostering the still feeble pulse as one mightguard a weak flame with a news-paper.

And so then, she concluded,addressing herself by bending silently in his direction to WilliamBankes—poor man! who had no wife, and no children and dined alone inlodgings except for tonight; and in pity for him, life being now strongenough to bear her on again, she began all this business, as a sailornot without weariness sees the wind fill his sail and yet hardly wantsto be off again and thinks how, had the ship sunk, he would havewhirled round and round and found rest on the floor of the sea."Did you find your letters? I told them to put them in the hall foryou," she said to William Bankes.Lily Briscoe watched her drifting into that strange no-man's land whereto follow people is impossible and yet their going inflicts such achill on those who watch them that they always try at least to followthem with their eyes as one follows a fading ship until the sails havesunk beneath the horizon.

How old she looks, how worn she looks, Lily thought, and how remote.Then when she turned to William Bankes, smiling, it was as if the shiphad turned and the sun had struck its sails again, and Lily thoughtwith some amusement because she was relieved, Why does she pity him?For that was the impression she gave, when she told him that hisletters were in the hall. Poor William Bankes, she seemed to besaying, as if her own weariness had been partly pitying people, and thelife in her, her resolve to live again, had been stirred by pity. Andit was not true, Lily thought; it was one of those misjudgments of hersthat seemed to be instinctive and to arise from some need of her ownrather than of other people's. He is not in the least pitiable. He hashis work, Lily said to herself. She remembered, all of a sudden as ifshe had found a treasure, that she had her work. In a flash she sawher picture, and thought, Yes, I shall put the tree further in themiddle; then I shall avoid that awkward space. That's what I shall do.That's what has been puzzling me. She took up the salt cellar and putit down again on a flower pattern in the table-cloth, so as to remindherself to move the tree.

"It's odd that one scarcely gets anything worth having by post, yet onealways wants one's letters," said Mr Bankes.What damned rot they talk, thought Charles Tansley, laying down hisspoon precisely in the middle of his plate, which he had swept clean,as if, Lily thought (he sat opposite to her with his back to the windowprecisely in the middle of view), he were determined to make sure ofhis meals. Everything about him had that meagre fixity, that bareunloveliness. But nevertheless, the fact remained, it was impossibleto dislike any one if one looked at them. She liked his eyes; theywere blue, deep set, frightening.

"Do you write many letters, Mr Tansley?" asked Mrs Ramsay, pitying himtoo, Lily supposed; for that was true of Mrs Ramsay—she pitied menalways as if they lacked something—women never, as if they hadsomething. He wrote to his mother; otherwise he did not suppose hewrote one letter a month, said Mr Tansley, shortly.

For he was not going to talk the sort of rot these condescended to bythese silly women. He had been reading in his room, and now he camedown and it all seemed to him silly, superficial, flimsy. Why did theydress? He had come down in his ordinary clothes. He had not got anydress clothes. "One never gets anything worth having by post"—thatwas the sort of thing they were always saying. They made men say thatsort of thing. Yes, it was pretty well true, he thought. They nevergot anything worth having from one year's end to another. They didnothing but talk, talk, talk, eat, eat, eat. It was the women's fault.Women made civilisation impossible with all their "charm," all theirsilliness."No going to the Lighthouse tomorrow, Mrs Ramsay," he said, assertinghimself. He liked her; he admired her; he still thought of the man inthe drain-pipe looking up at her; but he felt it necessary to asserthimself.

He was really, Lily Briscoe thought, in spite of his eyes, but thenlook at his nose, look at his hands, the most uncharming human beingshe had ever met. Then why did she mind what he said? Women can'twrite, women can't paint—what did that matter coming from him, sinceclearly it was not true to him but for some reason helpful to him, andthat was why he said it? Why did her whole being bow, like corn undera wind, and erect itself again from this abasement only with a greatand rather painful effort? She must make it once more. There's thesprig on the table-cloth; there's my painting; I must move the tree tothe middle; that matters—nothing else. Could she not hold fast tothat, she asked herself, and not lose her temper, and not argue; and ifshe wanted revenge take it by laughing at him?"Oh, Mr Tansley," she said, "do take me to the Lighthouse with you. Ishould so love it."

She was telling lies he could see. She was saying what she

did notmean to annoy him, for some reason. She was laughing at him. He was inhis old flannel trousers. He had no others. He felt very rough andisolated and lonely. He knew that she was trying to tease him for somereason; she didn't want to go to the Lighthouse with him; she despisedhim: so did Prue Ramsay; so did they all. But he was not going to bemade a fool of by women, so he turned deliberately in his chair andlooked out of the window and said, all in a jerk, very rudely, it wouldbe too rough for her tomorrow. She would be sick. It annoyed him that she should have made him speak like that, with MrsRamsay listening.

If only he could be alone in his room working, hethought, among his books. That was where he felt at his ease. And hehad never run a penny into debt; he had never cost his father a pennysince he was fifteen; he had helped them at home out of his savings; hewas educating his sister. Still, he wished he had known how to answerMiss Briscoe properly; he wished it had not come out all in a jerk likethat. "You'd be sick." He wished he could think of something to say toMrs Ramsay, something which would show her that he was not just a dryprig. That was what they all thought him. He turned to her. But MrsRamsay was talking about people he had never heard of to WilliamBankes.

"Yes, take it away," she said briefly, interrupting what she was sayingto William Bankes to speak to the maid. "It must have been fifteen—no, twenty years ago—that I last saw her," she was saying, turningback to him again as if she could not lose a moment of their talk, forshe was absorbed by what they were saying. So he had actually heardfrom her this evening! And was Carrie still living at Marlow, and waseverything still the same? Oh, she could remember it as if it wereyesterday—on the river, feeling it as if it were yesterday—going onthe river, feeling very cold. But if the Mannings made a plan theystuck to it. Never should she forget Herbert killing a wasp with ateaspoon on the bank! And it was still going on, Mrs Ramsay mused,gliding like a ghost among the chairs and tables of that drawing-roomon the banks of the Thames where she had been so very, very cold twentyyears ago; but now she went among them like a ghost; and it fascinatedher, as if, while she had changed, that particular day, now become verystill and beautiful, had remained there, all these years. Had Carriewritten to him herself? she asked.

"Yes. She says they're building a new billiard room," he said. No!No! That was out of the question! Building a new billiard room!It seemed to her impossible.

Mr Bankes could not see that there was anything very odd about it. They were very well off now. Should he give her love to Carrie?

"Oh," said Mrs Ramsay with a little start, "No," she added, reflecting that she did not know this Carrie who built a new billiard room. But how strange, she repeated, to Mr Bankes's amusement, that they should be going on there still. For it was extraordinary to think that they had been capable of going on living all these years when she had not thought of them more than once all that time. How eventful her ownlife had been, during those same years. Yet perhaps Carrie Manninghad not thought about her, either. The thought was strange anddistasteful.

"People soon drift apart," said Mr Bankes, feeling, however, somesatisfaction when he thought that after all he knew both the Manningsand the Ramsays. He had not drifted apart he thought, laying down hisspoon and wiping his clean-shaven lips punctiliously. But perhaps hewas rather unusual, he thought, in this; he never let himself get intoa groove. He had friends in all circles... Mrs Ramsay had to breakoff here to tell the maid something about keeping food hot. That waswhy he preferred dining alone. All those interruptions annoyed him.Well, thought William Bankes, preserving a demeanour of exquisitecourtesy and merely spreading the fingers of his left hand on thetable-cloth as a mechanic examines a tool beautifully polished andready for use in an interval of leisure, such are the sacrifices one'sfriends ask of one. It would have hurt her if he had refused to come.But it was not worth it for him.

Looking at his hand he thought thatif he had been alone dinner would have been almost over now; he wouldhave been free to work. Yes, he thought, it is a terrible waste oftime. The children were dropping in still. "I wish one of you wouldrun up to Roger's room," Mrs Ramsay was saying. How trifling it allis, how boring it all is, he thought, compared with the other thing—work. Here he sat drumming his fingers on the table-cloth when hemight have been—he took a flashing bird's-eye view of his work. Whata waste of time it all was to be sure! Yet, he thought, she is one ofmy oldest friends.

I am by way of being devoted to her. Yet now, atthis moment her presence meant absolutely nothing to him: her beautymeant nothing to him; her sitting with her little boy at the window—nothing, nothing. He wished only to be alone and to take up that book.He felt uncomfortable; he felt treacherous, that he could sit by herside and feel nothing for her. The truth was that he did not enjoyfamily life. It was in this sort of state that one asked oneself, Whatdoes one live for? Why, one asked oneself, does one take all thesepains for the human race to go on? Is it so very desirable?

Are weattractive as a species? Not so very, he thought, looking at thoserather untidy boys. His favourite, Cam, was in bed, he supposed.Foolish questions, vain questions, questions one never askedif one was occupied. Is human life this? Is human life that? Onenever had time to think about it. But here he was asking himself thatsort of question, because Mrs Ramsay was giving orders to servants, andalso because it had struck him, thinking how surprised Mrs Ramsay wasthat Carrie Manning should still exist, that friendships, even the bestof them, are frail things. One drifts apart. He reproached himselfagain. He was sitting beside Mrs Ramsay and he had nothing in theworld to say to her.

"I'm so sorry," said Mrs Ramsy, turning to him at last. He felt rigidand barren, like a pair of boots that have been soaked and gone dry sothat you can hardly force your feet into them. Yet he must force hisfeet into them. He must make himself talk. Unless he were verycareful, she would find out this treachery of his; that he did not carea straw for her, and that would not be at all pleasant, he thought. Sohe bent his head courteously in her direction.

"How you must detest dining in this bear garden," she said, making use,as she did when she was distracted, of her social manner. So, whenthere is a strife of tongues, at some meeting, the chairman, to obtainunity, suggests that every one shall speak in French. Perhaps it isbad French; French may not contain the words that express the speaker's thoughts; never the less speaking French imposes some order, someuniformity. Replying to her in the same language, Mr Bankes said, "No,not at all," and Mr Tansley, who had no knowledge of this language,even spoke thus in words of one syllable, at once suspected itsinsincerity.

They did talk nonsense, he thought, the Ramsays; and hepounced on this fresh instance with joy, making a note which, one ofthese days, he would read aloud, to one or two friends. There, in asociety where one could say what one liked he would sarcasticallydescribe "staying with the Ramsays" and what nonsense they talked. Itwas worth while doing it once, he would say; but not again. The womenbored one so, he would say. Of course Ramsay had dished himself by marrying a beautiful woman and having eight children. It would shapeitself something like that, but now, at this moment, sitting stuckthere with an empty seat beside him, nothing had shaped itself at all.It was all in scraps and fragments. He felt extremely, evenphysically, uncomfortable. He wanted somebody to give him a chance ofasserting himself. He wanted it so urgently that he fidgeted in hischair, looked at this person, then at that person, tried to break intotheir talk, opened his mouth and shut it again.

They were talkingabout the fishing industry. Why did no one ask him his opinion? Whatdid they know about the fishing industry?Lily Briscoe knew all that. Sitting opposite him, could she not see,as in an X-ray photograph, the ribs and thigh bones of the young man'sdesire to impress himself, lying dark in the mist of his flesh—thatthin mist which convention had laid over his burning desire to breakinto the conversation? But, she thought, screwing up her Chineseeyes, and remembering how he sneered at women, "can't paint, can'twrite," why should I help him to relieve himself?

There is a code of behaviour, she knew, whose seventh article says that on occasions of this sort it behoves the woman, whateverher own occupation might be, to go to the help of the young manopposite so that he may expose and relieve the thigh bones, the ribs,of his vanity, of his urgent desire to assert himself; as indeed it istheir duty, she reflected, in her old maidenly fairness, to help us,suppose the Tube were to burst into flames. Then, she thought, I shouldcertainly expect Mr Tansley to get me out. But how would it be, shethought, if neither of us did either of these things? So she sat theresmiling.

"You're not planning to go to the Lighthouse, are you, Lily," said MrsRamsay. "Remember poor Mr Langley; he had been round the world dozensof times, but he told me he never suffered as he did when my husbandtook him there. Are you a good sailor, Mr Tansley?" she asked.Mr Tansley raised a hammer: swung it high in air; but realising, as itdescended, that he could not smite that butterfly with such aninstrument as this, said only that he had never been sick in his life.But in that one sentence lay compact, like gunpowder, that hisgrandfather was a fisherman; his father a chemist; that he had workedhis way up entirely himself; that he was proud of it; that he wasCharles Tansley—a fact that nobody there seemed to realise; but one ofthese days every single person would know it. He scowled ahead of him.He could almost pity these mild cultivated people, who would be blownsky high, like bales of wool and barrels of apples, one of these daysby the gunpowder that was in him.

"Will you take me, Mr Tansley?" said Lily, quickly, kindly, for, ofcourse, if Mrs Ramsay said to her, as in effect she did, "I amdrowning, my dear, in seas of fire. Unless you apply some balm to theanguish of this hour and say something nice to that young man there,life will run upon the rocks—indeed I hear the grating and thegrowling at this minute. My nerves are taut as fiddle strings.Another touch and they will snap"—when Mrs Ramsay said all this, asthe glance in her eyes said it, of course for the hundred and fiftiethtime Lily Briscoe had to renounce the experiment—what happens if oneis not nice to that young man there—and be nice.

Judging the turn in her mood correctly—that she was friendly to himnow—he was relieved of his egotism, and told her how he had beenthrown out of a boat when he was a baby; how his father used to fishhim out with a boat-hook; that was how he had learnt to swim. One ofhis uncles kept the light on some rock or other off the Scottish coast,he said. He had been there with him in a storm. This was said loudlyin a pause. They had to listen to him when he said that he had beenwith his uncle in a lighthouse in a storm. Ah, thought Lily Briscoe,as the conversation took this auspicious turn, and she felt MrsRamsay's gratitude (for Mrs Ramsay was free now to talk for a momentherself), ah, she thought, but what haven't I paid to get it for you? She had not been sincere.

She had done the usual trick—been nice. She would never know him. Hewould never know her. Human relations were all like that, she thought,and the worst (if it had not been for Mr Bankes) were between men andwomen. Inevitably these were extremely insincere she thought. Thenher eye caught the salt cellar, which she had placed there to remindher, and she remembered that next morning she would move the treefurther towards the middle, and her spirits rose so high at the thoughtof painting tomorrow that she laughed out loud at what Mr Tansley wassaying. Let him talk all night if he liked it. "But how long do they leave men on a Lighthouse?" she asked. He toldher. He was amazingly well informed.

And as he was grateful, and ashe liked her, and as he was beginning to enjoy himself, so now, MrsRamsay thought, she could return to that dream land, that unreal butfascinating place, the Mannings' drawing-room at Marlow twenty yearsago; where one moved about without haste or anxiety, for there was nofuture to worry about. She knew what had happened to them, what toher. It was like reading a good book again, for she knew the end ofthat story, since it had happened twenty years ago, and life, whichshot down even from this dining-room table in cascades, heaven knowswhere, was sealed up there, and lay, like a lake, placidly between itsbanks. He said they had built a billiard room—was it possible?Would William go on talking about the Mannings? She wanted him to.But, no—for some reason he was no longer in the mood. She tried.He did not respond. She could not force him. She was disappointed.

"The children are disgraceful," she said, sighing. He said somethingabout punctuality being one of the minor virtues which we do notacquire until later in life.

"If at all," said Mrs Ramsay merely to fill up space, thinking what anold maid William was becoming. Conscious of his treachery, consciousof her wish to talk about something more intimate, yet out of mood forit at present, he felt come over him the disagreeableness of life,sitting there, waiting. Perhaps the others were saying somethinginteresting? What were they saying? That the fishing season was bad; that the men were emigrating. Theywere talking about wages and unemployment. The young man was abusingthe government. William Bankes, thinking what a relief it was to catchon to something of this sort when private life was disagreeable, heardhim say something about "one of the most scandalous acts of the presentgovernment." Lily was listening; Mrs Ramsay was listening; they wereall listening. But already bored, Lily felt that something was lacking;Mr Bankes felt that something was lacking. Pulling her shawl round herMrs Ramsay felt that something was lacking.

All of them bendingthemselves to listen thought, "Pray heaven that the inside of my mindmay not be exposed," for each thought, "The others are feeling this.They are outraged and indignant with the government about thefishermen. Whereas, I feel nothing at all." But perhaps, thought MrBankes, as he looked at Mr Tansley, here is the man. One was alwayswaiting for the man. There was always a chance. At any moment theleader might arise; the man of genius, in politics as in anything else.Probably he will be extremely disagreeable to us old fogies, thought MrBankes, doing his best to make allowances, for he knew by some curiousphysical sensation, as of nerves erect in his spine, that he wasjealous, for himself partly, partly more probably for his work, for hispoint of view for his science; and therefore he was not entirely open-minded or altogether fair, for Mr Tansley seemed to be saying, You havewasted your lives. You are all of you wrong. Poor old fogies, you'rehopelessly behind the times. He seemed to be rather cocksure, thisyoung man; and his manners were bad. But Mr Bankes bade himselfobserve, he had courage; he had ability; he was extremely well up inthe facts. Probably, Mr Bankes thought, as Tansley abused thegovernment, there is a good deal in what he says.

"Tell me now..." he said. So they argued about politics, and Lilylooked at the leaf on the table-cloth; and Mrs Ramsay, leaving theargument entirely in the hands of the two men, wondered why she was sobored by this talk, and wished, looking at her husband at the other endof the table, that he would say something. One word, she said toherself. For if he said a thing, it would make all the difference. Hewent to the heart of things. He cared about fishermen and their wages.He could not sleep for thinking of them. It was altogether differentwhen he spoke; one did not feel then, pray heaven you don't see howlittle I care, because one did care. Then, realising that it was becauseshe admired him so much that she was waiting for him to speak, shefelt as if somebody had been praising her husband to her and theirmarriage, and she glowed all over withiut realising that it wasshe herself who had praised him. She looked at him thinking to findthis in his face; he would be looking magnificent... But not in theleast!

He was screwing his face up, he was scowling and frowning, andflushing with anger. What on earth was it about? she wondered. Whatcould be the matter? Only that poor old Augustus had asked foranother plate of soup—that was all. It was unthinkable, it wasdetestable (so he signalled to her across the table) that Augustusshould be beginning his soup over again. He loathed people eating whenhe had finished. She saw his anger fly like a pack of hounds into hiseyes, his brow, and she knew that in a moment something violent wouldexplode, and then—thank goodness! she saw him clutch himself and clapa brake on the wheel, and the whole of his body seemed to emit sparksbut not words. He sat there scowling. He had said nothing, he wouldhave her observe. Let her give him the credit for that! But whyafter all should poor Augustus not ask for another plate of soup? Hehad merely touched Ellen's arm and said: "Ellen, please, another plate of soup," and then Mr Ramsay scowled like that.

And why not? Mrs Ramsay demanded. Surely they could let Augustus havehis soup if he wanted it. He hated people wallowing in food, Mr Ramsayfrowned at her. He hated everything dragging on for hours like this.But he had controlled himself, Mr Ramsay would have her observe, disgusting though the sight was. But why show it so plainly, MrsRamsay demanded (they looked at each other down the long table sendingthese questions and answers across, each knowing exactly what the otherfelt). Everybody could see, Mrs Ramsay thought. There was Rose gazingat her father, there was Roger gazing at his father; both would be offin spasms of laughter in another second, she knew, and so she saidpromptly:

"Light the candles," and they jumped up instantly and went and fumbled at the sideboard. Why could he never conceal his feelings? Mrs Ramsay wondered, and shewondered if Augustus Carmichael had noticed. Perhaps he had; perhapshe had not. She could not help respecting the composure with which hesat there, drinking his soup. If he wanted soup, he asked for soup.Whether people laughed at him or were angry with him he was the same.He did not like her, she knew that; but partly for that very reason sherespected him, and looking at him, drinking soup, very large and calmin the failing light, and monumental, and contemplative, she wonderedwhat he did feel then, and why he was always content and dignified; andshe thought how devoted he was to Andrew, and would call him into hisroom, and Andrew said, "show him things." And there he would lie allday long on the lawn brooding presumably over his poetry, till hereminded one of a cat watching birds, and then he clapped his pawstogether when he had found the word, and her husband said, "Poor oldAugustus—he's a true poet," which was high praise from her husband.

Now eight candles were stood down the table, and after the first stoopthe flames stood upright and drew with them into visibility the longtable entire, and in the middle a yellow and purple dish of fruit. Whathad she done with it, Mrs Ramsay wondered, for Rose's arrangement ofthe grapes and pears, of the horny pink-lined shell, of the bananas,made her think of a trophy fetched from the bottom of the sea, ofNeptune's banquet, of the bunch that hangs with vine leaves over theshoulder of Bacchus, among the leopard skins and thetorches lolloping red and gold... Thus brought up suddenly into thelight it seemed possessed of great size and depth, was like a world inwhich one could take one's staff and climb hills, she thought, and godown into valleys, and to her pleasure (for it brought them intosympathy momentarily) she saw that Augustus too feasted his eyes on thesame plate of fruit, plunged in, broke off a bloom there, a tasselhere, and returned, after feasting, to his hive. That was his way oflooking, different from hers. But looking together united them.

Now all the candles were lit up, and the faces on both sides of thetable were brought nearer by the candle light, and composed, as theyhad not been in the twilight, into a party round a table, for the nightwas now shut off by panes of glass, which, far from giving any accurateview of the outside world, rippled it so strangely that here, insidethe room, seemed to be order and dry land; there, outside, a reflectionin which things waved and vanished, waterily.

Some change at once went through them all, as if this had reallyhappened, and they were all conscious of making a party together in ahollow, on an island; had their common cause against that fluidity outthere. Mrs Ramsay, who had been uneasy, waiting for Paul and Minta tocome in, and unable, she felt, to settle to things, now felt heruneasiness changed to expectation. For now they must come, and LilyBriscoe, trying to analyse the cause of the sudden exhilaration,compared it with that moment on the tennis lawn, when solidity suddenly-vanished, and such vast spaces lay between them; and now the sameeffect was got by the many candles in the sparely furnished room, andthe uncurtained windows, and the bright mask-like look of faces seen bycandlelight. Some weight was taken off them; anything might happen,she felt. They must come now, Mrs Ramsay thought, looking at the door,and at that instant, Minta Doyle, Paul Rayley, and a maid carrying agreat dish in her hands came in together. They were awfully late; theywere horribly late, Minta said, as they found their way to differentends of the table.

"I lost my brooch—my grandmother's brooch," said Minta with a sound oflamentation in her voice, and a suffusion in her large brown eyes,looking down, looking up, as she sat by Mr Ramsay, which roused hischivalry so that he bantered her. How could she be such a goose, he asked, as to scramble about the rocks in jewels? She was by way of being terrified of him—he was so fearfully clever,and the first night when she had sat by him, and he talked about GeorgeEliot, she had been really frightened, for she had left the thirdvolume of MIDDLE-MARCH in the train and she never knew what happened inthe end; but afterwards she got on perfectly, and made herself out evenmore ignorant than she was, because he liked telling her she was afool.

And so tonight, directly he laughed at her, she was notfrightened. Besides, she knew, directly she came into the room that themiracle had happened; she wore her golden haze. Sometimes she had it;sometimes not. She never knew why it came or why it went, or if shehad it until she came into the room and then she knew instantly by theway some man looked at her. Yes, tonight she had it, tremendously; sheknew that by the way Mr Ramsay told her not to be a fool. She satbeside him, smiling.

It must have happened then, thought Mrs Ramsay; they are engaged. Andfor a moment she felt what she had never expected to feel again—jealousy. For he, her husband, felt it too—Minta's glow; he likedthese girls, these golden-reddish girls, with something flying,something a little wild and harum-scarum about them, who didn't"scrape their hair off," weren't, as he said about poor Lily Briscoe,"skimpy". There was some quality which she herself had not, somelustre, some richness, which attracted him, amused him, led him to makefavourites of girls like Minta. They might cut his hair from him,plait him watch-chains, or interrupt him at his work, hailing him, "Come along, Mr Ramsay; it's our turn to beat them now,"and out he came to play tennis. But indeed she was not jealous, only, now and then, when she madeherself look in her glass, a little resentful that she had grown old,perhaps, by her own fault. (The bill for the greenhouse and all therest of it.) She was grateful to them for laughing at him. ("How manypipes have you smoked today, Mr Ramsay?" and so on), till he seemed ayoung man; a man very attractive to women, not burdened, not weigheddown with the greatness of his labours and the sorrows of the world andhis fame or his failure, but again as she had first known him, gauntbut gallant; helping her out of a boat, she remembered; with delightfulways, like that (she looked at him, and he looked astonishingly young,teasing Minta). For herself—"Put it down there," she said, helpingthe Swiss girl to place gently before her the huge brown pot in whichwas the BOEUF EN DAUBE—for her own part, she liked her boobies. Paulmust sit by her.

She had kept a place for him. Really, she some times thought she liked the boobies best. They did not bother one with theirdissertations. How much they missed, after all, these very clever men!How dried up they did become, to be sure. There was something, shethought as he sat down, very charming about Paul. His manners weredelightful to her, and his sharp cut nose and his bright blue eyes. Hewas so considerate. Would he tell her—now that they were all talkingagain—what had happened?

"We went back to look for Minta's brooch," he said, sitting down byher. "We"—that was enough. She knew from the effort, the rise in hisvoice to surmount a difficult word that it was the first time he hadsaid "we." "We did this, we did that." They'll say that all theirlives, she thought, and an exquisite scent of olives and oil and juicerose from the great brown dish as Marthe, with a little flourish, tookthe cover off. The cook had spent three days over that dish. And shemust take great care, Mrs Ramsay thought, diving into the soft mass, tochoose a specially tender piece for William Bankes. And she peered intothe dish, with its shiny walls and its confusion of savoury brown andyellow meats and its bay leaves and its wine, and thought, This willcelebrate the occasion—a curious sense rising in her, at once freakishand tender, of celebrating a festival, as if two emotions were calledup in her, one profound—for what could be more serious than the loveof man for woman, what more commanding, more impressive, bearing in itsbosom the seeds of death; at the same time these lovers, these peopleentering into illusion glittering eyed, must be danced round withmockery, decorated with garlands.

"It is a triumph," said Mr Bankes, laying his knife down for a moment.He had eaten attentively. It was rich; it was tender. It was perfectlycooked. How did she manage these things in the depths of the country?he asked her. She was a wonderful woman. All his love, all hisreverence, had returned; and she knew it.

"It is a French recipe of my grandmother's," said Mrs Ramsay, speakingwith a ring of great pleasure in her voice. Of course it was French.What passes for cookery in England is an abomination. Itis putting cabbages in water. It is roasting meat till it is likeleather. It is cutting off the delicious skins of vegetables. "Inwhich," said Mr Bankes, "all the virtue of the vegetable is contained."And the waste, said Mrs Ramsay. A whole French family could live onwhat an English cook throws away. Spurred on by her sense thatWilliam's affection had come back to her, and that everything was allright again, and that her suspense was over, and that now she was freeboth to triumph and to mock, she laughed, she gesticulated, till Lilythought, How childlike, how absurd she was, sitting up there with allher beauty opened again in her, talking about the skins of vegetables.

There was something frightening about her. She was irresistible.Always she got her own way in the end, Lily thought. Now she hadbrought this off—Paul and Minta, one might suppose, were engaged. MrBankes was dining here. She put a spell on them all, by wishing, sosimply, so directly, and Lily contrasted that abundance with her ownpoverty of spirit, and supposed that it was partly that belief (for herface was all lit up—without looking young, she looked radiant) in thisstrange, this terrifying thing, which made Paul Rayley, sitting at herside, all of a tremor, yet abstract, absorbed, silent. Mrs Ramsay,Lily felt, as she talked about the skins of vegetables, exalted that,worshipped that; held her hands over it to warm them, to protect it,and yet, having brought it all about, somehow laughed, led her victims,Lily felt, to the altar. It came over her too now—the emotion, thevibration, of love. How inconspicuous she felt herself by Paul's side!He, glowing, burning; she, aloof, satirical; he, bound for adventure;she, moored to the shore; he, launched, incautious; she solitary,left out—and, ready to implore a share, if it were a disaster, inhis disaster, she said shyly:

"When did Minta lose her brooch?"

He smiled the most exquisite smile, veiled by memory,
Tinged by dreams.
He shook his head. "On the beach," he said.

"I'm going to find it," he said, "I'm getting up early." This being kept secret from Minta, he lowered his voice, and turned his eyes to where she sat, laughing, beside Mr Ramsay.

Lily wanted to protest violently and outrageously her desire to helphim, envisaging how in the dawn on the beach she would be the one topounce on the brooch half-hidden by some stone, and thus herself beincluded among the sailors and adventurers. But what did he reply toher offer? She actually said with an emotion that she seldom letappear, "Let me come with you," and he laughed. He meant yes or no—either perhaps. But it was not his meaning—it was the odd chucklehe gave, as if he had said, Throw yourself over the cliff if you like,I don't care. He turned on her cheek the heat of love, its horror, itscruelty, its unscrupulosity. It scorched her, and Lily, looking atMinta, being charming to Mr Ramsay at the other end of the table,flinched for her exposed to these fangs, and was thankful. For at anyrate, she said to herself, catching sight of the salt cellar on thepattern, she need not marry, thank Heaven: she need not undergo thatdegradation. She was saved from that dilution. She would move the treerather more to the middle. Such was the complexity of things. For what happened to her,especially staying with the Ramsays, was to be made to feel violentlytwo opposite things at the same time; that's what you feel, was one;that's what I feel, was the other, and then they fought together in hermind, as now. It is so beautiful, so exciting, this love, that Itremble on the verge of it, and offer, quite out of my own habit, tolook for a brooch on a beach; also it is the stupidest, the mostbarbaric of human passions, and turns a nice young man with a profilelike a gem's into a bully with a crowbar (hewas swaggering, he was insolent) in the Mile End Road.

Yet, she said toherself, from the dawn of time odes have been sung to love; wreathsheaped and roses; and if you asked nine people out of ten they wouldsay they wanted nothing but this—love; while the women, judging fromher own experience, would all the time be feeling, This is not what wewant; there is nothing more tedious, puerile, and inhumane than this;yet it is also beautiful and necessary. Well then, well then? sheasked, somehow expecting the others to go on with the argument, as ifin an argument like this one threw one's own little bolt which fellshort obviously and left the others to carry it on. So she listenedagain to what they were saying in case they should throw any light uponthe question of love.

"Then," said Mr Bankes, "there is that liquid the English call coffee.""Oh, coffee!" said Mrs Ramsay. But it was much rather a question (shewas thoroughly roused, Lily could see, and talked very emphatically) ofreal butter and clean milk. Speaking with warmth and eloquence, shedescribed the iniquity of the English dairy system, and in what statemilk was delivered at the door, and was about to prove her charges, forshe had gone into the matter, when all round the table, beginning withAndrew in the middle, like a fire leaping from tuft to tuft of furze,her children laughed; her husband laughed; she was laughed at, fire-encircled, and forced to veil her crest, dismount her batteries, andonly retaliate by displaying the raillery and ridicule of the tableto Mr Bankes as an example of what one suffered if one attacked theprejudices of the British Public. Purposely, however, for she had it on her mind that Lily, who hadhelped her with Mr Tansley, was out of things, she exempted her fromthe rest; said "Lily anyhow agrees with me," and so drew her in, alittle fluttered, a little startled. They were both out of things, Mrs Ramsay had been thinking,both Lily and Charles Tansley. Both suffered from the glow of theother two. He, it was clear, felt himself utterly in the cold; nowoman would look at him with Paul Rayley in the room. Poor fellow!Still, he had his dissertation, the influence of somebody uponsomething: he could take care of himself. With Lily it was different.She faded, under Minta's glow; became more inconspicuous than ever, inher little grey dress with her little puckered face and her littleChinese eyes.

Everything about her was so small. Yet, thought MrsRamsay, comparing her with Minta, as she claimed her help (for Lilyshould bear her out she talked no more about her dairies than herhusband did about his boots—he would talk by the hour about his boots)of the two, Lily at forty will be the better. There was in Lily athread of something; a flare of something; something of her own whichMrs Ramsay liked very much indeed, but no man would, she feared.Obviously, not, unless it were a much older man, like William Bankes.But then he cared, well, Mrs Ramsay sometimes thought that he cared,since his wife's death, perhaps for her. He was not "in love" ofcourse; it was one of those unclassified affections of which there areso many. Oh, but nonsense, she thought; William must marry Lily. Theyhave so many things in common. Lily is so fond of flowers. They areboth cold and aloof and rather self-sufficing. She must arrange forthem to take a long walk together.

Foolishly, she had set them opposite each other. That could be remediedtomorrow. If it were fine, they should go for a picnic. Everythingseemed possible. Everything seemed right. Just now (but this cannotlast, she thought, dissociating herself from the moment while they wereall talking about boots) just now she had reached security; she hoveredlike a hawk suspended; like a flag floated in an element of joy whichfilled every nerve of her body fully and sweetly, not noisily, solemnlyrather, for it arose, she thought, looking at them all eating there,from husband and children and friends; all of which rising in thisprofound stillness (she was helping William Bankes to one very smallpiece more, and peered into the depths of the earthenware pot) seemednow for no special reason to stay there like a smoke, like a fumerising upwards, holding them safe together. Nothing need be said;nothing could be said. There it was, all round them. It partook, shefelt, carefully helping Mr Bankes to a specially tender piece, ofeternity; as she had already felt about something different once beforethat afternoon; there is a coherence in things, a stability; something,she meant, is immune from change, and shines out (she glanced at thewindow with its ripple of reflected lights) in the face of the flowing,the fleeting, the spectral, like a ruby; so that again tonight she hadthe feeling she had had once today, already, of peace, of rest. Ofsuch moments, she thought, the thing is made that endures.

"Yes," she assured William Bankes, "there is plenty for everybody." "Andrew," she said, "hold your plate lower, or I shall spill it." (TheBOEUF EN DAUBE was a perfect triumph.) Here, she felt, putting thespoon down, where one could move or rest; could wait now listening; could then, like a hawk which lapses suddenly fromits high station, flaunt and sink on laughter easily, resting her wholeweight upon what at the other end of the table her husband was sayingabout the square root of one thousand two hundred and fifty-three.That was the number, it seemed, on his watch.

What did it all mean? To this day she had no notion. A square root?What was that? Her sons knew. She leant on them; on cubes and squareroots; that was what they were talking about now; on Voltaire andMadame de Stael; on the character of Napoleon; on the French system ofland tenure; on Lord Rosebery; on Creevey's Memoirs: she let it upholdher and sustain her, this admirable fabric of the masculineintelligence, which ran up and down, crossed this way and that, likeiron girders spanning the swaying fabric, upholding the world, so thatshe could trust herself to it utterly, even shut her eyes, or flickerthem for a moment, as a child staring up from its pillow winks at themyriad layers of the leaves of a tree. Then she woke up. It was stillbeing fabricated. William Bankes was praising the Waverly novels.

He read one of them every six months, he said. And why

should that makeCharles Tansley angry? He rushed in (all, thought Mrs Ramsay, becausePrue will not be nice to him) and denounced the Waverly novels when heknew nothing about it, nothing about it whatsoever, Mrs Ramsay thought, observing him rather than listening to what he said. She could see howit was from his manner—he wanted to assert himself, and so it wouldalways be with him till he got his Professorship or married his wife,and so need not be always saying, "I—I—I." For that was what hiscriticism of poor Sir Walter, or perhaps it was Jane Austen, amountedto.

"I—I—I." He was thinking of himself and the impression hewas making, as she could tell by the sound of his voice, and hisemphasis and his uneasiness. Success would be good for him. At anyrate they were off again. Now she need not listen. It could not last,she knew, but at the moment her eyes were so clear that they seemed togo round the table unveiling each of these people, and their thoughtsand their feelings, without effort likp a light stealing under water sothat its ripples and the reeds in it and the minnows balancingthemselves, aiid llie sudden silent trout are all lit up hanging,trembling. So she saw them; she heard them; but whatever they said hadalso this quality, as if what they said was like the movement of atrout when, at the same time, oue cau sec thc ripple and the gravel,something to the right, something to the left; and the whole is heldtogether; for whereas in active life she would be netting andseparating one thing from another; she would be saying she liked theWaverly novels or had not read them; she would be urging herselfforward; now she said nothing. For the moment, she hung suspended.

"Ah, but how long do you think it'll last?" said somebody. It was asif she had antennae trembling out from her, which, intercepting certainsentences, forced them upon her attention. This was one of them. Shescented danger for her husband. A question like that would lead,almost certainly, to something being said which reminded him of his ownfailure. How long would he be read—he would think at once. WilliamBankes (who was entirely free from all such vanity) laughed, and saidhe attached no importance to changes in fashion. Who could tell whatwas going to last—in literature or indeed in anything else?"Let us enjoy what we do enjoy," he said. His integrity seemed to MrsRamsay quite admirable. He never seemed for a moment to think, But howdoes this affect me? But then if you had the other temperament, whichmust have praise, which must have encouragement, naturally you began(and she knew that Mr Ramsay was beginning) to be uneasy; to wantsomebody to say, Oh, but your work will last, Mr Ramsay, or somethinglike that.

He showed his uneasiness quite clearly now by saying, withsome irritation, that, anyhow, Scott wouldlast him his lifetime. He said it irritably. Everybody, she thought,felt a little uncomfortable, without knowing why. Then Minta Doyle, whose instinct was fine, said bluffly, absurdly, that she did notbelieve that any one really enjoyed reading Shakespeare. Mr Ramsaysaid grimly (but his mind was turned away again) that very few peopleliked it as much as they said they did. But, he added, there isconsiderable merit in some of the plays nevertheless, and Mrs Ramsaysaw that it would be all right for the moment anyhow; he would laugh atMinta, and she, Mrs Ramsay saw, realising his extreme anxiety abouthimself, would, in her own way, see that he was taken care of, andpraise him, somehow or other. But she wished it was not necessary:perhaps it was her fault that it was necessary. Anyhow, she was freenow to listen to what Paul Rayley was trying to say about books one hadread as a boy. They lasted, he said.

He had read some of Tolstoi atschool. There was one he always remembered, but he had forgotten thename. Russian names were impossible, said Mrs Ramsay. "Vronsky," saidPaul. He remembered that because he always thought it such a good namefor a villain. "Vronsky," said Mrs Ramsay; "Oh, ANNA KARENINA," butthat did not take them very far; books were not in their line. No,Charles Tansley would put them both right in a second about books, butit was all so mixed up with, Am I saying the right thing? Am I makinga good impression? that, after all, one knew more about him thanabout Tolstoi, whereas, what Paul said was about the thing, simply, nothimself, nothing else. Like all stupid people, he had a kind ofmodesty too, a consideration for what you were feeling, which, once ina way at least, she found attractive. Now he was thinking, not abouthimself, or about Tolstoi, but whether she was cold, whether she felt adraught, whether she would like a pear.

No, she said, she did not want a pear. Indeed she had been keepingguard over the dish of fruit jealously, hopingthat nobody would touch it. Her eyes had been going in and out amongthe curves and shadows of the fruit, among the rich purples of thelowland grapes, then over the horny ridge of the shell, putting ayellow against a purple, a curved shape against a round shape, withoutknowing why she did it, or why, every time she did it, she felt moreand more serene; until, oh, what a pity that they should do it—a handreached out, took a pear, and spoilt the whole thing. In sympathy shelooked at Rose. She looked at Rose sitting between Jasper and Prue.How odd that one's child should do that!

How odd to see them sitting there, in a row, her children, Jasper,Rose, Prue, Andrew, almost silent, but with some joke of their owngoing on, she guessed, from the twitching at their lips. It wassomething quite apart from everything else, something they werehoarding up to laugh over in their own room. It was not about theirfather, she hoped. No, she thought not. What was it, she wondered,sadly rather, for it seemed to her that they would laugh when she wasnot there. There was all that hoarded behind those rather set, still,mask-like faces, for they did not join in easily; they were likewatchers, surveyors, a little raised or set apart from the grown-uppeople. But when she looked at Prue tonight, she saw that this wasnot now quite true of her. She was just beginning, just moving,just descending. The faintest light was on her face, as if theglow of Minta opposite, some excitement, some anticipation of happinesswas reflected in her, as if the sun of the love of men and women roseover the rim of the table-cloth, and without knowing what it was shebent towards it and greeted it. She kept looking at Minta, shyly, yetcuriously, so that Mrs Ramsay looked from one to the other and said,speaking to Prue in her own mind, You will be as happy as she is one ofthese days. You will be much happier, she added, because you are mydaughter, she meant; her own daughter must be happier than otherpeople's daughters. But dinner was over. It was time to go. Theywere only playing with things on their plates. She would wait untilthey had done laughing at some story her husband was telling. He washaving a joke with Minta about a bet. Then she would get up.

She liked Charles Tansley, she thought, suddenly; she liked his laugh.She liked him for being so angry with Paul and Minta. She liked hisawkwardness. There was a lot in that young man after all. And Lily,she thought, putting her napkin beside her plate, she always has somejoke of her own. One need never bother about Lily. She waited. Shetucked her napkin under the edge of her plate. Well, were they donenow? No. That story had led to another story. Her husband was ingreat spirits tonight, and wishing, she supposed, to make it all rightwith old Augustus after that scene about the soup, had drawn him in—they were telling stories about some one they had both known atcollege. She looked at the window in which the candle flames burntbrighter now that the panes were black, and looking at that outsidethe voices came to her very strangely, as if they were voices at aservice in a cathedral, for she did not listen to the words. Thesudden bursts of laughter and then one voice speakingalone, reminded her of men and boys crying out the Latin wordsof a service in some Roman Catholic cathedral. She waited. Herhusband spoke. He was repeating something, and she knew it was poetryfrom the rhythm and the ring of exultation, and melancholy in hisvoice:

Come out and climb the garden path, Luriana Lurilee.The China rose is all abloom and buzzing with the yellow bee.The words sounded as if they werefloating like flowers on water out there, cut off from them all, as ifno one had said them, but they had come into existence of themselves.And all the lives we ever lived and all the lives to beAre full of trees and changing leaves.

She did not know what they meant, but, like music, the words seemed tobe spoken by her own voice, outside her self, saying quite easily andnaturally what had been in her mind the whole evening while she saiddifferent things. She knew, without looking round, that every one atthe table was listening to the voice saying:I wonder if it seems to you, Luriana, Lurileewith the same sort of relief and pleasure that she had, as if thiswere, at last, the natural thing to say, this were their own voicespeaking.But the voice had stopped. She looked round. She made herself get up.Augustus Carmichael had risen and, holding his table napkin so that itlooked like a long white robe he stood chanting:To see the Kings go riding byOver lawn and daisy leaWith their palm leaves and cedarLuriana, Lurilee, and as she passed him, he turned slightly towards her repeating the last words:

Luriana, Lurileeand bowed to her as if he did her homage. Without knowing why, shefelt that he liked her better than he ever had done before; and with afeeling of relief and gratitude she returned his bow and passed throughthe door which he held open for her.It was necessary now to carry everything a step further. With her footon the threshold she waited a moment longer in a scene which wasvanishing even as she looked, and then, as she moved and took Minta'sarm and left the room, it changed, it shaped itself differently; it hadbecome, she knew, giving one last look at it over her shoulder, alreadythe past.

- Then indeed peace had come. Messages of peace breathed from the sea tothe shore. Never to break its sleep any more, to lull it rather moredeeply to rest, and whatever the dreamers dreamt holily, dreamt wisely, to confirm what else was it murmuring as Lily Briscoe laid her headon the pillow in the clean still room and heard the sea. Through theopen window the voice of the beauty of the world came murmuring, toosoftly to hear exactly what it said—but what mattered if the meaningwere plain? entreating the sleepers (the house/was full again; MrsBeckwith was staying there, also Mr Carmichael), if they would notactually come down to the beach itself at least to lift the blind andlook out. They would see then night flowing down in purple; his headcrowned; his sceptre jewelled; and how in his eyes a child might look.And if they still faltered (Lily was tired out with travelling andslept almost at once; but Mr Carmichael read a book by candlelight), ifthey still said no, that it was vapour, this splendour of his, and thedew had more power than he, and they preferred sleeping; gently thenwithout complaint, or argument, the voice would sing its song. Gentlythe waves would break; tenderly thelight fell (it seemed to come through her eyelids). And it all looked,Mr Carmichael thought, shutting his book, falling asleep, much as itused to look.

Indeed the voice might resume, as the curtains of dark wrappedthemselves over the house, over Mrs Beckwith, Mr Carmichael, and LilyBriscoe so that they lay with several folds of blackness on their eyes,why not accept this, be content with this, acquiesce and resign?

Thesigh of all the seas breaking in measure round the isles soothed them;the night wrapped them; nothing broke their sleep, until, the birdsbeginning and the dawn weaving their thin voices in to its whiteness, acart grinding, a dog somewhere barking, the sun lifted the curtains,broke the veil on their eyes, and Lily Briscoe stirring in her sleep.She clutched at her blankets as a faller clutches at the turf on theedge of a cliff. Her eyes opened wide. Here she was again, shethought, sitting bold upright in bed. Awake.

THE LIGHTHOUSE

- What does it mean then, what can it all mean? Lily Briscoe askedherself, wondering whether, since she had been left alone, it behovedher to go to the kitchen to fetch another cup of coffee or wait here.What does it mean?—a catchword that was, caught up from some book,fitting her thought loosely, for she could not, this first morning withthe Ramsays, contract her feelings, could only make a phrase resound tocover the blankness of her mind until these vapours had shrunk. Forreally, what did she feel, come back after all these years and MrsRamsay dead? Nothinnothing nothing that she could express at all.

She had come late last night when it was all mysterious, dark. Now shewas awake, at her old place at the breakfast table, but alone. It wasvery early too, not yet eight. There was this expedition—they weregoing to the Lighthouse, Mr Ramsay, Cam, and James. They should havegone already—they had to catch the tide or something. And Cam wasnot ready and James was not ready and Nancy had forgotten to order thesandwiches and Mr Ramsay had lost his temper and banged out of theroom.

"What's the use of going now?" he had stormed.

Nancy had vanished. There he was, marching up and down the terrace ina rage. One seemed to hear doors slamming and voices calling all overthe house. Now Nancy burst in, and asked, looking round the room, in aqueer half dazed, half desperate way, "What does one send to theLighthouse?" as if she were forcing herself to do what she despaired ofever being able to do.

What does one send to the Lighthouse indeed! At any other time Lilycould have suggested reasonably tea, tobacco, newspapers. But thismorning everything seemed so extraordinarily queer that a question likeNancy's—What does one send to the Lighthouse?—opened doors in one'smind that went banging and swinging to and fro and made one keepasking, in a stupefied gape, What does one send? What does one do?Why is one sitting here, after all?Sitting alone among the clean cups at thelong table, she felt cut off from other people, and able only to go onwatching, asking, wondering. The house, the place, the morning, allseemed strangers to her. She had no attachment here, she felt, norelations with it, anything might happen, and whatever did happen, astep outside, a voice calling ("It's not in the cupboard; it's on thelanding," some one cried), was a question, as if the link that usuallybound things together had been cut, and they floated up here, downthere, off, anyhow. How aimless it was,, how chaotic, how unreal itwas, she thought, looking at her empty coffee cup. Mrs Ramsay dead; Andrew killed; Prue dead too—repeat it as she might, it roused nofeeling in her. And we all get together in a house like this on amorning like this, she said, looking out of the window. It was abeautiful still day.

- [Macalister's boy took one of the fish and cut a square out of its side to bait his hook with. The mutilated body was thrown back into the sea.]
- "Mrs Ramsay!" Lily cried, "Mrs Ramsay!" But nothing happened. The painincreased. That anguish could reduce one to such a pitch ofimbecility, she thought! Anyhow the old man had not heard her. Heremained benignant, calm—if one chose to think it, sublime. Heaven bepraised, no one had heard her cry that ignominious cry, stop pain,stop! She had not obviously taken leave of her senses. No one hadseen her step off her strip of board into the waters of annihilation.She remained a skimpy old maid, holding a paint-brush.

And now slowly the pain of the want, and the bitter anger (to be calledback, just as she thought she would never feel sorrow for Mrs Ramsayagain. Had she missed her among the coffee cups at breakfast? not inthe least) lessened; and of their anguish left, as antidote, a reliefthat was balm in itself, and also, but more mysteriously, a sense ofsome one there, of Mrs Ramsay, relieved for a moment of the weight thatthe world had put on her, staying lightly by her side and then (forthis was Mrs Ramsay in all her beauty) raising to her forehead a wreathof white flowers with which she went. Lily squeezed her tubes again.She attacked that problem of the hedge. It was strange how clearly shesaw her, stepping with her usual quickness across fields among whosefolds, purplish and soft, among whose flowers, hyacinth or lilies, shevanished. It was some trick of the painter's eye. For days after shehad heard of her death she had seen her thus, putting her wreath to herforehead and going unquestioningly with her companion, a shade acrossthe fields. The sight, the phrase, had its power to console. Wherevershe happened to be, painting, here, in the country or in London, thevision would come to her, and her eyes, half closing, sought somethingto base her vision on. She looked down the railway carriage, theomnibus; took a line from shoulder or cheek; looked at the windowsopposite; at Piccadilly, lamp-strung in the evening. All had been partof the fields of death. But always something—it might be a face, avoice, a paper boy crying STANDARD, NEWS—thrust through, snubbed her,waked her, required and got in the end an effort of attention, so thatthe vision must be perpetually remade. Now again, moved as she was bysome instinctive need of distance and blue, she looked at the baybeneath her, making hillocks of the blue bars of the waves, andstony fields of the purpler spaces, again she was roused as usual bysomething incongruous. There was a brown spot in the middle of thebay. It was a boat. Yes, she realised that after a second. But whoseboat? Mr Ramsay's boat, she replied. Mr Ramsay; the man who hadmarched past her, with his hand raised, aloof, at the head of aprocession, in his beautiful boots, asking her for sympathy, whichshe had refused. The boat was now half way across the bay.

So fine was the morning except for a streak of wind here and there thatthe sea and sky looked all one fabric, as if sails were stuck high upin the sky, or the clouds had dropped down into the sea. A steamer farout at sea had drawn in the air a great scroll of smoke which stayedthere curving and circling decoratively, as if the air were a finegauze which held things and kept them softly in its mesh, only gentlyswaying them this way and that. And as happens sometimes when theweather is very fine, the cliffs looked as if they were conscious ofthe ships, and the ships looked as if they were conscious of thecliffs, as if they signalled to each other some message of their own.For sometimes quite close to the shore, the Lighthouse looked thismorning in the haze an enormous distance away."Where are they now?" Lily thought, looking out to sea. Where was he,that very old man who had gone past her silently, holding a brown paperparcel under his arm? The boat was in the middle of the bay.

- They don't feel a thing there, Cam thought, looking at the shore,which, rising and falling, became steadily more distant and morepeaceful. Her hand cut a trail in the sea, as her mind made the greenswirls and streaks into patterns and, numbed and shrouded, wandered inimagination in that underworld of waters where the pearls stuck inclusters to white sprays, where in the green light a change came overone's entire mind and one's body shone half transparent enveloped in agreen cloak.

Then the eddy slackened round her hand. The rush of the water ceased;the world became full of little creaking and squeaking sounds. Oneheard the waves breaking and flapping against the side of the boat asif they were anchored in harbour. Everything became very close to one.For the sail, upon which James had his eyes fixed until it had becometo him like a person whom he knew, sagged entirely; there they came toa stop, flapping about waiting for a breeze, in the hot sun, miles fromshore, miles from the Lighthouse. Everything in the whole world seemedto stand still. The Lighthouse became immovable, and the line of thedistant shore became fixed. The sun grew hotter and everybody seemedto come very close together and to feel each other's presence, whichthey had almost forgotten. Macalister's fishing line went plumb downinto the sea. But Mr Ramsay went on reading with his legs curled underhim.

He was reading a little shiny book with covers mottled like a plover'segg. Now and again, as they hung about in that horrid calm, he turneda page. And James felt that each page was turned with a peculiargesture aimed at him; now assertively, now commandingly; now with theintention of making people pity him; and all the time, as his fatherread and turned one after another of those little pages, James keptdreading the moment when he would look up and speak sharply to himabout something or other. Why were they lagging about here? he woulddemand, or something quite unreasonable like that. And if he does,James thought, then I shall take a knife and strike him to the heart.

He had always kept this old symbol of taking a knife and strikinghis father to the heart. Only now, as he grew older, and satstaring at his father in an impotent rage, it was not him, that oldman reading, whom he wanted to kill, but it was the thing thatdescended on him—without his knowing it perhaps: that fierce suddenblack-winged harpy, with its talons and its beak all cold and hard,that struck and struck at you (he could feel the beak on his bare legs,where it had struck when he was a child) and then made off, and therehe was again, an old man, very sad, reading his book. That he wouldkill, that he would strike to the heart. Whatever he did—(and hemight do anything, he felt, looking at the Lighthouse and the distantshore) whether he was in a business, in a bank, a barrister, a man atthe head of some enterprise, that he would fight, that he would trackdown and stamp out—tyranny, despotism, he called it—making peopledo what they did not want to do, cutting off their right to speak.

Howcould any of them say, But I won't, when he said, Come to theLighthouse. Do this. Fetch me that. The black wings spread, and thehard beak tore And then next moment, there he sat reading his book;and he might look up—one never knew—quite reasonably. He might talkto the Macalisters. He might be pressing a sovereign into some frozenold woman's hand in the street, James thought, and he might be shoutingout at some fisherman's sports; he might be waving his arms in the airwith excitement. Or he might sit at the head of the table dead silentfrom one end of dinner to the other. Yes, thought James, while theboat slapped and dawdled there in the hot sun; there was a waste ofsnow and rock very lonely and austere; and there he had come to feel,quite often lately, when his father said something or did somethingwhich surprised the others, there were two pairs of footprints only;his own and his father's. They alone knew each other.

What then wasthis terror, this hatred? Turning back among the many leaveswhich the past had folded in him, peering into the heart of thatforest where light and shade so chequer each other that all shapeis distorted, and one blunders, now with the sun in one's eyes,now with a dark shadow, he sought an image to cool and detach and roundoff his feeling in a concrete shape. Suppose then that as a childsitting helpless in a perambulator, or on some one's knee, he had seena waggon crush ignorantly and innocently, some one's foot? Suppose hehad seen the foot first, in the grass, smooth, and whole; then thewheel; and the same foot, purple, crushed. But the wheel was innocent.So now, when his father came striding down the passage knocking them upearly in the morning to go to the Lighthouse down it came over hisfoot, over Cam's foot, over anybody's foot. One sat and watched it.

But whose foot was he thinking of, and in what garden did all thishappen? For one had settings for these scenes; trees that grew there;flowers; a certain light; a few figures. Everything tended to setitself in a garden where there was none of this gloom. None of thisthrowing of hands about; people spoke in an ordinary tone of voice.They went in and out all day long. There was an old woman gossiping inthe kitchen; and the blinds were sucked in and out by the breeze; allwas blowing, all was growing; and over all those plates and bowls andtall brandishing red and yellow flowers a very thin yellow veil wouldbe drawn, like a vine leaf, at night. Things became stiller and darkerat night. But the leaf-like veil was so fine, that lights lifted it,voices crinkled it; he could see through it a figure stooping, hear, coming close, going away, some dress rustling, some chain tinkling.

It was in this world that the wheel went over the person's foot.Something, he remembered, stayed flourished up in the air, somethingarid and sharp descended even there, like a blade, a scimitar, smitingthrough the leaves and flowers even of that happy world and making itshrivel and fall."It will rain," he remembered his father saying. "You won't be able togo to the Lighthouse."

The Lighthouse was then a silvery, misty-looking tower with a yelloweye, that opened suddenly, and softly in the evening. Now—James looked at the Lighthouse. He could see the white-washed rocks;the tower, stark and straight; he could see that it was barred withblack and white; he could see windows in it; he could even see washingspread on the rocks to dry. So that was the Lighthouse, was it?No, the other was also the Lighthouse. For nothing was simply onething. The other Lighthouse was true too. It was sometimes hardly tobe seen across the bay. In the evening one looked up and saw the eyeopening and shutting and the light seemed to reach them in that airysunny garden where they sat.

But he pulled himself up. Whenever he said "they" or "a person," andthen began hearing the rustle of some one coming, the tinkle of someone going, he became extremely sensitive to the presence of whoevermight be in the room. It was his father now. The strain was acute.For in one moment if there was no breeze, his father would slap thecovers of his book together, and say: "What's happening now? What arewe dawdling about here for, eh?" as, once before he had brought hisblade down among them on the terrace and she had gone stiff all over,and if there had been an axe handy, a knife, or anything with a sharp point he would have seized it and struck his father through the heart.She had gone stiff all over, and then, her arm slackening, so that hefelt she listened to him no longer, she had risen somehow and gone awayand left him there, impotent, ridiculous, sitting on the floor graspinga pair of scissors. Not a breath of wind blew.

The water chuckled and gurgled in thebottom of the boat where three or four mackerel beat their tails up anddown in a pool of water not deep enough to cover them. At any momentMr Ramsay might rouse himself, shut hisbook, and say something sharp; but for the moment he was reading, sothat James stealthily, as if he were stealing downstairs on bare feet,afraid of waking a watchdog by a creaking board, went on thinking whatwas she like, where did she go that day? He began following her fromroom to room and at last they came to a room where in a blue light, asif the reflection came from many china dishes, she talked to somebody;he listened to her talking. She talked to a servant, saying simplywhatever came into her head. She alone spoke the truth; to her alonecould he speak it. That was the source of her everlasting attractionfor him, perhaps; she was a person to whom one could say what came intoone's head. But all the time he thought of her, he was conscious ofhis father following his thought, surveying it, making it shiver andfalter. At last he ceased to think.

There he sat with his hand on the tiller in the sun, staring at theLighthouse, powerless to move, powerless to flick off these grains ofmisery which settled on his mind one after another. A rope seemed tobind him there, and his father had knotted it and he could only escapeby taking a knife and plunging it... But at that moment the sailswung slowly round, filled slowly out, the boat seemed to shakeherself, and then to move off half conscious in her sleep, and then shewoke and shot through the waves. The relief was extraordinary. Theyall seemed to fall away from each other again and to be at theirease, and the fishing-lines slanted taut across the side of theboat. But his father did not rouse himself. He only raised his righthand mysteriously high in the air, and let it fall upon his knee againas if he were conducting some secret symphony.

- The sea without a stain on it, thought Lily Briscoe, still standingand looking out over the bay. The sea stretched like silk across thebay. Distance had an extraordinary power; they had been swallowed upin it, she felt, they were gone for ever, they had become part of thenature of things. It was so calm; it was so quiet. The steamer itselfhad vanished, but the great scroll of smoke still hung in the air anddrooped like a flag mournfully in valediction.]
- It was like that then, the island, thought Cam, once more drawing herfingers through the waves. She had never seen it from out at seabefore. It lay like that on the sea, did it, with a dent in the middleand two sharp crags, and the sea swept in there, and spread away formiles and miles on either side of the island. It was very small;shaped something like a leaf stood on end. So we took a little boat,she thought, beginning to tell herself a story of adventure aboutescaping from a sinking ship. But with the sea streaming through herfingers, a spray of seaweed vanishing behind them, she did not want totell herself seriously a story; it was the sense of adventure

andescape that she wanted, for she was thinking, as the boat sailed on,how her father's anger about the points of the compass, James'sobstinacy about the compact, and her own anguish, all had slipped, allhad passed, all had streamed away. What then came next? Where werethey going? From her hand, ice cold, held deep in the sea, therespurted up a fountain of joy at the change, at the escape, at theadventure (that she should be alive, that she should be there). Andthe drops falling from this sudden and unthinking fountain of joy fellhere and there on the dark, the slumbrous shapes in her mind; shapes ofa world not realised but turning in their darkness, catching here andthere, a spark of light; Greece, Rome, Constantinople. Small as itwas, and shaped something like a leaf stood on its end with the gold-sprinkled waters flowing in and about it, it had, she supposed, a placein the universe—even that little Island? Thc old gentlemen in thestudy she thought could have told her. Sometimes she strayed in fromthe garden purposely to catch them at it. There they were (it might beMr Carmichael or Mr Bankes who was sitting with her father) sittingop posite each other in their low arm-chairs. They weie crackling infront of them the pages of THE TIMES, when she came in from the garden,all in a muddle, about something some one had said about Christ, orhearing that a mammoth had been dug up in a London street, or wonderingwhat Napoleon was like. Then they took all this with their clean hands(they wore grey-coloured clothes; they smelt of heather) and theybrushed the scraps together, turning the paper, crossing their knees,and said something now and then very brief. Just to please herself shewould take a book from the shelf and stand there, watching her fatherwrite, so equally, so neatly from one side of the page to another, witha little cough now and then, or something said briefly to the other oldgentleman opposite. And she thought, standing there with her book open,one could let whatever one thought expand here like a leaf in water;and if it did well here, among the old gentlemen smoking and THE TIMEScrackling then it was right. And watching her father as he wrote inhis study, she thought he was not vain, nor atyrant and did not wish to make you pity him. Indeed, if he saw shewas there, reading a book, he would ask her, as gently as any onecould, Was there nothing he could give her?

Lest this should be wrong, she looked at him reading the little bookwith the shiny cover mottled like a plover's egg. No; it was right.Look at him now, she wanted to say aloud to James. (But James had hiseye on the sail.) He is a sarcastic brute, James would say. He bringsthe talk round to himself and his books, James would say. He isintolerably egotistical. Worst of all, he is a tyrant. But look! shesaid, looking at him. Look at him now. She looked at him reading thelittle book with his legs curled; the little book whose yellowish pagesshe knew, without knowing what was written on them. It was small; itwas closely printed; on the fly-leaf, she knew, he had written that hehad spent fifteen francs on dinner; the wine had been so much; he hadgiven so much to the waiter; all was added up neatly at the bottom ofthe page.

But what might be written in the book which had rounded itsedges off in his pocket, she did not know. What he thought they noneof them knew. But he was absorbed in it, so that when he looked up, ashe did now for an instant, it was not to see anything; it was to pindown some thought more exactly. That done, his mind flew back againand he plunged into his reading. He read, she thought, as if he wereguiding something, or wheedling a large flock of sheep, or pushing hisway up and up a single narrow path; and sometimes he went fast andstraight, and broke his way through the bramble, and sometimes itseemed a branch struck at him, a bramble blinded him, but he was notgoing to let himself be beaten by that; on he went, tossing over pageafter page. And she went on telling herself a story about escapingfrom a sinking ship, for she was safe, while he sat there; safe, as shefelt herself when she crept in from the garden, and took a bookdown, and the old gentleman, lowering the paper suddenly, saidsomething very brief over the top of it about the character of Napoleon.

She gazed back over the sea, at the island. But the leaf was losingits sharpness. It was very small; it was very distant. The sea wasmore important now than the shore. Waves were all round them, tossingand sinking, with a log wallowing down one wave; a gull riding onanother. About here, she thought, dabbling her fingers in the water, aship had sunk, and she murmured, dreamily half asleep, how we perished, each alone.

- So much depends then, thought Lily Briscoe, looking at the sea whichhad scarcely a stain on it, which was so soft that the sails and theclouds seemed set in its blue, so much depends, she thought, upondistance: whether people are near us or far from us; for her feelingfor Mr Ramsay changed as he sailed further and further across the bay.It seemed to be elongated, stretched out; he seemed to become more andmore remote. He and his children seemed to be swallowed up in thatblue, that distance; but here, on the lawn, close at hand, MrCarmichael suddenly grunted. She laughed. He clawed his book up fromthe grass. He settled into his chair again puffing and blowing likesome sea monster. That was different altogether, because he was sonear. And now again all was quiet. They must be out of bed by thistime, she supposed, looking at the house, but nothing appeared there.But then, she remembered, they had always made off directly a meal wasover, on business of their own. It was all in keeping with thissilence, this emptiness, and the unreality of the early morning hour.It was a way things had sometimes, she thought, lingering for a momentand looking at the long glittering windows and the plume of blue smoke:they became illness, before habits had spun themselves across thesurface, one felt that same unreality, which was so startling; feltsomething emerge. Life was most vivid then. One could be at one'sease. Mercifully one need not say, very briskly, crossing the lawn togreet old Mrs Beckwith, who would be coming out to find a corner to sitin, "Oh, good-morning, Mrs Beckwith! What a lovely day! Are you goingto be so bold as to sit in the sun? Jasper's hidden the chairs. Dolet me find you one!" and all the rest of the usual chatter. One neednot speak at all. One glided, one shook one's sails (there was a gooddeal of movement in the bay, boats were starting off) between things,beyond things. Empty it was not, but full to the brim. She seemed tobe standing up to the lips in some substance, to move and float andsink in it, yes, for these waters were unfathomably deep. Into themhad spilled so many lives. The Ramsays'; the children's; and all sortsof waifs and strays of things besides. A washer-woman with her basket;a rook, a red-hot poker; the purples and grey-greens of flowers: somecommon feeling which held the whole together.

It was some such feeling of completeness perhaps which, ten years ago,standing almost where she stood now, had made her say that she must bein love with the place. Love had a thousand shapes. There might belovers whose gift it was to choose out the elements of things and placethem together and so, giving them a wholeness not theirs in life, makeof some scene, or meeting of people, one ofthose globed compacted things over which thought lingers, and loveplays.

Her eyes rested on the brown speck of Mr Ramsay's sailing boat. Theywould be at the Lighthouse by lunch time she supposed. But the windhad freshened, and, as the sky changed slightly and the sea changedslightly and the boats altered their positions, the view, which amoment before had seemed miraculously fixed, was now unsatisfactory. The wind had blown the trail of smoke about; there was something displeasing about the placing of the ships.

The disproportion there seemed to upset some harmony

in her own mind.She felt an obscure distress. It was confirmed when she turned to herpicture. She had been wasting her morning. For whatever reason shecould not achieve that razor edge of balance between two oppositeforces; Mr Ramsay and the picture; which was necessary. There wassomething perhaps wrong with the design? Was it, she wondered, thatthe line of the wall wanted breaking, was it that the mass of the treeswas too heavy? She smiled ironically; for had she not thought, whenshe began, that she had solved her problem?

What was the problem then? She must try to get hold of something thtevaded her. It evaded her when she thought of Mrs Ramsay; it evadedher now when she thought of her picture. Phrases came. Visions came.Beautiful pictures. Beautiful phrases. But what she wished to get holdof was that very jar on the nerves, the thing itself before it has beenmade anything. Get that and start afresh; get that and start afresh;she said desperately, pitching herself firmly again before her easel.It was a miserable machine, an inefficient machine, she thought, thehuman apparatus for painting or for feeling; it always broke down atthe critical moment; heroically, one must force it on. She stared,frowning. There was the hedge, sure enough. But one got nothing bysoliciting urgently. One got only a glare in the eye from looking atthe line of the wall, or from thinking—she wore a grey hat. She wasastonishingly beautiful. Let it come, she thought, if it will come.

For there are moments when one can neither think nor feel. And ifone can neither think nor feel, she thought, where is one?Here on the grass, on the ground, she thought, sitting down, andexamining with her brush a little colony of plantains. For the lawnwas very rough. Here sitting on the world, she thought, for she couldnot shake herself free from the sense that everything this morning washappening for the first time, perhaps for the last time, as atraveller, even though he is half asleep, knows, looking out of thetrain window, that he must look now, for he will never see that town,or that mule-cart, or that woman at work in the fields, again. Thelawn was the world; they were up here together, on this exaltedstation, she thought, looking at old Mr Carmichael, who seemed (thoughthey had not said a word all this time) to share her thoughts. And shewould never see him again perhaps. He was growing old. Also, sheremembered, smiling at the slipper that dangled from his foot, he wasgrowing famous. People said that his poetry was "so beautiful." Theywent and published things he had written forty years ago. There was afamous man now called Carmichael, she smiled, thinking how many shapesone person might wear, how he was that in the newspapers, but here thesame as he had always been.

He looked the same—greyer, rather.Yes, he looked the same, but somebody had said, she recalled, that whenhe hac heard of Andrew Ramsay's death (he was killed in a seconc by ashell; he should have been a great mathematician) M Carmichael had"lost all interest in life." What did it mean— that? she wondered. Hadhe marched through Trafalgar Square grasping a big stick? Had heturned pages over and over without reading them, sitting in his roomin St. John's Wooc alone? She did not know what he had done, when heheard that Andrew was killed, but she felt it in him all the same.The only mumbled at each other on staircases; they looked up a thesky and said it will be fine or it won't be fine. But this wa one wayof knowing people, she thought: to know the outline not the detail, tosit in one's garden and look at the slopes of hill running purpledown into the distant heather. She kne him in that way. She knewthat he had changed somehow. Sh had never read a line of his poetry.She thought that she kne how it went though, slowly and sonorously.It was seasone and mellow. It was about the desert and the camel.

Itwas about the palm tree and the sunset. It was extreme impersonal;it said something about death; it said very litt about love. Therewas an impersonality about him. He wante very little of other people.Had he not always lurched rath awkwardly past the drawing-room windowwith som newspaper under his arm, trying to avoid Mrs Ramsay who forsome reason he did not much like? On that account, course, shewould always try to make him stop. He would bo to her. He would haltunwillingly and bow profoundl Annoyed that he did not want anythingof her, Mrs Rams would ask him wouldn't he likea coat, a rug, a newspaper? No, he wanted nothing. There was some quality in her which he did not much like. It wasperhaps her masterfulness, her positiveness, something matter-of-factin her. She was so direct.

(A noise drew her attention to the drawing-room window—the squeak of ahinge. The light breeze was toying with the window.)There must have been people who disliked her very much, Lily thought(Yes; she realised that the drawing-room step was empty, but it had noeffect on her whatever. She did not want Mrs Ramsay now.)—People whothought her too sure, too drastic.

Also, her beauty offended people probably. How monotonous, they wouldsay, and the same always! They preferred another type—the dark, thevivacious. Then she was weak with her husband. She let him make thosescenes. Then she was reserved. Nobody knew exactly what had happenedto her. And (to go back to Mr Carmichael and his dislike) one could notimagine Mrs Ramsay standing painting, lying reading, a whole morning onthe lawn. It was unthinkable. Without saying a word, the only token ofher errand a basket on her arm, she went off to the town, to the poor,to sit in some stuffy little bedroom. Often and often Lily had seenher go silently in the midst of some game, some discussion, with herbasket on her arm, very upright. She had noted her return. She hadthought, half laughing (she was so methodical with the tea cups), halfmoved (her beauty took one's breath away), eyes that are closing inpain have looked on you. You have been with them there.And then Mrs Ramsay would be annoyed because somebody was late, or thebutter not fresh, or the teapot chipped. And all the time she wassaying that the butter was not fresh one would be thinking of Greektemples, and how beauty had been with them there in that stuffy littleroom. She never talked of it—she went, punctually, directly.

It washer instinct to go, an instinct like the swallows for the south, theartichokes for the sun, turning her infallibly to the human race,making her nest in its heart. And this, like all instincts, was alittle distressing to people who did not share it; to Mr Carmichaelperhaps, to herself certainly. Some notion was in both of them aboutthe ineffectiveness of action, the supremacy of thought. Her going wasa reproach to them, gave a different twist to the world, so that theywere led to protest, seeing their own prepossessions disappear, andclutch at them vanishing. Charles Tansley did that too: it was part ofthe reason why one disliked him. He upset the proportions of one'sworld. And what had happened to him, she wondered, idly stirring theplatains with her brush. He had got his fellowship. He had married;he lived at Golder's Green.

She had gone one day into a Hall and heard him speaking during the war.He was denouncing something: he was condemning somebody. He waspreaching brotherly love. And all she felt was how could he love hiskind who did not know one picture from another, who had stood behindher smoking shag ("fivepence an ounce, Miss Briscoe") and making it hisbusiness to tell her women can't write, women can't paint, not so muchthat he believed it, as that for some odd reason he wished it? Therehe was lean and red and raucous, preaching love from a platform (therewere ants crawling about among the plantains which she disturbed withher brush—red, energetic, shiny ants, rather like Charles Tansley).She had looked at him ironically from her seat in the half-empty hall,pumping love into that chilly space, and suddenly, there was the oldcask or whatever it was bobbing up and down among the waves and MrsRamsay looking for her spectacle case among the pebbles. "Oh, dear!What a nuisance! Lost again. Don't bother, Mr Tansley. I losethousands every summer," at which he pressed his chin back against hiscollar, as if afraid to sanction such exaggeration, but could stand itin her whom he liked, and smiled very charmingly.

He must haveconfided in her on one of those long expeditions when people gotseparated and walked back alone. He was educating his little sister,Mrs Ramsay had told her. It was immensely to his credit. Her own ideaof him was grotesque, Lily knew well, stirring the plantains with herbrush. Half one's notions of other people were, after all, grotesque.They served private purposes of one's own. He did for her instead of awhipping-boy. She found herself flagellating his lean flanks when shewas out of temper. If she wanted to be serious about him she had tohelp herself to Mrs Ramsay's sayings, to look at him through her eyes.She raised a little mountain for the ants to climb over. She reducedthem to a frenzy of indecision by this interference in their cosmogony.Some ran this way, others that.

One wanted fifty pairs of eyes to see with, she reflected. Fifty pairsof eyes were not enough to get round that one woman with, she thought.Among them, must be one that was stone blind to her beauty. One wantedmost some secret sense, fine as air, with which to steal throughkeyholes and surround her where she sat knitting, talking, sittingsilent in the window alone; which took to itself and treasured up likethe air which held the smoke of the steamer, her thoughts, herimaginations, her desires. What did the hedge mean to her, what didthe garden mean to her, what did it mean to her when a wave broke?(Lily looked up, as she had seen Mrs Ramsay look up; she too heard awave falling on the beach.) And then what stirred and trembled in hermind when the children cried, "How's that? How's that?" cricketing?She would stop knitting for a second. She would look intent. Then shewould lapse again, and suddenly Mr Ramsay stopped dead in his pacing infront of her and some curious shock passed through her and seemed torock her in profound agitation on its breast when stopping there hestood over her and looked down at her. Lily could see him.

He stretched out his hand and raised her from her chair. It seemedsomehow as if he had done it before; as if he had once bent in the sameway and raised her from a boat which, lying a few inches off someisland, had required that the ladies should thus be helped on shore bythe gentlemen. An old-fashioned scene that was, which required,very nearly, crinolines and peg-top trousers. Letting herself behelped by him, Mrs Ramsay had thought the timehas come now. Yes, she would say it now. Yes, she would marry him.And she stepped slowly, quietly on shore. Probably she said oneword only, letting her hand rest still in his. I will marry you,she might have said, with her hand in his; but no more. Timeafter time the same thrill had passed between them—obviously ithad, Lily thought, smoothing a way for her ants. She was notinventing; she was only trying to smooth out something she had beengiven years ago folded up; something she had seen. For in the roughand tumble of daily life, with all those children about, all thosevisitors, one had constantly a sense of repetition—of one thingfalling where another had fallen, and so setting up an echo whichchimed in the air and made it full of vibrations.

But it would be a mistake, she thought, thinking how they walked offtogether, arm in arm, past the greenhouse, to simplify theirrelationship. It was no monotony of bliss—she with her impulses andquicknesses; he with his shudders and glooms. Oh, no. The bedroom doorwould slam violently early in the morning. He would start from thetable in a temper. He would whizz his plate through the window. Thenall through the house there would be a sense of doors slamming andblinds fluttering, as if a gusty wind were blowing and people scuddedabout trying in a hasty way to fasten hatches and make things ship-shape. She had met Paul Rayley like that one day on the stairs.They had laughed and laughed, like a couple of children, all becauseMr Ramsay, finding an earwig in his milk at breakfast had sent thewhole thing flying through the air on to the terrace outside. 'An earwig,Prue murmured, awestruck, 'in his milk.' Other people might findcentipedes. But he had built round him such a fence of sanctity, andoccupied the space with such a demeanour of majesty that an earwigin his milk was a monster.

But it tired Mrs Ramsay, it cowed her a little—the plates whizzingand the doors slamming. And there would fall between them sometimeslong rigid silences, when, in a state of mind which annoyed Lilyin her, half plaintive, half resentful, she seemed unable to surmountthe tempest calmly, or to laugh as they laughed, but in her wearinessperhaps concealed something. She brooded and sat silent. After atime he would hang stealthily about the places where she was—roamingunder the window where she sat writing letters or talking, for shewould take care to be busy when he passed, and evade him, and pretendnot to see him. Then he would turn smooth as silk, affable, urbane,and try to win her so. Still she would hold off, and now she wouldassert for a brief season some of those prides and airs the dueof her beauty which she was generally utterly without; would turnher head; would look so, over her shoulder, always with someMinta, Paul, or William Bankes at her side. At length, standingoutside the group the very figure of a famished wolfhound (Lily got upoff the grass and stood looking at the steps, at the window, where shehad seen him), he would say her name, once only, for all the world likea wolf barking in the snow, but still she held back; and he would sayit once more, and this time something in the tone would rouse her, andshe would go to him, leaving them all of a sudden, and they would walkoff together among the pear trees, the cabbages, and the raspberrybeds. They would have it out together. But with what attitudes andwith what words? Such a dignity was theirs in this relationship that,turning away, she and Paul and Minta would hide their curiosity andtheir discomfort, and begin picking flowers, throwing balls,chattering, until it was time for dinner, and there they were, he atone end of the table, she at the other, as usual.

"Why don't some of you take up botany?.. With all those legs and armswhy doesn't one of you...?" So they would talk as usual, laughing,among the children. All would be as usual, save only for some quiver,as of a blade in the air, which came and went between them as ifthe usual sight of the children sitting round their soup plateshad freshened itself in their eyes after that hour among the pears andthe cabbages. Especially, Lily thought, Mrs Ramsay would glance atPrue. She sat in the middle between brothers and sisters, alwaysoccupied, it seemed, seeing that nothing went wrong so that shescarcely spoke herself. How Prue must have blamed herself for thatearwig in the milk How white she had gone when Mr Ramsay threw hisplate through the window! How she drooped under those long silencesbetween them! Anyhow, her mother now would seem to be making it up toher; assuring her that everything was well; promising her that one ofthese days that same happiness would be hers. She had enjoyed it forless than a year, however.

She had let the flowers fall from her basket, Lily thought, screwing upher eyes and standing back as if to look at her picture, which she wasnot touching, however, with all her faculties in a trance, frozen oversuperficially but moving underneath with extreme speed.She let her flowers fall from her basket, scattered and tumbled them onto the grass and, reluctantly and hesitatingly, but without question orcomplaint—had she not the faculty of obedience to perfection?—wenttoo. Down fields, across valleys, white, flower-strewn—that washow she would have painted it. The hills were austere. It was rocky;it was steep. The waves sounded hoarse on the stones beneath. Theywent, the three of them together, Mrs Ramsay walking rather fast infront, as if she expected to meet some one round the corner.

Suddenly the window at which she was looking was whitened by some lightstuff behind it. At last then somebody had come into the drawing-room;somebody was sitting in the chair. For Heaven's sake, she prayed, letthem sit still there and not come floundering out to talk to her.Mercifully, whoever it was stayed still inside; had settled by somestroke of luck so as to throw an odd-shaped triangular shadow over thestep. It altered the composition of the picture a little. It wasinteresting. It might be useful. Her mood was coming back to her. Onemust keep on looking without for a second relaxing the intensity ofemotion, the determination not to be put off, not to be bamboozled.One must hold the scene—so—in a vise and let nothing come in andspoil it. One wanted, she thought, dipping her brush deliberately, tobe on a level with ordinary experience, to feel simply that's a chair,that's a table, and yet at the same time, It's a miracle, it's anecstasy. The problem might be solved after all. Ah, but what hadhappened? Some wave of white went over the window pane. The air musthave stirred some flounce in the room. Her heart leapt at her andseized her and tortured her.

"Mrs Ramsay! Mrs Ramsay!" she cried, feeling the old horror comeback—to want and want and not to have. Could she inflict that still?And then, quietly, as if she refrained, that too became part ofordinary experience, was on a level with the chair, with the table.Mrs Ramsay—it was part of her perfect goodness—sat there quitesimply, in the chair, flicked her needles to and fro, knitted herreddish-brown stocking, cast her shadow on the step. There she sat.And as if she had something she must share, yet could hardly leave hereasel, so full her mind was of what she was thinking, of what she wasseeing, Lily went past Mr Carmichael holding her brush to the edge ofthe lawn. Where was that boat now? And Mr Ramsay? She wanted him.

Mr Ramsay had almost done reading. One hand hovered over the page asif to be in readiness to turn it the very instant he had finished it.He sat there bareheaded with the wind blowing his hair about,extraordinarily exposed to everything. He looked very old. He looked,James thought, getting his head now against the Lighthouse, now againstthe waste of waters running away into the open, like some old stonelying on the sand; he looked as if he had become physically what wasalways at the back of both of their minds—that loneliness which wasfor both of them the truth about things.

He was reading very quickly, as if he were eager to get to the end.Indeed they were very close to the Lighthouse now. There it loomed up,stark and straight, glaring white and black, and one could see thewaves breaking in white splinters like smashed glass upon the rocks.One could see lines and creases in the rocks. One could see thewindows clearly; a dab of white on one of them, and a little tuft ofgreen on the rock. A man had come out and looked at them through aglass and gone in again. So it was like that, James thought, theLighthouse one had seen across the bay all these years; it was a starktower on a bare rock. It satisfied him. It confirmed some obscurefeeling of his about his own character. The old ladies, he thought,thinking of the garden at home, went dragging their chairs about on thelawn. Old Mrs Beckwith, for example, was always saying how nice it wasand how sweet it was and how they ought to be so proud and they oughtto be so happy, but as a matter of fact, James thought, looking at theLighthouse stood there on its rock, it's like that. He looked at hisfather reading fiercely with his legs curled tight. They shared thatknowledge. "We are driving before a gale—we must sink," he begansaying to himself, half aloud, exactly as his father said it. Nobody seemed to have spoken for an age.

Cam was tired of looking atthe sea. Little bits of black cork had floated past; the fish weredead in the bottom of the boat. Still her father read, and Jameslooked at him and she looked at him, and they vowed that they wouldfight tyranny to the death, and he went on reading quite unconscious ofwhat they thought. It was thus that he escaped, she thought. Yes,with his great forehead and his great nose, holding his little mottledbook firmly in front of him, he escaped. You might try to lay hands onhim, but then like a bird, he spread his wings, he floated off tosettle out of your reach somewhere far away on some desolate stump.She gazed at the immense expanse of the sea. The island had grown sosmall that it scarcely looked like a leaf any longer. It looked likethe top of a rock which some wave bigger than the rest would cover.Yet in its frailty were all those paths, those terraces, those bedrooms—all those innumberable things. But as, just before sleep, thingssimplify themselves so that only one of all the myriad details haspower to assert itself, so, she felt, looking drowsily at the island,all those paths and terraces and bedrooms were fading and disappearing,and nothing was left but a pale blue censer swinging rhythmically thisway and that across her mind. It was a hanging garden; it was avalley, full of birds, and flowers, and antelopes... She was fallingasleep.

"Come now," said Mr Ramsay, suddenly shutting his book.Come where? To what extraordinary adventure? She woke with a start.To land somewhere, to climb somewhere? Where was he leading them? Forafter his immense silence the words startled them. But it was absurd.He was hungry, he said. It was time for lunch. Besides, look, hesaid. "There's the Lighthouse. We're almost there."

"He's doing very well," said Macalister, praising James. "He's keeping her very steady."

But his father never praised him, James thought grimly.

Mr Ramsay opened the parcel and shared out the sandwiches among them. Now he was happy, eating bread and cheese with these fishermen. He would have liked to live in a cottage and lounge about in the harbour spitting with the other old men, James thought, watching him slice his cheese into thin yellow sheets with his penknife.

This is right, this is it, Cam kept feeling, as she peeled her hard-boiled egg. Now she felt as she did in the study when the old men were reading THE TIMES. Now I can go on thinking whatever I like, and I shan't fall over a precipice or be drowned, for there he is, keeping his eye on me, she thought.

At the same time they were sailing so fast along by the rocks that it was very exciting—it seemed as if they were doing two things at once; they were eating their lunch here in the sun and they were also making for safety in a great storm after a shipwreck. Would the water last? Would the provisions last? she asked herself, telling herself a story but knowing at the same time what was the truth.

They would soon be out of it, Mr Ramsay was saying to old Macalister;but their children would see some strange things. Macalister said hewas seventy-five last March; Mr Ramsay was seventy-one. Macalister saidhe had never seen a doctor; he had never lost a tooth. And that's theway I'd like my children to live—Cam was sure that her father wasthinking that, for he stopped her throwing a sandwich into the sea andtold her, as if he were thinking of the fishermen and how they lived,that if she did not want it she should put it back in the parcel. Sheshould not waste it.

He said it so wisely, as if he knew so well allthe things that happened in the world that she put it back at once, andthen he gave her, from his own parcel, a gingerbread nut, as if he werea great Spanish gentleman, she thought, handing a flower to a lady at awindow. He was shabby, and simple,eating bread and cheese; and yet he was leading them on a greatexpedition where, for all she knew, they would be drowned. "That was where she sunk," said Macalister's boy suddenly. Three men were drowned where we are now, the old man said. He had seen them clinging to the mast himself.

And Mr Ramsay taking a look at the spot was about, James and Cam were afraid, to burst out:

But I beneath a rougher sea, and if he did, they could not bear it; they would shriek aloud; they could not endure another explosion of the passion that boiled in him; but to their surprise all he said was "Ah" as if he thought to himself.

But why make a fuss about that? Naturally men are drowned in a storm,but it is a perfectly straightforward affair, and the depths of the sea(he sprinkled the crumbs from his sandwich paper over them) are onlywater after all. Then having lighted his pipe he took out his watch.He looked at it attentively; he made, perhaps, some mathematicalcalculation. At last he said, triumphantly:

"Well done!" James had steered them like a born sailor.

There! Cam thought, addressing herself silently to James. You've gotit at last. For she knew that this was what James had been wanting,and she knew that now he had got it he was so pleased that he would notlook at her or at his father or at any one. There he sat with his handon the tiller sitting bolt upright, looking rather sulky and frowningslightly. He was so pleased that he was not going to let anybody sharea grain of his pleasure. His father had praised him. They must thinkthat he was perfectly indifferent. But you've got it now, Cam thought.

They had tacked, and they were sailing swiftly, buoyantly on longrocking waves which handed them on from one to another with anextraordinary lilt and exhilaration beside the reef. On the left arow of rocks showed brown through the water which thinned andbecame greener and on one, a higher rock, a wave incessantly brokeand spurted a little column of drops which fell down in a shower. Onecould hear the slap of the water and the patter of falling drops and akind of hushing and hissing sound from the waves rolling and gambollingand slapping the rocks as if they were wild creatures who wereperfectly free and tossed and tumbled and sported like this for ever.

Now they could see two men on the Lighthouse, watching them and making ready to meet them.

Mr Ramsay buttoned his coat, and turned up his trousers. He took thelarge, badly packed, brown paper parcel which Nancy had got ready andsat with it on his knee. Thus in complete readiness to land he satlooking back at the island. With his long-sighted eyes perhaps hecould see the dwindled leaf-like shape standing on end on a plate ofgold quite clearly. What could he see? Cam wondered. It was all ablur to her. What was he thinking now? she wondered. What was it hesought, so fixedly, so intently, so silently? They watched him, bothof them, sitting bareheaded with his parcel on his knee staring andstaring at the frail blue shape which seemed like the vapour ofsomething that had burnt itself away. What do you want? they bothwanted to ask. They both wanted to say, Ask us anything and we willgive it you. But he did not ask them anything. He sat and looked atthe island and he might be thinking, We perished, each alone, or hemight be thinking, I have reached it. I have found it; but he saidnothing.

Then he put on his hat: "Bring those parcels," he said, nodding his head at the things Nancyhad done up for them to take to the Lighthouse. "The parcels for theLighthouse men," he said. He rose and stood in the bow of the boat,very straight and tall, for all the world, James thought, as if he weresaying, "There is no God," and Cam thought, as if he were leaping intospace, and they both rose to follow him as he sprang, lightly like ayoung man, holding his parcel, on to the rock.

- "He must have reached it," said Lily Briscoe aloud, feeling suddenlycompletely tired out. For the Lighthouse had become almost invisible,had melted away into a blue haze, and the effort of looking at it andthe effort of thinking of him landing there, which both seemed to beone and the same effort, had stretched her body and mind to the utmost.Ah, but she was relieved. Whatever she had wanted to give him, when heleft her that morning, she had given him at last."He has landed," she said aloud. "It is finished." Then, surging up,puffing slightly, old Mr Carmichael stood beside her, looking like anold pagan god, shaggy, with weeds in his hair and the trident in his hand. He stood by her on the edge of thelawn, swaying a little in his bulk and said, shading his eyes with hishand: "They will have landed," and she felt that she had been right.They had not needed to speak. They had been thinking the same thingsand he had answered her without her asking him anything. He stoodthere as if he were spreading his hands over all the weakness andsuffering of mankind; she thought he was surveying, tolerantly andcompassionately, their final destiny. Now he has crowned the occasion,she thought, when his hand slowly fell, as if she had seen him let fallfrom his great height a wreath of violets and asphodels which,fluttering slowly, lay at length upon the earth.

Quickly, as if she were recalled by something over there, she turned toher canvas. There it was—her picture. Yes, with all its greens andblues, its lines running up and across, its attempt at something. Itwould be hung in the attics, she thought; it would be destroyed. Butwhat did that matter? she asked herself, taking up her brush again.She looked at the steps; they were empty; she looked at her canvas; itwas blurred. With a sudden intensity, as if she saw it clear for asecond, she drew a line there, in the centre. It was done; it wasfinished. Yes, she thought, laying down her brush in extreme fatigue,I have had my vision.

Chapter 11

Summary and Analysis of To the Lighthouse

Summary and Analysis of The Window: Chapters I-IV

Chapter I

The novel opens with Mrs. Ramsay assuring her son James that the weather will be nice enough tomorrow for a trip to the Lighthouse. As James entertains himself by cutting out pictures, Mr. Ramsay asserts that the weather will not be fine, which provokes James to want to impale and kill his father.

Mrs. Ramsay knits a stocking for the Lighthouse keeper's little boy, who has a tuberculous hip. Charles Tansley agrees with Mr. Ramsay about the unlikelihood of going to the Lighthouse the next day, and Mrs. Ramsay reflects on the fact that neither she nor her children find him agreeable; he is odious and self-centered.

After dinner, the eight Ramsay children go to their rooms. Mrs. Ramsay considers them too critical, noting that they focus too much on the differences between people. She has errands to run in town and invites Charles Tansley to join her. On the lawn, they pass Mr. Carmichael.

Mrs. Ramsay and Charles Tansley enjoy each other's company on the walk, although Mrs. Ramsay pities him. They walk out onto the quay and gaze at the Lighthouse before Mrs. Ramsay stops in to run an errand at a house in town. Charles Tansley waits for her there, and as she silently comes down the stairs, he finds her exceptionally beautiful. He feels proud to accompany her back to the house, holding her bag.

Chapters II-III

Back at home, Mr. Ramsay again tells James that a trip to the Lighthouse will not be possible. Mrs. Ramsay is angry that he is continuing to disappoint their son.

In an attempt to console James, Mrs. Ramsay looks through a magazine to find a picture of a rake or a mowing-machine for him to cut out as an engaging challenge. She hears the sound of men talking in the background, and their voices soothe her. She compares their voices to the sound of the waves beating against the shore—guarding, supportive, and constant. She also muses, however, that the sound of the waves represents destruction and ephemerality.

Mrs. Ramsay comes across a picture of a pocket-knife for James to cut. She then looks out the window and notices Lily Briscoe on the lawn, remembering that Lily is painting her portrait and that she is supposed to keep her head steady.

Chapter IV

Out on the lawn, Lily Briscoe stands alert by her painting, keeping "a feeler on her surroundings" to prevent people from looking at it. She is extremely finicky about having her work viewed by anyone but William Bankes, who approaches her. Lily and Mr. Bankes reside in the village, and they have developed an alliance out of their brief conversations and their frequent encounters. Mr. Bankes respects Lily's good sense and orderliness.

Suddenly, Mr. Bankes and Lily notice Mr. Ramsay, in a private moment, glaring and saying, "Someone had blundered." At this moment, Mr. Bankes suggests that he and Lily take a stroll. It is with difficulty that she turns her eyes from the picture, contemplating with quiet desperation the difficulty of translating her artistic vision directly to the canvas. The two companions stroll off in "the usual direction" toward the break in the hedge at which they can see the bay, the place where they walk every evening.

Watching the waves, Lily is saddened by the realization that distant views outlast the people who gaze upon them. Mr. Bankes reflects on his friendship with Mr. Ramsay, and on a past time on Westmorland Road when Mr. Ramsay had showed his simplicity by admiring a group of small chicks. It was at this time that their friendship had ceased and had become dependent on repetition. He considers Mr. Ramsay's life and how his children both add something to his life and destroy part of it. Lily urges Mr. Bankes to "think of [Mr. Ramsay's] work," for which she has the utmost admiration. Ever since Andrew told her to think of the subject of his work by imagining a kitchen table when no one is there to see it, she sees a scrubbed kitchen table when she thinks of Mr. Ramsay's work. Mr. Bankes believes that Mr. Ramsay is among the men who have finished their best work by the time they are forty. Indeed, Mr. Ramsay made a serious contribution to the field of philosophy at the age of 25 and has merely amplified or repeated this work since. Though Lily has a keen respect for Mr. Ramsay's intelligence, she finds him vain and believes that Mr. Bankes is a finer man.

Arousing them from their thoughts, Jasper shoots a gun, scattering a flock of birds into the sky. Again, Mr. Ramsay proclaims, "Some one had blundered!" with intense and tragic emotion that causes him both shame and indulgent revelry.

Analysis

The opening chapters of the novel firmly establish several of the main characters. Mrs. Ramsay immediately appears as a nurturing and domestic woman whose beauty is of particular interest to those who know her. Her roles as wife and mother form the centre of her universe, and she has a burning desire to please her family and guests. Mr. Ramsay, on the other hand, is guided strictly by rationality and intellect. To his wife's dismay, he can be inconsiderate in his desire to live by truth. He is infinitely practical and self-absorbed, and his repeated expostulation that "someone had blundered" initiates his pattern of loudly and publicly voicing his cerebral anguish. He lives very much inside his own head, not even noticing

Lily and Mr. Bankes on the lawn. These opening chapters also provide a thorough initial portrait of Lily. She is very private and somewhat anxious, and despite her recognition of Mr. Ramsay's vanity, she loves the family very deeply and feels very loyal.

One of the great innovations of modernist novels is the stream of consciousness technique, whereby the writer tries to capture a character's unbroken flow of internal thoughts. Thus an author can describe the unspoken thoughts and feelings of a character without the devices of objective narration or dialogue. In To the Lighthouse, Virginia Woolf makes constant use of this technique, and it is established as the predominant style from the beginning. In this novel, the action occurs not in the outside world but in the thoughts and feelings of the characters as exhibited by the ongoing narrative. Although there is a narrative voice apart from any of the characters, a large portion of the narrative consists of the exposition of each characters' consciousness. Some sections use entire pages without letting an objective voice interrupt the flow of thoughts of a single character.

As a literary device, stream of consciousness was perhaps the most fitting counterpart to contemporary work being done by Sigmund Freud regarding the existence and function of the human unconscious. Freud newly posited the theory that there is a portion of the mind to which we do not have complete access, with the implication that we cannot know all of our own thoughts, fears, motivations, and desires. Writers and artists of this period were intrigued by this concept, and they sought in various ways to depict and illuminate the human unconscious. Although stream of consciousness is the illumination of thoughts and feelings that characters consciously experience, Woolf reaches much further into the human mind than a conventional narrative about the past, providing an intimate view of a character's interiority.

Woolf not only expresses the flow of each character's thoughts, but she also weaves them together into a narrative that flows seamlessly from one character's thoughts to another's without any obvious break or disruption.

Woolf was also a master of a related literary form called free indirect discourse, in which the identity of the narrator is not entirely clear. The novel abounds with dialogue that is not demarcated by quotation marks, as well as phrases and passages that could easily be spoken or merely thought. This form of narration is told in the third person, but it conveys a sense of the character's internal thoughts from the character's own experience, thereby expressing these thoughts somewhere between a first-person and third-person mode of narrative.

Woolf's use of stream of consciousness and free indirect discourse enhance the themes of the novel. To the Lighthouse forcefully conveys the subjective experience of reality, and the proliferation of stream of consciousness indicates that a person's experience cannot be truly viewed through the objective lens of a third party. Instead, Woolf suggests that reality is more like the accumulation of the various perspectives and experiences of individuals. Mrs. Ramsay, for instance, cannot be accurately described by one person. She can only be fully understood as the collection of different impressions of her.

Similarly, the narrative chain that Woolf creates, linking the consciousness of various characters in an unbroken flow, emphasizes the connections between people that Mrs. Ramsay always tries to establish. Though each character is separate, their influence and dependence on one other is undeniable. Their interwoven thoughts form the narrative quilt, and they both propel one another's experiences and emerge from one another's perspectives.

Summary and Analysis of The Window: Chapters V-VII

Chapter V

As Mrs. Ramsay watches Lily Briscoe and William Bankes pass by outside, she tries to calm James by suggesting that the weather may, in fact, be nice enough to go to the Lighthouse. She uses James as a model against which to measure the stocking that she is knitting for the Lighthouse keeper's boy. As she measures the stocking, her mind is occupied by several domestic thoughts. She believes that Lily and Mr. Bankes should marry. She then considers the house and its state of disrepair. The children love it nevertheless—and it removes Mr. Ramsay from the realm of academia—and it is spacious enough to entertain guests. Though she laments its increasing shabbiness, she accepts the notion that "Things must spoil."

Mrs. Ramsay suddenly emerges from her thoughts to scold James, telling him that he must stand still, and he obeys. The stocking, she determines, is too short, and the narrator twice comments that "Never did anybody look so sad."

The narrative voice then shifts to incorporate many different views concerning Mrs. Ramsay's beauty. Some people doubt that there is anything substantial behind her incomparable, silent beauty. Mr. Bankes's reflections on her beauty predominate; he observes that "she's no more aware of her beauty than a child."

Mrs. Ramsay calms herself and kisses James on the forehead, proposing that they find another picture for him to cut out.

Chapter VI

Looking back at Mr. Ramsay, Mrs. Ramsay senses that "someone had blundered"—her husband's vanity is deflated, and he appears outraged and anguished. When Mr. Ramsay veils his torment and playfully tickles James's foot, Mrs. Ramsay delights in the triumph of domesticity. James, however, pushes his father away with hatred, and Mr. Ramsay then reiterates that there is absolutely no possiblity of traveling to the Lighthouse the next day. When Mrs. Ramsay protests that the weather might be fine for traveling, Mr. Ramsay is enraged by his wife's diversion from rationality and fact. Though Mr. Ramsay pursues truth without any consideraton for the feelings of others, Mrs. Ramsay reveres him and feels inferior to him.

Mr. Ramsay resumes his private walk, glancing in at his wife and son through the window as he returns to contemplation. He knows that his intellectual achievements surpass those of most other men, yet he is dissatisfied and longs to achieve the next level of greatness. He draws a parallel between the scope of intellectual greatness and the alphabet. He feels that he has achieved as far as the letter "Q"—which is relatively astounding—yet he fears that he will be a failure if he cannot reach "R." He considers that only about one man in an entire generation ever reaches "Z," and he consoles himself by accepting that it is not his fault that he is not the "chosen" one. He also finds consolation in the thought that even intellectual greatness is ephemeral; even an insignificant pebble will outlast the most revered works of Shakespeare.

Chapter VII

The chapter opens as a continuation of the focus on Mr. Ramsay, with James's thoughts of hatred for him. James hates his "exactingness," his egotism, and his demands for sympathy and need to be reassured of his genius—interfering with James's relationship with Mrs. Ramsay. From James's point of view, Mrs. Ramsay has all of the energy and life, and Mr. Ramsay takes it from her. She protects and surrounds those whom she loves, living for them and leaving nothing of herself by which she can even know herself anymore. In fact, Mrs. Ramsay never wants to feel finer than Mr. Ramsay; she wants always to feel subservient, and she allows him to be more important than she is although he depends upon her.

Mr. Carmichael suddenly passes by as she considers the frailty of human relations; he casts a shadow over the page of the book that she is reading to James. For a reason unclear even to Mrs. Ramsay, she calls out to him to ask if he is going indoors.

Analysis

The major adult characters in To the Lighthouse each have unique ways of creating a sense of stability and permanence admist the chaos and ephemerality of life. In contrast to Mrs. Ramsay's search for stability in the realms of emotion and domesticity, Mr. Ramsey finds stability in the rational domain of philosophical thought. This is the domain in which he also seeks to make a contribution that will transcend his lifetime, providing him with a sense of eternal relevance, though he recognizes the improbability of this aim, knowing that "he would never reach R."

Mr. Ramsay glorifies the idea of the genius and the idea of an individual, like himself, devoting his life to the discovery of truly significant and enduring ideas. Despite the fact that he grasps this notion as his real chance to create something permanent in his lifetime, he cannot deny the fact that he will most likely never achieve this goal. What is more, he acknowledges the meaninglessness and impermanence of any significant contribution to human culture, through his revelation that "The very stone that one kicks with one's boot will outlast Shakespeare." Mr. Ramsay surely understands the ultimate impossibility of permanence in this world, yet he is unable to free himself from this desire to make a lasting impression on it.

He repeatedly mutters the words, "Someone had blundered," which is a line from a poem by Alfred Lord Tennyson called "The Charge of the Light Brigade." The poem itself recalls a disastrous battle during the Crimean War in which Britain lost many men and jeopardized its forward defenses. In its popular interpretation, the poem is a tribute to heroism and courage in the face of crushing defeat, and thus it bears acute significance for Mr. Ramsay's plight. As he confronts his imminent failure, he searches for ways to glorify the heroic effort instead of the success—after all, philosophers seek but do not achieve wisdom—and he longs for the level of respect and admiration after his death that was granted to the soldiers who lost their own lives fighting valiantly. His preoccupation with glory and his persistence, though seemingly indications of his strength, are actually manifestations of his insecurity and neediness.

In additon to further character development, these chapters also continue the patterns established in the novel's opening by remaining loyal to the idea of reality as subjective. Chapter V incorporates a collection of views about Mrs. Ramsay's beauty, suggesting that as a person, she is truly the sum of all of the different perspectives about her. Also, the text further subordinates action in the external world to the processes of the mind. Dialogue and events are often presented merely parenthetically, as insignificant ornaments for a text dominated by descriptions of thoughts and feelings. The novel asserts that life and reality, in essence, are defined by and created out of people's intimate internal existence.

Summary and Analysis of The Window: Chapters VIII-X

Chapter VIII

Augustus Carmichael is an unhappy opium user who visits the Ramsays' house each year as an escape. He does not trust Mrs. Ramsay. Though she goes out of her way to be friendly to him, he does not respond, and Mrs. Ramsay knows that this is because of his wife, who is "odious" and controlling, causing Mr. Carmichael to shrink from Mrs. Ramsay. This rejection causes Mrs. Ramsay emotional injury, for it forces her to consider that all of her generous impulses are only an indication of her self-satisfying vanity. It makes her "aware of the pettiness of some part of her," as well as of the self-serving aspect of human relationships.

Mrs. Ramsay turns her thoughts back to James, her most sensitive child, and decides that she should continue reading the story to him. As she reads, her thoughts wander to her husband, who has stopped at the hedge in front of the house.

As Mr. Ramsay looks through the window at his wife and son, the narrative shifts to his speculation on an article in the Times about the Americans who visit William Shakespeare's house every year. He reflects on greatness and progress, and he tries to imagine how different the world would have been without Shakespeare. In order to assuage his own sense of failure, he wants to believe that "the world exists for the average human being; that the arts are merely a decoration imposed on the top of human life; they do not express it: Nor is Shakespeare necessary to it." He tries to disparage greatness and exalt the ordinary man in order to protect his own pride in the event that he never achieves the success that he wants.

As he ponders, Mr. Ramsay takes his habitual walk,

pausing to stand alone on a piece of land being eroded by the sea and thinking that this erosion to nonexistence is also his own fate. He believes that it is his fate to confront the ephemerality and superfluity of human existence, and it is his very tendency to acknowledge his own insignificance that inspires reverence in others. However, as he looks at Mrs. Ramsay, he deprecates his own sense of domestic comfort, feeling personally unjustified and nonsensical in his method of finding happiness in a world of misery. Lily Briscoe and William Bankes, however, see Mr. Ramsay's self-deprecation as the disguise of a man afraid to confront his own feelings, though Lily admits that the shift from Mr. Ramsay's thoughts to the preoccupations of the domestic world must be great. Mr. Ramsay looks at the sea and turns away.

Chapter IX

Mr. Bankes regrets that Mr. Ramsay behaves so unusually. For her part, though Lily Briscoe does not mind his self-importance, she is bothered by his narrowness of mind. The two friends watch Mr. Ramsay, and Mr. Bankes tries to extract Lily's agreement that Mr. Ramsay is "a bit of a hypocrite," but as he advances towards them, Lily feels that he is sincere and true, and she reflects upon the flood of love that she feels for the Ramsays.

Just as Lily is about to offer a criticism of Mrs. Ramsay to balance the criticism of her husband, she turns to Mr. Bankes and sees a youthful and powerful love in his eyes as he watches Mrs. Ramsay through the window. This rapture makes Lily forget what she was going to say, and she feels eased and grateful for such depth of emotion.

Lily then looks back at her painting and becomes upset, feeling that her own work is "infinitely bad," and she considers how she might have painted it differently. As she focuses her thoughts again on Mrs. Ramsay's loveliness, she muses that women are less capable of worship than men are. She thinks of how Mrs. Ramsay has tried to convince her that "an unmarried woman has missed the best of life," but Lily does not want to marry, for she enjoys her solitude and her work.

Lily now recollects a time when she sat on the floor with her arms around Mrs. Ramsay's knees, feeling that Mrs. Ramsay had some sacred knowledge about the world. In that moment, Lily longed for unity with Mrs. Ramsay, convinced that intimacy was indeed knowledge. She feels a new sense of intimacy with Mr. Bakes when he turns his gaze on Lily's painting, though she has to remind herself that she must let someone see it. When Mr. Bankes asks her what she has intended to portray with the triangular purple shape, Lily replies that it is a depiction of Mrs. Ramsay reading to James.

Chapter X

Mrs. Ramsay's daughter Cam dashes past Mr. Ramsay and Lily's painting, and she does not stop running until Mrs. Ramsay calls her name for the second time. Her mother sends her to ask Mildred whether or not Andrew, Minta Doyle, and Paul Rayley have returned yet. When Cam returns to tell her that they have not returned, Mrs. Ramsay suspects that Paul has proposed and Minta has accepted. James tugs at Mrs. Ramsay to ask that she continue reading.

As she reads, Mrs. Ramsay thinks about having urged Paul and Minta, after lunch, to take a walk together. She considers that it would be unacceptable for Minta to be out with Paul for so long if they were not engaged, and she thinks about Minta's parents, who are far different from their tomboyish daughter. Minta's mother, among others, had accused Mrs. Ramsay of being domineering and of robbing them of Minta's affections, but Mrs. Ramsay thinks the charges are untrue. Mrs. Ramsay thinks of James and Cam, lamenting the fact that they must grow up.

Though she believes that all of her children are gifted, she is most impressed with James, and she is sure that he will never be this happy again. Mr. Ramsay thinks that it is nonsensical to take such a "gloomy" view of life, and Mrs. Ramsay believes that despite his gloom and desperation, Mr. Ramsay is truly happier and more hopeful than she is. She feels that she is in a constant battle with life, which looms terrible before her.

Though Mrs. Ramsay persuades people to marry and have children, she recognizes that she might have made these same choices too early. She wonders whether she and Mr. Ramsay share the unnamed element essential to marriage. As it grows later and darker, Mrs. Ramsay becomes anxious that Andrew, Minta, and Paul have not returned. She looks at James and then at the three strokes of the Lighthouse as it is being lit, two short and one long. Mildred enters to take James to bed before he has a chance to ask about going to the Lighthouse again, but Mrs. Ramsay can see that he is thinking about it, and she suspects that he will remember this disappointment for the rest of his life.

Analysis

This section of the novel begins a discourse on art that will continue through to the end. Woolf explicitly offers Lily Briscoe's somewhat rough and vague artistic philosophy as the painter stands before her canvas, unable to formulate or enact her vision. Looking at the various objects in her visual field ("hedges and houses and mothers and children"), she is at a loss about how to connect them. Her painting must be mainly about unity, about the drawing together of disparate elements to create a unified and cohesive work.

The art of unity and cohesion is a theme that resonates throughout the text and is strengthened in later chapters with Mrs. Ramsay's attempts at drawing together the people and moments that are separated from one another. Coherence (of people, paintings, and moments) is an issue of central importance throughout the novel. Mrs. Ramsay is principally concerned with the merging of people, as she demonstrates in the dinner scene. She hates the fact that her children notice people's differences and distinctions, while she wants only to focus on points of connection and coherence.

In this way, Mrs. Ramsay is an artist of the social realm. Mr. Ramsay, though highly intellectual by nature and concerned with distinctions and categorizations (his physical domain, after all, is by the hedge, which is a symbol of divison and distinction), is also ultimately concerned with merging and coherence. To make a lasting contribution is to bring a common element to all the time periods where the contribution is appreciated. Later, wanting to reconnect to his dead wife and her living wishes, he will draw past and present moments together by finally enacting the Lighthouse trip.

These chapters also solidify some latent feminist themes that persist throughout the novel. Though Mrs. Ramsay is a fairly typical feminine wife-mother, the novel abounds with women who do not behave conventionally and who demand a level of control and independence that would have been seen, at the time, as quite masculine. Despite Mrs. Ramsay's pleadings and warnings, Lily refuses to marry. Like Mr. Ramsay, she is committed to her work and longs for recognition. She is an independent and solitary figure who remains unmarried by choice and not by necessity, which stands in direct contradiction to the social norms in Britain at the time. When Charles Tansley, a more exreme upholder of misogynist views, tells Lily that women can neither write nor paint, Lily resists the pressure to shrink under his offensive reprimands. Even so, Lily is not entirely free from the pressure to fulfill conventional expectations about her gender role, for she often feels guilt or that she has failed when she does not meet these expectations. Later, she will not be able to offer Mr. Ramsay the sympathy that he so desperately wants, which will lead her to feel ineffective as a woman.

Mrs. Ramsay's four daughters, Prue, Rose, Nancy, and Cam, also rebel against the traditional female model. For Prue and Rose, the rebellion is mainly silent. Though they behave as others expect of them, they secretly long for a very different existence than the one that their mother leads. They are uninterested in being entirely consumed by fulfilling the role of wife-mother. For Nancy and Cam, the rebellion is somewhat more evident. Nancy is to reveal her independence during her walk with Paul and Minta. At the end of the novel, she will reveal that she is not a domestic woman when she forgets to order sandwiches for the expedition to the Lighthouse. Cam is seen devilishly darting across the lawn, ignoring the stereotypical female characteristics of being soft, quiet, and obedient. She does not comply with Mrs. Ramsay's first request for her to return, and she puts up great resistance against her father at the end of the novel.

Minta is also an independent woman with stereotypically male characteristics. Mrs. Ramsay remembers that Minta used to walk around with a hole in her stocking and marvels at how different she is from her parents. She describes Minta as a "tomboy." Even Mrs. Ramsay herself, despite her seemingly complete contentment with her feminine role and her encouragement to others to marry early, sometimes wonders if she made a mistake by choosing this path so quickly. She wonders if other women should postpone such important choices.

Chapter X directly addresses the phenomenon of consciousness, demonstrating (and even explicitly commenting upon) Mrs. Ramsay's capacity to read to James and, simultaneously, to be engaged in a constant stream of thought and speculation. The novel captures the idea of layered consciousness and explores the ways in which thought occurs at different levels.

Summary and Analysis of The Window: Chapters XI-XIV

Chapter XI

Mrs. Ramsay muses that, because children have an exceptional memory, one must always be cautious about what one does in front of them, and now Mrs. Ramsay is glad to have some time alone. She draws a parallel between a solitary person and a "wedge-shaped core of darkness"—an image that is reminiscent of the purple triangle in Lily's painting that represents Mrs. Ramsay—in that, because it is invisible to others, it is limitless. It is only this invisible self, she believes, that finds peace and stability, representing a triumph over the force of life that she battles. As she stares out the window, she feels united with the long, steady third stroke of the Lighthouse. She reflects on the idea that people, when they are alone, attach themselves to inanimate objects and feel that the object both expresses and is the person viewing it. She finds herself thinking and taking comfort in the Lord and is immediately frustrated with herself because she does not believe in God, reason, order or justice and sees this thought as a silly indulgence. Mr. Ramsay passes by his wife on the way over to the hedge and is disheartened by her aloof expression of sadness. As Mrs. Ramsay continues to stare at the light, she thinks of all the happiness that she has had and decides that "It is enough!" Though Mr. Ramsay finds her beautiful and is hurt by her distance, he resolves not to disturb her. However, as he passes by her again she senses that, though he would never ask it of her, he wants to be able to protect her, and she offers a gesture of love and generosity by calling to him.

Chapter XII

Mrs. Ramsay takes her husband's arm and they walk together, though she is unable to tell him about the fifty-pound cost of work to be done to the greenhouse. Instead she talks about Jasper shooting birds, about Charles Tansley, and about the flowers in the garden. They discuss their children. Mrs. Ramsay talks of Prue's blossoming beauty, and Mr. Ramsay expresses his hope that Andrew will work hard enough to receive a scholarship. Finally, Mr. Ramsay summons the courage to tell his wife that he does not like to see her looking as sad as she did earlier, and they both become uncomfortable when she is upset by the realization that he watched her thinking.

Mr. Ramsay reflects wistfully on the days of his youth, when he could walk by himself all day long, spending all of his hours thinking and working. He reprimands himself, however, for thinking this way, reminding himself that having eight children is indeed an accomplishment. Though they begin to argue, Mr. Ramsay kisses Mrs. Ramsay's hand with great affection and intensity, bringing tears to her eyes and revealing the depth of feeling that they share.

As they walk back to the house, she thinks that though he is blind to many of the ordinary pleasures of life, he has a clear vision of the extraordinary things, and she feels that a mind like his must necessarily be different from the minds of most people. She looks at the first evening star with a surge of joy, wanting to show it to him but knowing that "He never looked at things." She sees Lily and Mr. Bankes walking together and decides, with excitement, that they should marry each other.

Chapter XIII

Lily Briscoe and William Bankes discuss which European countries and museums they have visited. Lily suggests that it is preferable not to see the pictures of others because "they only made one hopelessly discontented with one's own work." Mr. Bankes points out that the greatness of some would not be possible without the humbleness of many as a contrast. Lily has an impulse to compliment him, but she restrains herself, realizing that unlike most other people he does not want flattery.

They see Mr. and Mrs. Ramsay watching Prue and Jasper playing catch, and Lily decides that marriage is just this: "a man and a woman looking at a girl throwing a ball." This moment impresses Lily as a pure symbol of marriage, though this dramatic viewing renders each member of the Ramsay family hard-edged and separate. When Mr. Ramsay speaks, a spell seems to be broken, and Mr. Ramsay retreats to his study. Mrs. Ramsay asks if Nancy has been on the walk with Paul and Minta.

Chapter XIV

This chapter is a flashback from the perspective of the objective narrator, who answers Mrs. Ramsay's question by describing Nancy's setting off with Paul, Minta, and Andrew on their walk to the beach. Minta has a powerful effect on Nancy, who feels elated whenever Minta takes her hand and downtrodden whenever Minta drops her hand.

At the beach, they separate, and Nancy and Andrew are both conscious of allowing the couple to be alone. Nancy wades out to small pools of water, looking over at the horizon and ruminating on the simultaneous vastness and smalleness of things. Running onto the shore to avoid the incoming tide, she takes refuge behind a rock only to find Paul and Minta kissing, and she is outraged.

As the party climbs up the cliff, Minta realizes with a start that she lost her grandmother's brooch. She is severely distraught, and they all return to the beach in search of it. Because the tide is too high, they decide to return later when they might be able to find it. Paul and Minta walk ahead, and he tries to comfort her by explaining that he is famous for finding things. He silently resolves to leave the house at dawn to find the brooch and, if unsuccessful, to buy her another from Edinburgh. As they approach the house and Paul sees that the windows are lit, he knows that they are ready for dinner and his eyes "feel full."

Analysis

Mrs. Ramsay feels certain that every experience is truly transient, yet she remains compelled to connect herself with symbols of permanence. She reflects on this tension as she sits at the window knitting (also a manifestation of her desire to weave and stick everything together into a cohesive whole) and staring at the Lighthouse. For Mrs. Ramsay, the steady stroke of the Lighthouse represents stability and permanence. For this reason, she connects herself to it, unites herself with it, in hopes of gaining a similar sense of connection to the present and to eternity. Mesmerized, Mrs. Ramsay figuratively attaches herself to and becomes the light, assimilating her own existence into this radiating energy and thereby asserting its creative force. Ironically, although this light is steady and enduring, it is also broken into pulses, which undermines its supposed stability. In addition, she refers to the inanimate things to which she unites herself in order to share in their permanence, yet none of these things is actually inanimate or permanent. Trees, streams, and flowers are all objects or systems that change or die. Once again, these tensions undermine Mrs. Ramsay's gesture of unity with symbols of endurance, and therefore the novel suggests the futility of her attempts.

Even the rhythm of Mrs. Ramsay's thoughts changes to mimic the rhythm of the pulsating light, capturing the three-stroke pattern in her thought structure. As she looks up to "meet the stroke of the Lighthouse," her thoughts proceed in three subsequent phrases of almost equal length, ending with "the long steady stroke, the last of the three, which was her stroke." In additionn the repetition of the phrase "sitting and looking" embodies the rhythmic pulses of light, indicating not only that Mrs. Ramsay senses a deep personal connection with the light, but also that she is inhabited by its energy and rhythm. It becomes her life force, reaching her from the Lighthouse at a great distance.

Mrs. Ramsay's vision of the essence of the individual as a "wedge-shaped core of darkness" is interesting in its resonance with Lily's abstract depiction of Mrs. Ramsay as a purple triangle in her painting.

This image potentially reveals some of Mrs. Ramsay's underlying feelings about human relations and their frailty, for though she tries to draw people together, a wedge is an emblem of separation. Instead of finding peace and stability in the idea of social communion, she suggests that true stability can only be reached by this invisible core self, which is entirely private and removed from the reflections and influence of others. In this very perrsonal moment, Mrs. Ramsay's stream of consciousness reveals a fundamental dissonance with her most prominent values, and its complexity adds depth to her character.

In Chapter XIII, Lily's work emerges as the novel's expression of the unique power of an artist (a characterization of Lily and her work that the final chapter will complete). Though Mr. Ramsay struggles to gain control and immortality through his intellectual endeavors, he is unable to attain this level of success. Lily, however, makes obvious the almost magical ability of an artist to come close to attaining this goal by creating a product of universal significance. As she sees Mr. and Mrs. Ramsay watching Jasper and Prue playing catch, she views them through an artist's lens and, in the space of a few moments, envisions them as symbols: of husband and wife, of marriage. She makes these individuals abstract representations of one of the most significant social relationships, and in so doing, she hints at her intense powers of creation.

Chapter XIV is a flashback entirely enclosed within parentheses. At the end of Chapter XIII, Mrs. Ramsay asks if Nancy has followed Paul and Minta on their walk, and this question is followed by the narrator's descripton of Nancy's decision to accompany them, as well as a description of their walk. This section is taken out of real time—exploring the subjectivity of time and experience—and out of the context of the progressing narrative. In fact, Chapter XV will be a jolt back into the present, when Prue responds directly to her mother's question.

Summary and Analysis of The Window: Chapters XV-XVII

Chapters XV-XVI

Prue responds to Mrs. Ramsay's question from the end of chapter XIII, saying that she thinks that Nancy did go with Minta and Paul on their walk.

Mrs. Ramsay considers that Paul is less likely to have proposed with Nancy present. Suddenly, Jasper and Rose enter the room, relaying Mildred's question about postponing dinner until all of the guests have returned, and Mrs. Ramsay declines to do so. She is irritated by the tardiness of the four who set out on their walk, feeling that this is a special occasion on account of Mr. Bankes's final willingness to attend.

Mrs. Ramsay charges the children with the task of choosing her necklace, knowing that Rose particularly appreciates this privilege. Mrs. Ramsay once again thinks of her children growing up, and she is saddened by the prediction that Rose will grow and suffer.

As Mrs. Ramsay watches the birds through the window and broaches the topic of Jasper shooting them, Jasper feels rebuked. He then feels ignored as Mrs. Ramsay turns her attention to a noise in the hall indicating that the four tardy adventurers have returned.

Mrs. Ramsay walks downstairs, accepting her guests' quiet "tribute to her beauty" as though she were a queen, and she wonders if Paul has proposed. The clamor of a gong announces dinner.

Chapter XVII

Sitting at the head of the table, Mrs. Ramsay instructs her guests where to sit, indicating that Mr. Bankes should sit beside her. She notices Mr. Ramsay at the other end of the table, frowning, but she feels indifferent to him at the moment, feeling that it had all "come to an end." She silently laments that the room is shabby and that "nothing seemed to have merged," knowing that "the whole of the effort of flowing and creating rested on her."

This thought brings her to action. She makes small talk with Mr. Bankes, feeling a sense of pity for him that Lily Briscoe detects. Lily remains removed from the conversation, thinking of her painting and deciding that she will fix it tomorrow by moving the tree more toward the middle. Mr. Tansley is disgusted by the "rot" they all talk. He avoids participating in the conversation and considers that the silliness of women makes civilization "impossible." He asserts himself toward Mrs. Ramsay by reiterating that they will not go to the Lighthouse the next day.

Lily questions her concern for Mr. Tansley's chauvinistic opinions about women, and when she addresses him, Mr. Tansley is well aware of the fact that she is doing so only to annoy him, because it is clear to him that she despises him. Mr. Tansley wishes to be alone in his room, working, but he also wants to prove to Mrs. Ramsay that he is not a "dry prig." However, when he turns to speak to her, Mrs. Ramsay is already talking with William Bankes about an old friend, Carrie Manning, with whom she has lost touch. Mr. Bankes tells her that "people soon drift apart," and he reflects on his own frustration at his feeling of obligation to attend this dinner on account of his friendship with Mrs. Ramsay although he has nothing to say to her and would rather be working. He and Mrs. Ramsay make small talk as a way of imposing order and uniformity on the situation, and Mr. Tansley notices its insincerity, feeling that it is all nonsense and longing to assert himself again. They speak of going to the Lighthouse, and Mr. Tansley feels resentful that none of them recognizes his significance. Noticing Mrs. Ramsay's desperation about how the members of the party are getting along, Lily decides to help her by being nice to Mr. Tansley, asking him to take her to the Lighthouse. Feeling that she has made a sizable sacrifice by being insincere, Lily thinks of the weakness of human relations. Her spirits are raised only by the thought of moving the tree to the middle of her painting.

Mrs. Ramsay thinks back twenty years to her friendship with the Mannings, while she realizes that Mr. Bankes no longer wants to talk about them. Mr. Bankes, Lily, and Mrs. Ramsay feel that something is lacking in the party. Indeed each person at the table fears that he or she is the only one who is not interested in the conversation. Wishing that her husband would say something, Mrs. Ramsay looks over at Mr. Ramsay, who is scowling at Augustus Carmichael's request for more soup. Mr. and Mrs. Ramsay shoot knowing glances across the table, having a silent argument about the disgracefulness or harmlessness of asking for more soup. She respects Mr. Carmichael for doing what he wishes, even given that he does not like her.

Mrs. Ramsay asks Rose and Roger to light the candles. Mrs. Ramsay and Mr. Carmichael are fixated on the dish of fruit at the centre of the table, and Mrs. Ramsay feels that this unites them. She also imagines that the candlelight unites them all against the wavering, watery, ethereal world outside.

Minta and Paul arrive, explaining that they were held up by the lost brooch. Mrs. Ramsay decides that he must have proposed and is suddenly jealous of Minta's glowing attractiveness. Mrs. Ramsay directs Paul to sit by her, hoping that he will fill her in. When he uses the word "we" with a sense of meaning, she knows that he has proposed.

As Lily asks Paul about the lost brooch, she has an impulse to help him find it and to be included in their life, but she knows that he is indifferent to her help. She is divided between feeling that love is a beautiful, exciting thing, and conversely that it is the "stupidest, most barbaric of human passions." Appropriately, Mrs. Ramsay, at this moment, is trying to devise a plan to match Lily with Mr. Bankes. Mrs. Ramsay finally feels a sense of eternity and coherence, which causes her immense joy, peace, and a feeling of stillness. She feels as though she is hanging suspended over the party as the men discuss novels, easily unveiling their thoughts and feelings while she observes them.

She continues to watch over the fruit bowl as well, deriving a sense of serenity from the arrangement. She is therefore disturbed when someone takes a piece of fruit. She looks over at her children, who remain removed from the party and seem to be amused by a joke of their own. At the other end of the table, Mr. Ramsay is telling a story and reciting a poem, and as Mrs. Ramsay looks out the window, she hears only their laughter and voice inflections. When the story is over, she stands and sees her guests out of the dining room, watching as the scene becomes "already the past."

Analysis

As a woman very concerned with creating a warm and domestic atmosphere, Mrs. Ramsay attempts to create unity among the family and guests who are visiting the summer home. She desperately wants to create lasting and beautiful moments among her guests at the dinner table, but she is forced to recognize the ultimate brevity of this experience even if merging occurs.

She despairs at the state of disunity at the beginning of dinner: "Nothing seemed to have merged. They all sat separate. And the whole of the effort of merging and flowing and creating rested on her." She wants to eliminate any distance or separations of consciousness between the people at the table, and she feels fully responsible for the creation of something meaningful.

Mrs. Ramsay's goal is finally achieved after she and Augustus Carmichael unite by looking together at the basket of fruit on the table. In this moment, Mrs. Ramsay's vision of unity seems fulfilled, and she revels in the abstract nearness of the people at the meal. She even compares this unified and stable image to the wavering, unsteady, and quickly changing world outside of the window.

This comparison serves as an indication that her sense of impermanence in the moment is, in fact, misguided; the dinner will end and the outside environment will continue on as usual. She fully realizes this tension as her guests are leaving; she watches as the scene becomes "already the past."

She is no longer able to indulge in the sense of beauty and transcendence by which she earlier had been overcome. She allows herself to confront the fact that the experiences that comprise her conscious reality move so quickly into the past that they almost cease to exist in the present. While Mrs. Ramsay believes in the inescapably ephemeral nature of reality, she is unable to fully release herself from the need to find permanence in her creations of beauty and unity. Thus, her ability to draw people together in a moment of complete unity is not something permanent; it is Mrs. Ramsay's power of art, as Lily later realizes.

If art, as Lily defines it, is about coherence and the joining of disparate elements, Mrs. Ramsay is indeed a masterful artist. Her joy when this moment is finally achieved is a resolution of her disappointment and anxiety at the beginning of the dinner, when coherence was utterly lacking.

Though she recognizes, at the end of the meal, that even these most meaningful moments are fleeting, she later finds comfort in the idea that the meal will be remembered by all of her guests and, in that way, she has created a lasting if not permanent work of art.

The dinner scene also draws a parallel between Lily Briscoe and Mrs. Ramsay, for they both reveal their highest powers of human comprehension. Through the narratives of their streams of consciousness during the dinner, the reader becomes aware of how quickly and thoroughly these women are able to comprehend the unspoken thoughts and feelings of those around them. They both are extremely perceptive of the mental lives of others.

Summary and Analysis of The Window: Chapters XVIII-XIX

Chapter XVIII

As soon as Mrs. Ramsay dismisses herself from the party, Lily senses that "a sort of disintegration set in"—all of the others start going their separate ways. The subject of conversation reverts from poetry to politics. Mrs. Ramsay walks upstairs, wanting a moment to herself after all of the dinner chatter. She wants to extract one thing from the dinner, perhaps the very essence of this gathering of people, to separate from the rest of her collection of memories, and she looks out the window at the branches of an elm tree to gain an impression of stillness, order, and stability.

She feels as though the world is changing and, like the stroke of the Lighthouse, she uses the elm tree to ground herself in a feeling of constancy. She then finds the one thought of the dinner party, as fleeting as the party was, that provides the sense of stability she was looking for: she knows that the guests, for the rest of their lives, will have this memory of the party—Paul and Minta will revive their memory of the special evening even after Mrs. Ramsay has died. In this way, the party has a life extending far beyond its immediate and passing existence, and this comforts Mrs. Ramsay.

She enters the children's room, annoyed that Cam and James are still awake. Cam cannot fall asleep because she is frightened by a pig skull on the wall that James insists on keeping in the bedroom. Mrs. Ramsay covers the skull with her own shawl and lays in bed with Cam, speaking rhythmically to her of beautiful and comforting things until she falls asleep. She then walks over to James's bed, assuring him that the skull is still there. He asks her if they will go to the Lighthouse tomorrow, and she answers that they will go soon, on the next nice day. She is upset even with herself for raising his hopes, probably just for those hopes to be crushed by Mr. Ramsay and Charles Tansley.

As she walks to the stairs, she engages in an inner dialogue about her mixed feelings for Charles Tansley. When Mrs.

Ramsay arrives at the top of the stairs, Prue looks up at her, proudly and reverently thinking, "That's my mother." Prue tells her that they will go down to the beach to watch the waves, and Mrs. Ramsay is suddenly filled with gaiety. Though she wants to accompany them, she feels a strong and undefinable need to stay at home. She goes into the other room, where Mr. Ramsay is reading.

Chapter XIX

Mrs. Ramsay has the sense of having entered the room for something that she wants, but she does not know what. She notices that her husband does not want to be disturbed. He is engrossed in a book by Sir Walter Scott (whom Charles Tansley had discussed over dinner, saying that no one read him anymore), obvously moved by it and rapidly flipping the pages. She knows that Mr. Ramsay is troubled by the idea that no one will read his own books, and this troubles her in turn. She resumes her knitting of the stocking.

Mrs. Ramsay thinks to herself that fame does not matter, and she once again feels that she has come here for something, not knowing what that thing is. She remembers the lines of a poem recited at dinner ("And all the lives we ever lived/And all the lives to be,/Are full of trees and changing leaves." She picks up a book, reading from different pages at random. She is roused by the sound of her husband slapping his thigh, and they look up at each other, silently communicating.

Mr. Ramsay, utterly engaged with the story, suddenly forgets his own failures and his quest for personal greatness. He is moved to tears by the death and sorrow of the characters. Stifling a desire to complain to his wife that young men did not admire him, he feels determined not to bother her and notices how peaceful she looks as she is reading. He reprimands himself for this feeling of domestic comfort and returns to his book.

As Mrs. Ramsay reads, she senses that Mr. Ramsay is watching her. He is glad that she no longer looks sad, and he is astonished by her beauty—but he doubts that she comprehends what she is reading.

Mrs. Ramsay finishes reading, and they begin a sparse conversation about Paul and Minta's engagement. During the moments of silence, Mrs. Ramsay wishes that her husband would say something, though she does sense their growing intimacy. He tells her that she will not finish the stocking tonight, and she agrees. In silence again, she realizes that he wants her to tell him that she loves him, but this is something that she finds herself unable to say. She stands and looks out the window, feeling that he is watching her and finding her beautiful. She turns to him and smiles, knowing that, although she has said nothing, he knows that she loves him. She tells him that he was right—it will be too wet tomorrow for a trip to the Lighthouse—and she knows that he can feel her love.

Analysis

Mrs. Ramsay's reliance on the tree outside the window (standing tall like the Lighthouse, but much closer) to offer her a sense of stability and order is immediately reminiscent of the tree in Lily's painting, which has been an object of thought throughout the dinner. For Lily, this tree also represents order and stability. By moving it to the middle, she will create a composition of unity and balance, and this composition will be more likely to endure. She will combine all of the elements into a coherent picture, and her ability to do this expresses her artist's sense of control and order. This connection between Lily and Mrs. Ramsay, both looking to trees as representations of stability, is particularly important in light of the novel's conclusion, when it seems that only Lily's ability to fulfill her artistic vision from ten years earlier can save the Ramsays. Lily's later completion of the painting is evidence that something from the night of the dinner party has staying power, just as Mrs. Ramsay had wished, even if that permanence exists only through memory and artistic representation.

The symbolic power of the tree gains further resonance through Mrs. Ramsay's recitation of lines from Charles Elton's poem, "Luriana Lurilee"—"And all the lives we ever lived/

And all the lives to be,/Are full of trees and changing leaves." Trees (like water and like nature in general) dichotomously represent both stability and change. Though the deciduous tree itself remains fixed, the leaves on its branches annually repeat the life-death cycle.

Water, too, is a common symbol of the tension between constancy and change. Mrs. Ramsay is comforted by the water's rhythmic lapping against the shore, yet it is also the force that causes the erosion of land over time. Its constancy gives it the power to cause decay. The dual representative purpose of the tree and of water indicates, more generally, that the Ramsays cannot escape the realities of human existence, where the greatest moments last only as long as memory keeps them.

The boar skull in the nursery, in particular the fact that Mrs. Ramsay covers it with her shawl, provides deep and immediate symbolism as this section of the novel nears its conclusion. "The Window" is in large part about the characters' fear of the passage of time and the disappointment, suffering, and destruction that naturally accompany the process of aging. The skull is a clear symbol of the decay of time. The animal from which it came is now nothing more than a skull hanging in the children's room, without meaning or purpose. Its placement in the nursery is significant given Mrs. Ramsay's preoccupation with wanting her children to stay young and to avoid all of the suffering of age and experience. This skull, which so frightens Cam, represents the inevitable end of life and meaning. The animal itself is not remembered through the skull anymore, and Mrs. Ramsay cloaks the skull and its awful significance with her own protective clothing.

When Mrs. Ramsay covers it with her shawl, it parallels her attempts to soothe her children with her warmth and beauty. Just as she tries to shield them from harsh reality (the fact James will not go to the Lighthouse, for instance), she tries to shield them from this grotesquely realistic image. Even so, as she tells James, the skull still hangs beneath the shawl; she can hide it, but she cannot fully erase its looming presence, since the skull still takes up its share of space in the room and in their lives. Later, in the "Time Passes" interlude, the shawl slowly unravels from the skull as the ravages of time take over, with no one to resist or hide the decay. As the house is taken over by natural life processes such as overgrowth and decay, the skull as symbol of death and disintegration is slowly exposed. The silent communication that occurs between Mr. and Mrs. Ramsay throughout the book (and at the end of Chapter XIX, in particular) is perhaps the most compelling expression in the novel of the fluidity of consciousness. The married couple seem to ask and answer one another's silent questions without any conscious effort. It is fitting that Mrs. Ramsay should retreat into her self as a silent and invisible wedge-shaped darkness, not able to express or openly reveal her feelings, during these times of deepest expression.

Summary and Analysis of Time Passes: Chapters I-X

Chapter I

Mr. Bankes, Andrew, Paul, Minta, Prue, and Lily return from their walk on the beach and then retire to their rooms. All of the lamps are slowly extinguished except that of Mr. Carmichael, who customarily lies awake reading Virgil.

Chapter II

Once everyone is asleep and all the lamps are put out, an "immense darkness" envelops the house, seeming to swallow and obliterate everything in it. Everything becomes indistinguishable and entirely still except for a breeze, the "certain airs" that enter the house. The breeze seems to ask each thing in the house how long it will endure. The airs, directed by "some random light" perhaps emanating from the Lighthouse, now enter the bedrooms and cease, for the bedrooms and the people in them are steadfast and the airs have no need to question when they will "perish and disappear." The airs then move through the rest of the house and then cease again, slamming a door in the kitchen with a final sigh. At this moment, at midnight, Mr. Carmichael blows out his candle.

Chapter III

The days pass, and autumn arrives as night "succeeds to night," lengthening and darkening. Through all of the foreboding and life-crushing darkness, the yellow moonlight provides a mellowing influence and keeps the waves lapping against the shore without fail. It seems that "divine goodness" looks upon the house and its characters—but it is not pleased, and it closes the curtain again, confusing them and making it seem that their calm will never return.

An era of desolation and erosion follows. The world seems out of order and full of confusion. It becomes useless to ask the night "as to what, and why, and wherefore."

One dark morning, Mr. Ramsay stumbles along a passage with his arms outstretched for Mrs. Ramsay—but she had suddenly died the night before.

Chapters IV-V

The narrator indicates that time has passed by declaring that the Ramsays' house is now empty "and the doors locked and the mattresses rolled round." The "stray airs" that entered the house in Chapter II of this section appear again, meeting no resistance from anyone. They bluster around the house, its belongings now aged and unused, revealing that there was life in the house's past. The light from the Lighthouse still enters through the window, leaving its image on the opposite wall.

Even during this time of uninhabited desolation, something of the Ramsays pervades the house. The sea airs seem to reiterate their questions: "Will you fade"—"Will you perish"—and some force in the house answers, "We remain." The integrity of the almost entirely undisturbed silence gives the house a noble presence—until Mrs. McNab, the housekeeper, comes as directed to open the windows and dust the bedrooms.

Mrs. McNab makes her way through the house, cleaning it free of age and decay. She is world-weary and life-trodden. She hums a song that she has sung for twenty years. She feels that life is "one long sorrow and trouble," and she wonders, "how long shall it endure?" Then, some recollection brings her joy, for she grins and resumes singing her old song.

Chapter VI

Spring arrives, and Prue Ramsay (looking quite beautiful, people say) marries. But Prue dies that summer in an illness connected with childbirth.

The house continues to be overtaken by time and age, and the Lighthouse continues to shed its authoritative light on the house through the windows. It illuminates Mrs. Ramsay's shawl, which slowly unravels off the skull in the nursery. Mrs. McNab continues to enter and clean the house for a time, until complete silence falls again, disturbed only by the occasional sense that something is falling.

Andrew Ramsay dies instantaneously in France while fighting in World War I. The war revives people's interest in poetry, and as a result, a volume published by Mr. Carmichael has unexpected success.

Chapters VII-VIII

Time wears on with no one to witness it at the Ramsay home. The chaos of storms and lightning batter the house. Days, nights, months, and years run "shapelessly together," bringing a sense of "brute confusion." The house remains desolate and empty.

Mrs. McNab picks a bunch of flowers from the house's garden, thinking it will do no harm since it seems that the family will never come again and the house will probably be sold. Despite her efforts at cleaning the house, its years of disuse and the difficulty of getting help during the war made it impossible for her to do as much as she would have liked. She thinks of Mrs. Ramsay, now dead, and Mrs. Ramsay's clothes, which she will never wear again. She imagines Mrs. Ramsay coming up the drive with one of the children in her grey cloak, and it is clear that Mrs. Ramsay's presence still lingers in the house. She remembers how Mrs. Ramsay used to tend to the garden and the pleasant way she had about her. Mrs. McNab surveys the work—it is too great for one old woman—and she leaves the house to its quiet solitude.

Chapter IX

The house has been deserted, left to rot and ruin, and the airs that enter the house and nibble away at it seem to be triumphant. Toads and swallows have nestled in, and the plants are overgrown. Mrs. McNab now feels powerless to prevent nature from overtaking the abandoned home. The job of reviving the house is too great for one woman. Nothing now withstands the forces of decay and destruction that replace every indication of previous life here. There is none left to watch over the house but the Lighthouse, whose beams enter and survey the rooms.

Finally the Ramsays write Mrs. McNab, telling her of their intention to return to the house for the summer. Mrs. McNab, Mrs. Bast, and Mrs. Bast's son George restore the house as best they can, groaning about the tremendous task. Mrs. McNab remembers Mr. Ramsay and his odd solitude and blindness to others. Sitting with a cup of tea, Mrs. McNab unwinds her ball of memories of the Ramsays. After days of cleaning inside the house and tending to the mess of a garden outside, the task is complete. Then Lily Briscoe arrives late one evening in September.

Chapter X

The house is full again, with Lily, Mr. Carmichael, and Mrs. Beckwith there to visit. Lily lies in bed listening to the ocean, feeling quite peaceful. Mr. Carmichael stays up late reading as he used to. He thinks, as he shuts his book, that it all looks "much as it used to look" ten years ago. In the morning, Lily awakes sitting bolt upright in bed.

Analysis

The rhythm of the novel changes drastically in this middle section. In "The Window," time is subjective and extended, with the events and thoughts occuring essentially over the course of a single day. Time there is not strictly chronological;

it is dictated by the consciousness of a particular character at a particular time, and a moment can elapse in a single sentence or it can take several pages. Time is not linear in that chapters move backwards and forwards, and reality bends to fit the narrative.

In "Time Passes," however, the pace of the novel rapidly accelerates, and ten years elapse over the course of about twenty pages. Linear chronological time replaces subjective time as the consciousness of characters disappears almost entirely from the narrative, while objective reality takes over. Almost nothing of the Ramsays remains. Three family members, including Mrs. Ramsay, die unexpectedly, and the house is now frequented by a character who had been completely absent from the first section of the novel.

Death and destruction take over, just like the characters had always feared. The narrative gives a sense of great potential lost. Amdist the chaos of merciless time, however, the Lighthouse beams still enter the house.

The elusiveness of the Lighthouse is matched by its permanence and everpresence, and this characteristic is explored in the narrative of "Time Passes." In this section, since the house remains empty for ten years, the narrator has complete sovereignty over the text, except for brief interludes by Mrs. McNab. Like the Lighthouse, the narrator presides over the abandoned house. Here the function of the Lighthouse is firmly solidified; its immovable endurance becomes obvious, and it illuminates the ravages of time.

Though the stroke of the Lighthouse lays itself with "authority upon the carpet in the darkness, tracing its pattern," it still cannot exert its influence over the changing world of the Ramsays. The Lighthouse bears witness to these happenings, but it does not interfere with or inhibit them. It is incapable of withstanding or denying the effects of time or the paths of individual consciousness.

Thus the Lighthouse is neither partial nor invasive, merely drawing attention to the changes taking place and making them perceptible to the reader by illuminating them. This function of the Lighthouse again parallels a main role of the narrator in the novel. The narrator chooses to witness, comment upon, and render the story, making it perceptible to the reader, while maintaining the distance of an outside observer who does not interfere. This distance gives readers the sense that the various consciousnesses of the characters determine the shape and rhythm of the text without intervention by the narrator (or even, if we are caught up in the story, without intervention by the author). Woolf creates a reality that, from within the novel, is determined solely by subjective consciousness.

The depiction of subjective consciousness and subjective reality is further achieved in "Time Passes" through the spasmodic, bracketed announcements of the deaths of Mrs. Ramsay, Prue, and Andrew. The narrator's lack of objective, informative, or creative authority is apparent not only in the narrative's reflections and impressions of the characters, but also in these scattered accounts of distinctly factual events in the novel. For example, here is the news of Prue's death: "[Prue Ramsay died that summer in some illness connected with childbirth, which was indeed a tragedy, people said, everything, they said, had promised so well."

The abrupt, isolated accounts read almost as news briefs or short interruptions of the narrative to convey information of which the narrator has just become aware. They are parenthetical and disruptive of the narrative rhythm, suggesting an element of surprise even for the narrator, thereby indicating that the narrator is neither omniscient nor prescient of the various elements of the plot.

In addition, this narrator does not even have complete knowledge of the events themselves; like a third-party observer, some of the knowledge is secondhand. Prue Ramsay died "in some illness connected with childbirth," but the narrator is apparently not aware of the details. Most of the information provided between brackets simply relays the impression of an unspecified "people," and this detail emphasizes the uncertainty of facts that have been garnered from an unrevealed source.

Readers who prefer ominiscient, reliable narrators will

be disappointed that there is no objective certainty even regarding information as factual and significant as the death of the Ramsays. The narrator is characterized as the unknowing, inactive witness and recorder of the fictional world. In this sense the pulse of the Lighthouse is like the flash of a camera, illuminating for the record but not interfering with the Ramsays' house, and illuminating the inside of the house only through selected windows.

Summary and Analysis of The Lighthouse: Chapters I-III

Chapter I

Lily Briscoe sits alone at the breakfast table early in the morning, unable to understand or express her own feelings about Mrs. Ramsay's death. Today, there will be an expedition—Mr. Ramsay, Cam, and James are going to the Lighthouse, though the children are late to depart and Mr. Ramsay has lost his temper because Nancy forgot to order the sandwiches. Lily feels "cut off from other people" and like a stranger in this house, lacking attachments and relations. The world seems aimless and chaotic now that Mrs. Ramsay, Prue, and Andrew are dead, and she feels strangely numb to these changes.

When Mr. Ramsay passes by, Lily pretends to drink from her empty coffee cup to avoid his penetrating gaze. Suddenly, Lily remembers that the last time she sat at this table, ten years ago, she resolved to complete her painting by moving the tree closer to the middle. She did not, however, complete it, so she decides to finish it now. She sets up her chair and easel on the lawn in what she believes to be the exact location of her previous setup, and she suddenly knows what she wants to do with the painting.

But Mr. Ramsay's presence on the terrace paralyzes her and makes her unable to paint. She stalls, trying to avoid his gaze and his declaration—much as he had declared the night before—that she would find them "much changed." He also appears as domineering toward his children, for he essentially demanded that James and Cam go with him on this trip to the Lighthouse, and Lily feels that their spirits are being subdued.

Setting her clean canvas on the easel, she hopes to ward off Mr. Ramsay, but she finds it simply impossible to work while he is at such a close distance. He silently demands something of her that she cannot give, something that Mrs. Ramsay had given. Suddenly, she feels a surge of anger directed at Mrs. Ramsay for dying, for having left her here, and for leaving behind a feeling of emptiness. Nevertheless, she is convinced that she is, in fact, numb to Mrs. Ramsay's death, and she wonders why she tries to make herself feel emotions that are not real. Finally, she decides that the cost of insincerity is worth placating and dismissing Mr. Ramsay, so she decides to recreate the look of rapture, sympathy, and delight that Mrs. Ramsay had demonstrated so many times. Mr Ramsay approaches Lily, and she resolves to give him what she can.

Chapter II

Mr. Ramsay notes that Lily looks somewhat shrivelled, and he approaches her, not really conscious of his hope to evoke her sympathy. Irritated that Lily avoids direct interaction by looking at the sea and speaking of the Lighthouse, Mr. Ramsay emits a loud groan, and Lily feels guilt and self-hatred for not responding to it with the sympathy that she thinks other women would.

Mr. Ramsay begins to explain the significance and difficulty of this trip to the Lighthouse, for Mrs. Ramsay used to send gifts to the men and children who lived there. He talks of how exhausting and painful such trips are, and Lily feels overwhelmed and tortured by his need for her sympathy. She becomes anxious for him and the children to take off on their expedition. She stands in silence, feeling herself an ineffectual woman for not being able to fulfill the emotional duties traditionally expected of women; she is failing to console him in his self-pity.

Grasping for something to say, she comments on his

beautiful boots, and he is pleased. This restorative interaction leads them to a peaceful reconciliation. Suddenly Lily is overcome with genuine sympathy for him, but just as she is finally able to express it, Cam and James solemnly emerge from the house. Lily feels frustrated, wishing that they would provide the sympathy that she almost entirely failed to give. The three travelers proceed to the boat with the brown paper parcels, leaving Lily feeling impressed by the melancholy troupe, inferring that they are bound by some common feeling. Lily now sees Mr. Ramsay's unornamented beauty and newly appreciates his commitment to bare truth.

Chapter III

Lily is both relieved and disappointed that the three Ramsays have left. As she looks at her canvas, she sheds the "disorderly sensations" of the previous several minutes and tries to remember how she originally envisioned this painting. She has extreme difficulty actually making the first stroke, knowing that "one line placed on the canvas committed her to innumerable risks, to frequent and irrevocable decisions," but she knows it must be done, and she executes a quick stroke. She paints rthymically, stepping back to survey the brown lines. She always feels a sense of complete vulnerability before painting, "like an unborn soul." She speculates that her work will only be hung in the servants' bedrooms or stuffed under a sofa. She feels insecure, wondering why she should paint if no one will view her work. She tells herself that she is not, in fact, capable of creating. Suddenly, her artistic faculties take over and she begins painting almost unconsciously, without any disturbance from thoughts of the outer world. She remembers Charles Tansley's discouragement, but she feels a rising tenderness for him as she recalls a day that she spent on the beach with him and Mrs. Ramsay. Mrs. Ramsay was writing letters and watching as Lily and Mr. Tansley skipped stones across the water, getting along quite well. Lily imagines that Mrs. Ramsay was somehow responsible for this scene, as well as for Lily and Mr. Tansley's brief episode of communion. Mrs. Ramsay's simple presence stripped an individual of anger and irritation and brought people together. This recollection refashions Lily's memory of Mr. Tansley more sympathetically, and Lily realizes that, in a sense, this refashioning represents Mrs. Ramsay's own persisting creation of a work of art. Both Lily and Mrs. Ramsay were, in their separate ways, "making of the moment something permanent." This revelation offers Lily a sense of shape and stability amidst chaos, and she feels that she owes it all to Mrs. Ramsay. Walking to the end of the lawn, she sees a boat apart from the others with its sail being hoisted. She knows that this is the Ramsays' boat, and she watches as it passes the other boats as it sails out to sea.

Analysis

In the section called "The Lighthouse," time returns to its original pace in the novel and reality is, once again, defined by the consciousness of the characters. In fact, the first and third parts of the novel seem to collapse into each other, completely obliterating the middle section. The novel has moved from subjective time to linear chronological time and back again. "The Window" ended at night, with the characters going to sleep and entering a period of darkness.

Now, "The Lighthouse" opens with Lily sitting at the breakfast table, and the reader almost feels as though this could be the very next day. However, it is not the very next day—the period of darkness has lasted not for one night but for ten years—and the life of the Ramsays has been irrevocably altered, now that three members of the family, including Mrs. Ramsay, are dead.

Despite Mrs. Ramsay's physical absence, her presence remains in the house and in the memories of those who knew her best. During "Time Passes," Mrs. McNab often vividly envisioned Mrs. Ramsay walking toward the house, tending to her garden. Now, in "The Lighthouse," Lily keeps looking over at the drawing-room steps, imagining and sensing Mrs. Ramsay's seemingly permanent presence. The novel is infused with her consciousness throughout "The Window," and this final section reveals that her consciousness has persisted as a central consciousness even after her death. Though Mrs. Ramsay's thoughts are not directly expressed anymore, her influence is apparent, especially her influence on Lily. Some essential, invisible aspect of her character is imparted through Lily, who even begins to feel a sympathy for Mr. Ramsay that she was never able to feel while Mrs. Ramsay was alive. In this way, Lily embodies some of the beloved woman's "wedge-shaped core of darkness" in its most positive construal. In a sense, this reproduction of Mrs. Ramsay's individual creative power represents the fulfillment of Mrs. Ramsay's wish for permanence and stability.

Just as Mr. Ramsay's anxiety centers around the regret that his life's work will never bring him a sense of lasting recognition, Lily Briscoe worries about the long-term status of her paintings. She is generally considered a rather mediocre artist, and her concerns that her paintings will be thrown into attics and otherwise forgotten are not unfounded. Her emotional investment in the endurance of her own work produces the same general sense of unfulfillment for Lily that their own anxieties and efforts do for the Ramsays. However, unlike the Ramsays, Lily is eventually able to abandon the desire for permanence, and she comes to embrace the uncertainty and instability of experience. Somehow, the distant sight of the Ramsays on the boat sparks a pivotal epiphany, when Lily's creative energy swells to outpouring. The process of removal from them and relinquishment of her anxiety results in the unveiling of Lily's most sympathetic feelings for the Ramsays, and these feelings inspire her vision.

Summary and Analysis of The Lighthouse: Chapters IV-VII

Chapter IV

In the boat, Mr. Ramsay is sitting between Cam and James, fidgeting and becoming impatient with the lack of wind to speed them along. Macalister and Macalister's boy have also come along to help. Cam and James, feeling angry that their father forced them to come along on this trip, hope that the breeze will never rise. Desiring to thwart the entire expedition, they had made a silent pact "to resist tyranny to the death."

Meanwhile, Lily's reflection on Mrs. Ramsay's preoccupation with marriage produces a degree of scorn and resentment for the dead woman. Though Lily has chosen not to marry, the memory of Mrs. Ramsay's presence now compels her to second-guess her decision. But when she considers the flaws in the Ramsays' past relationship, as well as the problems facing other married couples, she suddenly feels triumphant.

Once the boat gets a little farther out into the water, the sails catch the breeze and the boat takes off. Mr. Ramsay and Macalister smoke a pipe, and Macalister recounts the story of the great storm last winter. Mr. Ramsay reprimands James whenever the sail slackens. In their anger, James and Cam only catch a word here and there of Macalister's story, for they are focused on their father and his reactions. Cam is suddenly filled with a sense of pride for her father, knowing that if he had been caught in the storm, he would have been an adventurous hero. But then she remembers her pact with James and suppresses this feeling, remembering that Mr. Ramsay has subdued them once again with his authority and has forced them to do his bidding.

In any case, the speed of the boat fills both James and Cam with a sudden sense of excitement and escape. Mr. Ramsay is also invigorated, suddenly exclaiming, "We perished... each alone," and then, in a gesture of repentance, indicates the shore and their house, which is now too far away for Cam to distinguish. Mr. Ramsay curiously crouches in the centre of the boat, succumbing to self-pity and reflecting on the exquisite pleasure of women's sympathy. He recites poetry despondently so that all can hear. Cam becomes enraged.

Cam thinks of their house and of their lives, realizing how much of it is in the past, and she too murmurs her father's words,"we perished, each alone." Mr. Ramsay begins to tease her about not knowing the points of the compass, and he marvels at the vagueness of women's minds. However, he finds women endearing for this very reason, and he resolves to make Cam smile. James fears that Cam will succumb to Mr.

Ramsay and that he will be left to fight the tyranny alone. Cam does try to resist her father's entreaty, seeking to remain on the side of justice. She longs, nevertheless, to pass on a silent token of her love for her father without upsetting James, who now remembers that his mother also used to give in to Mr. Ramsay's whims. Cam is tempted by his words, his oddity, and his passion, but she finds his blindness and tyranny intolerable. Torn between father and brother, between feelings of love and bitterness, she says nothing.

Chapter V

Lily sees the boat just as the sail catches the breeze and speeds up. In contrast, she feels weighed down by the sympathy that she failed to offer to Mr. Ramsay. She has always found it difficult to praise him, which has made their relationship feel neutral. As she walks back to her canvas, she wonders why her recollection of that day with Mrs. Ramsay and Mr. Tansley on the beach is so vivid, and she resumes her painting. She feels as though she is sitting beside Mrs. Ramsay on the beach. She imagines Mrs. Ramsay sitting silent by her side, the two women resting in the "extreme obscurity of human relationships." As she dips into the paint, she feels she is dipping into the past.

Lily turns her thoughts to the Rayleys, collecting her impressions of them. Her efforts at painting and at "tunnelling her way" into the past become a single endeavor, and she feels triumphant at the thought of telling Mrs. Ramsay that the Rayleys' marriage was not a success (Paul fell in love with another woman). Feeling a hint of contempt for the dead Mrs. Ramsay, Lily celebrates the facts that she has not married and that the Rayleys' marriage failed, for these facts signify some form of victory for Lily and her choice not to marry. She still, however, feels a burning, celebratory surge when she remembers Paul looking for Minta's brooch. She considers the notion of being "in love."

Because she can move the tree to the middle of the painting, however, she feels indivdually centered; she has no need for marriage. Her work is her companion in a different sense, and it endows her life with significance and feeling. Surfacing from her dream-state of memories about William Bankes and Mrs. Ramsay, Lily looks at Mr. Carmichael, who is basking in the sun.

She wants to get his attention, to speak to him, but she does not know what to say. Looking over at the drawing-room steps, she feels that they are unbearably empty without Mrs. Ramsay's presence, and she is suddenly overcome by an intense longing for the deceased woman. She thinks of the ephemerality of life, of how everything vanishes and nothing stays—except art. Words and paint, she decides, do persist—even if they are shoved under a sofa. The moment that is captured in a work of art, in a sense, remains forever. She begins to cry, and as she aches for an understanding of life in all of its brief miraculousness, she calls Mrs. Ramsay's name aloud.

Chapter VI

Macalister's boy cuts a square of flesh out of the side of a fish to use for bait, and the fish, stlll alive, is thrown back into the sea.

Chapter VII

Lily is grateful that her cries have not commanded Mr. Carmichael's attention, for it would have ashamed her for anyone to hear this "ignominious cry." Her pain and anger subside, and Lily returns to her painting. She is trying to depict the hedge. She again feels the soothing perception of Mrs. Ramsay's presence. She imagines Mrs. Ramsay, as she often does when she is painting, raising a wreath of white flowers to her forehead and walking across fields. She looks out across the bay and sees the boat, which is now halfway across. The Lighthouse appears a great distance from the shore this morning, and Lily continues to watch the boat with curiosity.

Analysis

The bracketed presentation of Chapter VI immediately recalls the brief parenthetical reports of the death of the

Ramsays in "Time Passes," and it, too, concerns mutilation and death. In this case, however, the act of cutting out a piece of a fish's flesh for bait and throwing it, still alive, back into the sea, represents survival in the face of difficulties.

A being can persist for a while in this undoubtedly cruel and constantly changing world, though one must frequently expect, through one's experience, to be largely or permanently altered. Just as the death of the Ramsays and the decay of their house were painful manifestations of change and the passage of time, the remaining characters, like the fish, are able to exist mainly as they did before. Unlike the death announcements in the previous section, though, the ultimate survival of the fish seems to be a good omen for the remainder of their lives.

Lily's reflection on Mrs. Ramsay's preoccupation with marriage produces scorn and resentment for the dead woman. Though Lily has chosen not to marry, even the memory of Mrs. Ramsay's presence compels her to second-guess her decision. But marriage is also a difficult experience. When she considers the flaws in the Ramsays' past relationship, adding to them the problems facing other married couples, she feels suddenly triumphant. She honestly confronts the tension between the advantages and disadvantages of marriage, rather than simply fulfilling a traditional role or simply rejecting it.

Their lives had not all turned out the way that Mrs. Ramsay had hoped, and Lily's amusement in considering that fact slowly gives way to her scorn for Mrs. Ramsay. Lily's feelings of negativity, however, are quite possibly a displaced fear of being without Mrs. Ramsay for the rest of her life. She is filled with a desperate longing for Mrs. Ramsay, crying out to her across the lawn and allowing tears to stream down her face. Though James and Cam silently agree upon their pact to undermine their father's efforts and to withhold from him as much of what he wants from them as they are able, neither of them is capable of suppressing the feelings of sympathy and pride that arise on their boat ride to the Lighthouse. Despite his demanding nature and his poetic murmurings, he is old, and he makes Cam feel ultimately very safe.

Cam even echoes some of the lines of poetry that he dictates, such as "we all perished, each alone," illuminating how influenced she has been by her father, if unwittingly. By its very nature, the quotation therefore represents a way in which humans are unified—through mutual influence—in addition to expressing the common experience of facing one's individuality. More explicitly, the words describe an inevitable, lonely, separate reality, the opposite of what Mrs. Ramsay has tried to weave and merge together.

Summary and Analysis of The Lighthouse: Chapters VIII-XIII

Chapter VIII

As they progress toward the Lighthouse, Cam looks at the shore and feels that it has become "more distant and more peaceful." When the boat slows down, the world seems to stand still, with both the Lighthouse and the shore seeming immovable and fixed. At this moment, they all feel closer to one another. As Mr. Ramsay reads, James remains fearful that his father will become impatient and speak sharply to him, demanding something impossible. James feels a surge of violence again at the thought of tyranny and despotism, at the thought of his father demanding that he do something he does not want to do. He decides that if Mr. Ramsay does scold him, he will strike him in the heart with a knife.

James tries to understand the source of this anger, and he recalls a time in the past when his father told him that it would rain tomorrow and they would not be able to go to the Lighthouse. He also remembers how his mother would stiffen at Mr. Tansley's demands, leaving James's side in order to tend to Mr. Ramsay's needs, which made James feel impotent and ridiculous. His father's presence is still oppressive to him. James stops thinking, the wind finally picks up, and everyone feels relieved as the boat continues toward the Lighthouse.

Chapters IX-X

Looking out over the bay, Lily considers the extraordinary

power of distance. She contemplates how the bay seemed to swallow up the Ramsays. Cam looks at the island where the Ramsays' house is, seeing the island for the first time from the sea. She tells herself a story of adventure about escaping from a sinking ship. She feels liberated by the passing away of her father's anger, James's obstinacy, and her own anguish. She thinks back to the times when she would come in from the garden to find her father talking with another old gentleman in the study, reading the Times and conversing. Remembering his kindness at these times, Cam now thinks that her father is not vain or tyrannical. She wants James to see it, too, but she knows that he would be unconvinced. As the island becomes blurry in the distance, Cam realizes that she feels incredibly safe in Mr. Ramsay's presence, and she again murmurs, "how we perished, each alone."

Chapter XI

Looking at the sea, Lily meditates further on the effects of distance, thinking about how distance can change how people feel about each other. She notices that she feels differently about Mr. Ramsay, who now is far away and remote, than she does about Mr. Carmichael. The house remains still, and this early morning quiet makes the situation seem unreal to Lily. She supposes that the boaters will reach the Lighthouse by lunchtime, and she suddenly becomes distressed to note the disproportionate arrangement of ships on the sea. Lily returns to her painting, wanting to start afresh with a new and invigorating impulse, and she urges herself to wait for it. She looks over at Mr. Carmichael, thinking about his newfound fame and imagining what his poetry must be like, and then thinking about Mr. Carmichael's dislike of Mrs. Ramsay. She thinks of Charles Tansley, his fellowship, his marriage, and the time that she heard him denouncing the war and advocating brotherly love, which seemed entirely inconsistent with the man whom she had known.

Lily determines that, in order to truly see and understand Mrs. Ramsay, a person would need fifty pairs of eyes. She considers the Ramsays' marriage, concluding that it did not constitute matrimonial bliss, what with her impulses and his temper. Lily recalls their brooding silences and the way that Mrs. Ramsay would evade her husband, pretending not to see him. Suddenly, a figure appears fleetingly at the drawing-room window, causing Lily to feel a sense of torture and a longing for Mrs. Ramsay. She cries out the woman's name, horrified by gripping desperation. She wonders where the boat is; she now desires Mr. Ramsay's presence.

Chapter XII

James notices that his father, who is still reading, looks very old. He thinks that the two of them share a sense of loneliness as truth. They are approaching the Lighthouse, and James is pleased with its "stark and straight" appearance. Mr. Ramsay grows hungry and announces that it is lunchtime.

Macalister's boy points out the location where three men drowned, frightening James and Cam. Finally, Mr. Ramsay praises James, telling him that he has steered them successfully, and Cam knows that this support is exactly what James has wanted. From their boat, they can see two men at the Lighthouse ready to meet them. James and Cam watch Mr. Ramsay as he watches the distant island, both wondering what he is thinking. As they approach, Mr. Ramsay jumps up with parcels for the Lighthouse men in his hands, and his children join him.

Chapter XIII

Though she is tired from the effort of looking at the distant Lighthouse and the Ramsays' boat, Lily decides that "He must have reached it" and feels relieved. She believes that she has now given Mr. Ramsay what she was incapable of giving him earlier that morning. Mr. Carmichael stands beside her, and a silent understanding passes between them.

Suddenly, Lily turns back to her painting. She is no longer concerned about what will happen to it once it is finished. Looking at the empty steps and the blurred canvas, she paints a single line down the centre. She finally feels that she is finished—she has had her vision.

Analysis

In a novel that succeeds at distancing itself so fully from the tradition of standard, omniscient narrative, it is no wonder that it ends at the very moment when the characters merge with the key symbol of the narrator. Reaching the Lighthouse is symbolic of closing the divide that allowed subjective consciousness to thrive; entering the realm of the Lighthouse draws the characters into a place where they cannot independently exist. (They never quite could, since the author was always behind the narrator; the Lighthouse always did reach the Ramsays' house with its light.) This passage to the non-conscious and permanent witness is not a full closing of the divide, since the island and Lily Briscoe remain outside of the union, Lily with paintbrush in hand.

As the Ramsays move closer and closer to the Lighthouse, Lily is progressively more prepared to achieve her artistic vision. Ten years after she made her first attempt, she is finally able to complete her endeavor, in large part because this novel constructs distance as crucial for the creation of art. Lily's declaration that "it was finished" refers both to her painting and to Woolf's book, now that Lily herself claims the title of artist-creator. She now encompasses both the figures of Mrs. Ramsay and the Lighthouse, watching the family from a distance. She has become their witness and the one who makes their lives perceptible to the reader.

The conclusion of the novel also portrays Lily relinquishing her need for stabilty and permanence. She now is content to exist solely in and for the present. Since it has been a symbol of stability and endurance, the Lighthouse is no longer needed for this purpose; it becomes completely obscured by distance and haze. It seems to melt into the haze, suggesting the instability of the Lighthouse even as a distinct physical object.

When Mr. Ramsay reaches the Lighthouse, the unity is not just literal (in that the boat physically converges with the Lighthouse) and symbolic (in that the objective source of light merges with subjective consciousness), but it is also an abstract unity that relates this moment in time with the events of ten years before. Although unity has served as a symbol of permanence throughout the novel (even for Lily, who wishes to unite herself with Mrs. Ramsay), Lily releases herself from the need for unity, permanence, and stability. She is still on the island, and she does not require complete assurance that Mr. Ramsay has reached the Lighthouse. She is exhausted with the effort involved with meeting her need for symbolic stability, and her new perspective permits her to relinquish this need entirely.

Lily's final artistic gesture is also a representation of this general relinquishing of control. Throughout the novel, Lily has intended to find stability and order not in marriage, as Mrs. Ramsay suggests, but in the simple act of moving the tree in her painting more to the middle of the canvas. Like the Lighthouse, the tree is a symbol of stability and permanence, although its ability to be moved undermines its position and lends it an undeniable transience. In the final moments of the novel, Lily is inspired to complete the painting that she has been struggling with for over ten years, and she fully comes to terms with the fact that it will be hung in attics and destroyed. She no longer feels a need to use her art to tie her to the vast expanses of reality.

Instead she is able simply to embrace the ephemeral and beautiful nature of this moment, the moment when distance allows her to be inspired by form and shape. She has no further need of imagining Mrs. Ramsay's shadow on the steps, now that she can do without ideas of stability. She no longer needs even to see her own canvas clearly. Indeed, the tree that she has long intended to draw is represented in her vision as a simple, perfunctory line. The Lighthouse and the tree, which were the ultimate symbols of stability and permanence in the novel, are now made completely unrecognizable. Lily is able to embrace the unstable transience of this moment and finally find artistic and personal fulfillment.

Chapter 12

Study Questions and Answers

Q. "These Emotions of the Body": intercorporeal narrative in 'To the Lighthouse.'-book by Virginia Woolf "Women's Time." Feminist Theory: A Critique of Ideology.

"The Child's Relation with Others." The Primacy of Perception. James Edie, ed. Evanston, Northwestern UP, 1964. As Lily Briscoe gazes at the drawing-room steps in the third section of To the Lighthouse, she thinks they look "extraordinarily empty." She asks, "How could one express in words these emotions of the body? express that emptiness there?". We more clearly understand Lily's questions when we recall that "that emptiness" is the space once filled by a mother's body, by Mrs. Ramsay. This once female-occupied space may well be understood as the "absent centre" that feminist deconstructive critics locate at the core of language. For Mrs. Ramsay's marriage is a relationship in which "he could say things; she never could," and in this sense Mrs. Ramsay represents an absent or unspeaking presence in the text. Moreover, for Lily, Mrs. Ramsay's absence constitutes the problem at the centre of her attempts to express, to paint. Woolf herein anticipates both the general deconstructive skepticism about language as a vehicle of "reality" and the more specific feminist arguments for such skepticism — that a silencing objectification of women rather than a scientific objectivity about "reality" generates the terms of language.

But Woolf's project also moves us beyond these critical insights. I will argue that, beneath her explorations of both of these layers of philosophical doubt, Woolf reveals that the "emotions of the body" which Lily feels in response to that "emptiness there" are precisely the means whereby the text can turn inside out the unnamed, body-transcending core of traditional Western philosophy and narrative. While Woolf's characters vacillate between vertigo and exhilaration as they stand on the edge of "that emptiness there," Woolf's narrator moves into and within that emptiness, both discovering already within it a phenomenological fullness and further filling it herself. Specifically, in To the Lighthouse the narrator stations herself within the objects which situate the mother's and the other characters' presence in the world; she can therein reincarnate and even extend the mother's phenomenality insofar as it is carried silently within those objects; but in doing so she not only breaks the mother's silence, evincing the "emotions of the body," but also revises the patriarchal coding of bodily emotions, in which the traditional mother is complicit. By extending the mother's embeddedness in things, in other words, the narrator transgresses the patriarchal and traditional motherly frame for that embeddedness and creates a site of uncoded embodiment.

More broadly, by literalizing and spatializing "that emptiness there," by casting it as a dimension of physical and emotional existence rather than as an ineluctable metaphysical condition, Woolf corporealizes the spaces rendered empty by patriarchal culture and thought. She constitutes narrative not according to what Edward Said once characterized as its "celibate enterprise" of forming "individuals" who mark their own "beginnings," but as an entrance into what Helene Cixous calls the "in-between" of self and self created by the physical world. Woolf attends, as her narrator says, to "all sorts of waifs and strays of things.... A washer-woman with her basket; a rock; a red-hot poker; the purples and grey-greens of flowers" to get at what Lily Briscoe calls "the common feeling that held the whole". But neither Woolf's nor Lily's "common feeling" is a naive humanist "fantasy of totality" of the kind that Julia Kristeva warns feminists against. Her narrative includes ironies, alarms, and disruptions as hinted by the double meaning of the red-hot poker inserted into the preceding series of images. Woolf's prose moves into the fleshy "in-between" of her characters' fictional world, discovers its folds and ruptures, embraces its curves and arabesques. In short, far from maintaining the prudery or ethereality with which Woolf has often been identified, her narrative sensualizes metaphysical questions — of death and presence, speech and silence, time and space.

To the Lighthouse will serve here as an example of what I will somewhat awkwardly yet nonetheless precisely call Woolf's "intercorporeal" narrative strategies. I borrow the term from the French phenomenologist Maurice Merleau-Ponty, whose ideas indicate the direction of Woolf's experiments more fully, as I will discuss in the first section of this essay, than either the German phenomenology or the deconstructive criticism that has been used to read and critique modernism.

Phenomenological conceptions of duration or time-in-process served for earlier critics of Woolf to explain her concentrated "moments of being"—which provisionally protect her characters from the erosions of time and death. As is well known, under the influence of Henri Bergson and other disseminators of phenomenology, midcentury critics of Woolf and of modernist fiction studied temporal flux and simultaneity as elements of the fluid subjectivity represented in experimental novels.

- "Being" in novels by Proust, Faulkner, Joyce, and Woolf was elusive and contingent, never fixed and often fragmented, yet full and buoyant, because it was caught up in the phenomenological flux of time. Including modernism, into question. Along with the demotion of phenomenology to a philosophy of the falsely integrated subject went the demotion of modernism to naive precursor to postmodernism.
- One flaw in this automatic chain of demotions was, as more critics have come to recognize, a too strong dependence on somewhat oversimplified new critical uses of phenomenology to explain modernist experimentation. The multiple dimensions and attitudes of modernism are now seen to obtrude in

several directions beyond the scaffolding provided by universalized phenomenological conceptions of time and subjectivity.

- This essay also rereads modernism outside of such conceptions, but it does so by foregrounding another phenomenology and reconfiguring the relations among phenomenology, feminism, modernism, and postmodernism.

For an important, often obscured choice underlies the postmodern demystification of the phenomenology of modernism: that of postmodernist thinkers' selective critique of phenomenology as a philosophy. In focusing its critique of phenomenology — I have in mind, particularly, Jacques Derrida's seminal readings of Edmund Husserl and Martin Heidegger — on transcendental German phenomenologists, postmodernist thinkers have focused on the phenomenology most vulnerable to deflation by a postmodern ethos of instability and fragmentation. It is not the case, of course, that Derrida and others overlook this tradition's anti-transcendental rereadings of itself. Heidegger does, as Derrida recognizes, explore the phenomenality of a concrete "being in the world" in his revision of Husserl's conception of a pure transcendental consciousness. Heidegger also, as Derrida acknowledges, uncovers a decentering principle in consciousness when he notes that "the forgetting of Being is a part of the very esence of Being." Derrida himself borrows Heidegger's term "trace," building on Heidegger's description of the way in which the "presence of the present" remains "sealed in a trace".

Nonetheless, Derrida composes his project in counterpoint to German phenomenology, attempting to dismantle its transcendental assumptions further, yet at the same time perpetuating the honored romance with that transcendental tradition and obscuring other traditions of phenomenology. Deconstruction thus discredits phenomenology on the basis of a critique of the German tradition, and in the wake of that critique modernist novels suddenly appear as narrative embraces of presence. Or they appear to need rereadings attentive to their subtextual fragmentedness. On the one hand, both kinds of reading seem to me valid, in that modernism similarly debated both sides of those questions of time and presence which postmodernism considers its special arena.

Yet, on the other hand, I would suggest that modernism can now be re-encountered with another phenomenology. The phenomenology of Merleau-Ponty, in particular, though temporarily obscured by recent currents of intellectual history, can powerfully inform the contemporary discussion of a historical body. In the terms of this discussion, as I see it, presence accumulates and leaves its "trace" not as an ontological mythology but as a historical marking which relegates to different bodies distinct postures, clothes, labors, neighborhoods, goods, pleasures, and so on. Scrutinizing the line where body meets its surround and where consciousness cleaves to body, Merleau-Ponty begins to lay the foundation for discussing the embeddedness of ideology in the body, and for further understanding Western logocentrism's "absent centre" as the effaced materiality of history.

His work can supplement discussions of the body not as a fixed or positivistic referent, not as that which escapes history and contingency, but as that which continually infringes on transhistorical meta-narratives of the body's world. I would add immediately, too, that the notion that the body infringes does not necessarily mean either that the body marks the limits and contours of discourse only through its pain, as Elaine Scarry suggests, or that its joy becomes manifest in language only as semiotic rupture, as in Julia Kristeva's notion of a pre-Oedipal embodiment. The body does not survive only beyond and against language and narrative; it survives with and in language and narrative, partly because language's physicality extends the phenomenal world's physicality, and vice-versa, as both Woolf and Merleau-Ponty recognize.

The single most important point of intersection between Woolf and Merleau-Ponty is their attention to the palpable rather than the impalpable as the source of coherence and continuity — or, more precisely in Woolf's case, the source of narrative. Resisting the traditional urge to sweep upward toward spirit, toward objective law, or toward Stephen Dedalus's "father artificer" in order to generate narrative and triumph over time, both Merleau-Ponty and Woolf recognize random inanimate and nonhuman phenomena as alternative grounds of human narrative and temporality: human triumph, if it exists, best manifests itself in the recognition of those objects that stand outside human bodies and endure beyond the temporality of individual humans yet nonetheless inhabit the same orders of temporality and spatiality. Language itself, for both thinkers, depends on this delicate balance of difference and sameness or, more exactly for both Merleau-Ponty and Woolf, the dance of distance and nearness among human and nonhuman phenomena.

Merleau-Ponty formulates an "identity without superposition" between the body and the sensible world. His phrase "without superposition" may at first appear idealized, but he means only to highlight the literal, physical impossibility of the "superposition" of two bodies — two bodies cannot occupy the same place: and yet their ability to touch responsively, whether in violence, kindness, or whatever feeling, signals their "identity," their shared phenomenality. Focusing minutely on the site of physical encounter between the human and nonhuman phenomenal worlds, he traces the "horizons of the flesh" in contact with the world:

> How does it happen that I give to my hands, in particular, that degree, that rate, and that direction of movement that are capable of making me feel the textures of the sleek and the rough? Between the exploration and what it will teach me, between my movements and what I touch, there must exist some... kinship.... This can only happen if my hand, while it is felt from within, is also accessible from without, itself tangible... if it takes its place among the things it touches, is in a sense one of them, opens finally upon a tangible being of which it is also a part.

"Opens finally upon a tangible being of which it is also a part": we will see that this phrase characterizes Mrs. Ramsay's mode of being, as it characterizes the narrational posture of To the Lighthouse, which nevertheless uses this ontology, this opening onto, to expose the physical self-sacrifice enacted by Mrs. Ramsay within a patriarchy which feeds on her ontological resources while devaluing their power.

A contrast may be useful in clarifying this "intercorporeality" among bodies and things, as Merleau-Ponty calls it. Merleau-Ponty shares with Jean-Paul Sartre, with whom he had a lifelong friendship and intellectual dialogue, an emphasis on the seeable thisness of the individual human. But while Sartre pursues the transcendentalist and time-honored path of identifying the import for an autonomous consciousness of this thingness of ourselves, culminating in his philosophy of human existential "otherness," Merleau-Ponty sustains a contemplation of the mutual "access" engendered by the "kinship" among things and bodies in the world. Sartre assumes the essential deadness of objects and focuses his philosophy on a distinction between being-for-itself and being-in-itself, exhorting humans to denounce mere in-itself existences and forge meaning for-themselves. Merleau-Ponty, by contrast, explores the ways in which our in-itselfness in conjunction with the in-itselfness of the object world contains the means for constructing worlds for-ourselves.

Importantly, the "ourselves" here is not exclusively human; the object world is itself dynamic and forceful and a part of the "worlds" we create. While Sartre continued the deep division between human and nonhuman, and Heidegger, too, speaks of "the world" humans inhabit in a monolithic, if resonant, language, Merleau-Ponty traces more closely the ways we live, think, feel in discrete interdependence with innumerable things, in an involuntary intercorporeal connection with them. Thus "the thickness of my body, far from rivaling that of the world, is on the contrary the sole means I have to go unto the heart of things".

For Woolf the "thick" or materially embedded body such as that of Mrs. MacNab in "Time Passes" or the wandering woman in Mrs. Dalloway is indeed a vehicle for entering the "heart of things"; but importantly for her "the heart of things" is not only a realm of joy or community it is death, as J. Hillis Miller and others have recognized; it is "that emptiness there."

Yet, at the same time, for her as for Merleau-Ponty, "that emptiness" inhabits a fullness, a phenomenality.

Q. "The Spirit of the Age": Virginia Woolf's response to second wave psychology

Or

Q. Virginia Woolf was the most adamant of the modernists. Discuss

Let us always remember—influences are infinitely numerous; writers are infinitely sensitive. Virginia Woolf was the most adamant of the modernists in her claim that "We are sharply cut off from our predecessors". However, she also believed in the continuity of culture, and in writers' role as "receptacles" of cultural currents. S. P. Rosenbaum has examined some of the currents operating on Woolf herself, but his claim that Woolf's "writing was shaped by a series of intellectual assumptions about reality, perception, morality, government, and art" needs to be extended to include human psychology. Woolf was influenced by psychologists' working hypotheses about many aspects of personality, and her extraordinarily sensitive antennae picked up psychological ideas in the air. In her own ambivalent, idiosyncratic way, Woolf acknowledged both of these sources in a draft of "Character in Fiction", a paper given before the Cambridge Heretics Society. She wrote:

No generation since the world began has known quite so much about character as our generation.... The average man or woman today thinks more about character than his or her grandparents; character interests them more; they get closer, they dive deeper in to the real emotions and motives of their fellow creatures. There are scientific reasons why this should be so. If you read Freud you know in ten minutes some facts—or at least some possibilities—which our parents could not have guessed for themselves. <That is a very debatable point. But how much we can learn from science that is real... & make our own from science>. And then there is a... vaguer force at work—a force which is sometimes called the Spirit of the Age or the Tendency of the age. This mysterious power is taking us by the hand, I think, and making us look much more closely into the reasons why people do a. nd say and think things. Here Woolf chooses Freud as representative of scientists of the mind, perhaps not surprisingly, since by 1924 he had the highest profile of psychologists whose ideas were discussed by the Bloomsbury group.

Understandably, those few critics who have examined psychological influence on Woolf limit themselves to analysis of her problematic attitude to Freud. Woolf's claim that she knew psychoanalysis "only in the way of ordinary conversation" certainly does represent a severe understatement. Whether she fully realized it or not, the conversations she had about psychoanalysis were far from ordinary, since they took place with those who were at the forefront of the psychoanalytic movement in Britain, as critics Jan Goldstein, Elizabeth Abel, and Douglass Orr have demonstrated. However, prior to her exposure to psychoanalysis during the years 1914-1918, Woolf was aware of ideas of earlier proponents of "new" or what I have termed second wave psychology, and it is these neglected influences that I plan to examine in more detail before tracing a few of these strands primarily in her first two novels, The Voyage Out and Night and Day.

Second wave psychology provoked a paradigm shift in psychology by positing that mind consisted of psychic energy in perpetual movement, unlike the first wave, which had viewed mind as essentially mechanistic, passive, and divisible into elementary contents. In the early nineteenth century Johann Herbart had prefigured the new dynamic approach through his suggestions about thresholds of consciousness and momentary repressions. He posited that the mind had three layers, a narrow, conscious one, separated by what he called the threshold of consciousness from two larger ones, in which representations were inhibited or repressed, but not destroyed.

Despite Herbart's pioneering efforts, however, the second wave of psychology gathered momentum only in the late 1880s through the work of Pierre Janet, William James, Theodule Ribot, Frederic Myers, and, later, Henri Bergson, William McDougall, Freud, and Jung, among others. These psychologists made several important contributions. They explored the pathological in order to gain insight into the normal and thus broke down rigid distinctions between the two conditions. Their discovery of multiple selves in hysterics and other subjects under hypnosis led to more fluid or shifting conceptions of self and to a more sophisticated understanding of the relation between conscious and unconscious processes. These psychologies included an unmasking trend that "searched for hidden unconscious motivations, mainly of instincts and conflicts of instincts". Second wave psychology fostered a new method of treatment, psychotherapy, in which doctors attended to the statements, feelings, and dreams of their patients.

In Britain, the main vehicle for the early dissemination as well as development of the new ideas was the Society for Psychical Research. The Society was formed in 1882 by Cambridge intellectuals influenced by the revival of philosophical idealism in the 1870s. They sought evidence in abnormal psychology and psychical phenomena to support the hypothesis that personality survived bodily death. Not only did the Society consequently introduce to a varied English audience the latest European developments in psychiatry and psychology, including Janet's and Freud's, but it shaped the perceived significance and interpretation of this material. As well, mainly through the work of a prominent member, Frederic Myers, it proposed a fairly comprehensive dynamic psychology well before Freud's reached Britain.

By 1893 Myers had developed his influential theory of the subliminal self. Through Meyers's and other psychical researchers' work and their organization of the first four International Congresses of Experimental Psychology, psychical research very nearly became part of the psychological orthodoxy. It attracted both prominent psychologists and the elite of British society, including Prime Minister Arthur Balfour, titled persons and writers (such as Tennyson, Ruskin, "Lewis Carroll," A. Conan Doyle, and Virginia Woolf's friends James Strachey, Goldsworthy Lowes Dickinson, and Roger Fry). Despite the enormous influence of the Society, historians of psychology typically ignore it, partly because its researches are no longer considered within the realm of the scientifically acceptable.

Having briefly sketched the nature of second wave psychology and the various roles of the Society for Psychical Research in disseminating it, we can now turn to an examination of Virginia Woolf's awareness of this field of inquiry. My intention here is not primarily to argue for direct influence, but to evoke the milieu, or as Woolf calls it. "The Spirit of the Age" and place in which Woolf first encountered psychological ideas. In her case, an atmosphere in which questioning of formal psychological ideas occurred was established in her early youth through the influence of her father, Leslie Stephen. Through her brothers—Thoby and Adrian—and friends—Lytton and James Strachey—her connection with the psychological thought originating at Cambridge further advanced her psychological knowledge.

By the period during which she wrote her first novel, The Voyage Out, these two sources had already helped shape her fundamental assumptions about personality and the individual's relation to the group. It must be kept in mind throughout that this discussion is not meant to devalue Woolf's highly creative personal vision, but to suggest the nature of some of the more important, though neglected, base materials submitted to the crucible of her imagination.

Though underemphasized, Leslie Stephen's intellectual legacy to his daughter Virginia included his knowledge of philosophical psychology. After all, his literary theory included the tenet that "literature is the highest imaginative embodiment of a period's philosophy". Stephen himself was fully aware of philosophical tradition and kept abreast of contemporary intellectual developmentsHis most important, though completely ignored, source of information about psychology was James Sully, a leading luminary of psychology at the end of the century. Through his extensive connections and varied talents, Sully also provided a link between psychological, philosophical, and literary thought for his and Leslie Stephen's generations Sully introduced himself to

Stephen and became a close friend through writing a series of articles for Cornhill Magazine under Stephen's editorship. These included "serious" ones on self-esteem and self-admiration and "The Laws of Dream-fancy."The latter provoked Stephen to convey to Sully several of his dreams, and Sully said that Stephen generally

brought his own experiences and his reading to bear upon what I was writing about. Among the subjects which drew him out in this way, I remember dreams, children's ways, and the precocity of genius. According to Sully, his participation in the intimate Scratch Eight walking excursions, organized by Stephen, provided "rich opportunities of increasing our mutual knowledge." Since one of the members of the Scratch Eight, Edmund Gurney, was the Secretary of the Society for Psychical Research, this topic, along with philosophy, would likely have been discussed. After these excursions ended in 1891, Sully records that he took tramps with Stephen alone. Sully even visited the Stephens summer house at St. Ives around this time. That experience apparently had an effect. on him similar to Virginia Woolf's experience there (transformed into fiction in To the Lighthouse), as he said, "This visit to St. Ives was one of the memorable experiences of my life

While the extent of the intimacy between the two men should now be clear, it is not as easy to summarize the impact of Sully's thought on Stephen. For purposes of brevity I will focus on Sully's knowledge of the workings of the mind. In his memoir Sully rhetorically and modestly asks, "Were we [Sully and Stephen] not, despite the differences in our years and status, scribblers who were supremely interested in the processes of thought?"). Sully believed that "psychology proper" was "the science which has to disentangle and reduce to simplicity the web of consciousness". To this end he followed the tradition of dividing the functions of the mind into three—thinking, feeling, and willing—and traced their separate development. In considering the role of feeling, he stressed the relationship between pain and pleasure, and quoted Leslie Stephen's belief that pleasure is a state of equilibrium In his Outlines of Psychology, Sully devoted considerable space to classifying different types of association and examining their effect on memory. He refers to trains of images and of movements in this connection. He also showed that mind was active and acknowledged the importance of unconscious processes:

At any time there is a whole aggregate or complex of mental phenomena, sensations, impressions, thoughts, etc., most of which are obscure, transitory, and not distinguished. With this wide obscure region of the subconscious, there stands contrasted the narrow luminous region of the clearly conscious. An impression or thought must be presumed to be already present in the first or subconscious region before the mind by an effort of attention can draw it into the second region.

Furthermore, Sully was particularly interested "in the borderland between the normal and abnormal, in the imaginative and the fanciful", perhaps partly owing to his associations with psychical researchers Gurney and Myers He elaborated on his ideas about dreams, which so fascinated Stephen, in Illusions and in "The Dream as Revelation". These ideas are cited with approval by Freud from the 1914 edition of Interpretation of Dreams onward, not surprisingly since they represent the earliest British example of the second wave approach to dreams. They even pre-date Havelock Ellis's exploration.(First, in the words of Freud, Sully "was more firmly convinced, perhaps, than any other psychologist that dreams have a disguised meaning" and were not utter nonsense Sully was thus an early proponent of the unmasking trend in second wave psychology.

Second, Sully argued that these meanings were often related to long-past experiences. He stated that our dreams are a means of conserving these successive personalities. When asleep we go back to the old ways of looking at things and of feeling about them, to impulses and activities which long ago dominated us.

Third, Sully asserted that the interpretative function of dreams was similar to that by which sense is made of events in the waking state. Finally, in Illusions, Sully made the then controversial point that "our normal mental life is thus intimately related to insanity, and graduates away into it by such fine transactions", an attitude which anticipates a fundamental development of second wave psychology. Thus, through Sully, Leslie Stephen certainly had the opportunity of acquainting himself with the latest developments in English psychology.

Q. Virginia Woolf's Novel To The Lighthouse as a Feminist Text:

Or

Q. Woolf's work challenges representation and treatment of women; and the social relationship between men and women, this is shown most poignantly within the novel To The Lighthouse. Discuss

When looking at To The Lighthouse we see the conventional usage of feminism's challenged. Woolf uses many different styles and techniques, and although the term feminist is never used within the novel, it clearly is a feminist text. Woolf's work challenges representation and treatment of women; and the social relationship between men and women, this is shown most poignantly within the novel To The Lighthouse. I intend to investigate the usage of feminist writing within this text.

Mrs. Ramsay and Lily Briscoe are the two main female characters in the novel. Women, Mrs. Ramsay believes are there to care for others, marry people off and harmonize everyone. They are also there (shown within her inner monologue) to protect men, and to nurture their ego.

'She had the whole of the other sex under her protection; for reasons she could not explain, for their chivalry and valour.' To The Lighthouse is a novel that is fascinated by women, as the perspectives of Mrs. Ramsay and Lily are the most fully developed narratives within the text. Woolf's To The Lighthouse asks the question of the sexuality of women, and questions the women's role within the family. Lily does represent Woolf's 'ideal women' and Mrs. Ramsay in direct contrast is portrayed as the 'angel of the house.'

Woolf's essay 'Professions For Women' attacks Victorian

institutions, she writes about 'killing the angel of the house', which she successfully manages through Mrs. Ramsay's death in To The Lighthouse. Mrs. Ramsay is a product of the Victorian era, she is described in terms of delicateness of feminity and Woolf, romanticizes her and uses passive language to portray her. Woolf's theory in 'A Room Of One's Own' is significant because it helps to understand her issues with gender and feminist politics set by patriarchies.

'Whether there are sexes in the mind corresponding to the two sexes in the body, and whether they also require to be united in order to get complete satisfaction and happiness.... In each of us two powers reside, one male andfemale...It is fatal to be a man or woman pure and simple, one must be women Manly or man womanly.

Woolf attempts to show these differences through her portrayal of Lily and Mrs. Ramsay, and again through Mr. And Mrs. Ramsay. Woolf believed that patriarchy always tried to silence and repress women and women's experiences, this is why she rejects the series of feminine characteristics set by patriarchy; sweetness, modesty, humility and subservience..., and shows these qualities in direct contrast to Mr. Ramsay, and his masculine rationality that has reason, order and lucidity. In keeping with Woolf's 'Angel Of the House' figure, Mrs. Ramsay is projected more as a symbol as the 'earth mother' than as an individual, as she is never called by her first name, she represents an era of Victorian values and Lily Briscoe represents the feminist figure as she rejects irrationality, chaos and fragmentation, which has come to represent feminity.

This is shown more clearly in Charles Tansley's treatment of Lily and her painting; as an artist Lily is sensitive about the role of women and feels constantly pressurized by Mrs. Ramsay into bolstering the male ego. This draining effect Lily feels when she is expected to boost Tansley's ego is connected with the sensation she has when he is around, that he is constantly deprecating her work: 'Women can't write, Women can't paint' Through creating Lily, Woolf is representing a different kind of women; she is investigating the variety of experiences accessible to women, the constraints and the possibilities..

Mrs. Ramsay's character at times does seem confused, on one hand she is trying to marry people off and maintain all the attributes that we have come to expect from 'the angel of the house', but there are times when we are ale to experience her inner thoughts through her stream of consciousness. When Mrs. Ramsay sits everyone down, we have first her thoughts, then her words and actions. In her thoughts she feels weary, as if her life has produced nothing, while her words to others are quite directing:

'But what have I done with my life? Thought Mrs. Ramsay, taking her place at the head of the table, and looking at all the plates making white circles on it..only this – an infinitely long table and plates and knives...'

Her female experiences translate into seeing the endless table with plates and cutlery – a very solid, concrete, domestic example. Her moods, responses and the slant she puts on the interactions between them all, move around and differ. In particular, how Mrs. Ramsay views others is with a polarized gender expectation, particularly with William Bankes and Lily Briscoe: 'Smiling, for it was an admirable idea, that had flashed upon her this very second – William and Lily should marry.' As her defined role of wife and mother to everyone, Mrs. Ramsay believes she is there to care for others, harmonize everyone, marry people off and be protected by men. She also believes that women are there to protect the men, to nurture their egos, and to smooth over any awkward moments. Lily's character however breaks many conventional gender roles, she is an independent, educated women who has a talent to paint, and is not confined to the home domestically. At times Mrs. Ramsay appears to want to curtail Lily's independence, through attempting to marry her off to William. Mrs. Ramsay appears to feel persecuted when people do not conform to marriage and escape their gender roles.

Woolf does highlight the absence of women from higher education through oppressive protocol within To The Lighthouse; this does enforce the difference of gender roles.

The male figures within the novel are educated, are studying for degrees and admire each other for their academic achievements. Science within the novel is seen objectively, and is portrayed as a masculine image: 'Her husband, however, is one of the clever people, a distinguished philosopher with an acute intellect that was incapable of untruth; never tampered with a fact.'

Mrs. Ramsay's gender roles are shown in soft response to Mr. Ramsay, Mr. Ramsay emerges as a heroic tyrant and appears to represent the 'typical male'. He is compared to sharp instruments, knives, axe, poker with which his son wants to hit him: 'Had there been an axe handy, or a poker, any weapon that would have killed him, there and then James would have seized it.' The language the surrounds Mr. Ramsay is assertive, opinionated, slightly patronizing and shows his philosophical prowess. He has reached the level of 'ordinary experience'; as Lily calls it: he feels simply; 'that's a chair, that's a table', however in Mr. Ramsay's term he has managed to reach Q, but not R. The use of the alphabet shows the male mind; logical, chronological and linear but also child like: 'Still, if he could reach R it would be something. Here at least was Q. He dug his heels in at Q. Q he was sure of. Q he could demonstrate... Then R. He braced himself. He clenched himself.'

R to Mr. Ramsay is a failure, as it represents knowledge, achievement and aspirations. Rachel Bowlby illustrates how Mr. Ramsay's world view is logical and linear but it is limiting, rigid, despairing, she continues stating: 'The step from one logical step to the next is compared to letters of the alphabet, and contrasts with women's outsider position. However, women are seen as offering a kind of tour through life, through thought patterns, which are more flexible and fluid, various and able to hold opposition in harmony.'

However, Woolf show how the prioritization of the domestic space has repressed women and prevented them from taking part in everyday activities – Commerce, Travel, Work and Education. This is seen in To The Lighthouse in the public and private realms; Mrs. Ramsay and Lily find that oppression in the public realm is linked to that of the private. This illustrates how Woolf can deal with material and economic, historic conditions, which effect men and women's lives, and their ways of viewing the world, their perceptions and imaginative response's that differ. This is highlighted in To The Lighthouse with the constant comparisons between Mr. And Mrs. Ramsay, this is shown through the inner monologue of the characters and the inter subjectivity. Woolf investigates gender and the power of men and women, she explores the way in which we are constructed as gendered beings, and how culture, and society, restricts our actions, opportunities, and speech. Mrs. Ramsay eases us into this: '...For the fact that they negotiated treaties, ruled India, controlled finance, finally for an attitude towards herself which no women could fail to feel or to find agreeable...pray heaven it was none of her daughters!'

Although at times Mrs. Ramsay does appear to be a idealized version of a women, being 'the angel of the house', thorough her inner monologue it is seen that inwardly she questions male and female roles and that in her inner thoughts an independent thinking women is trying to eradicate the presence of the Victorian female ideal. Although as an idealized perfect mother figure, she has greater aspirations for her female daughters: 'Her daughters, Prue, Nancy, Rose-could sport with infidel ideas which they had brewed for themselves of a life different from hers; in Paris, perhaps; a wilder life; not always taking care of some man or other; for there was in all their minds a mute questioning of deference and chivalry, of the Bank Of England and the Indian Empire, of ringed fingers and lace....which called out the manliness in their girlish hearts.'

However Lily portrays Mrs. Ramsay outwardly, within a painting as Madonna with child, she displays the strength in the representation of women. Lily's painting of mother and child is painted in abstract because she is painting the inner thoughts; her painting is in opposition to gender and creates an oppositional act. The men in the novel cannot understand what Lily's painting stands for, Lily is welcoming a loss of personality and is shredding her responsibilities and her cares through retreat (social pressures and responsibilities). Her painting challenged convention because it is abstract and is painted by a woman. Perhaps, one of the most important running themes within the novel is self-deception, Virginia Woolf does not intervene on her characters, nor does she give objective views, their chains of thoughts question their identity. Woolf uses the automatic expectation of conforming to gender that society demands certain institiunal behaviour.

The symbolism in the novel is poignant to out entire understanding of To The Lighthouse. The Lighthouse represents symbolically Mrs. Ramsay as the guiding force, this symbolizes her gender role and that the social construction of womanhood is one of protection and guidance. The waves symbolize women and their duties and responsibilities, as the waves are about constant repetition and the metaphor of the depths of women's consciousness. Routine and duties are portrayed through the ticking of the watch, this contrasts the automatic and mechanical behaviour of women. Mrs. Ramsay appears to panic when she is silent, as she has no public role, just internalized feelings.

The old familiar pulse began beating, as the watch begins ticking – one, two, three. One, two, three. And so on and so on, she repeated, listening to it,sheltering and fostering the still feeble pulse as one might guard a weak flame with a newspaper.

Mrs. Ramsay finds the silence terrifying, as the clock stopping seems to show her identity falling apart. Mrs. Ramsay's ambitions can only be achieved when she is dead, and through Mrs. Ramsay's death, Lily achieves Mrs. Ramsay's unconscious desires. Yet unconsciously Mrs. Ramsay wants the freedom that Lily has, she rebuffs it because she cannot have the freedom:

'She could never marry: one could not take her painting very seriously; she was an independent little creature, and Mrs. Ramsay liked her for it; so remembering her promise, she bent her head.' The painting is the one thing that holds the novel together, and reconciles everything that has happened, through Mrs. Ramsay; Lily has clarity and is able to have clear vision; 'She must escape somewhere, be alone somewhere. Suddenly she remembered. when she had sat there last ten years ago there had been a little sprig or leaf pattern on the tablecloth, which she had looked at in a moment of revelation... She would paint that picture now:' The painting orders life and unifies, it shows how everything is related to each other: All were related,'

As they finally reach the lighthouse, it ends on a woman achieving her vision with negotiating the pitfalls and expectations of gender. The ending of To The Lighthouse, is significant in relation to the essay title because Lily is unable to make the self-sacrifices that Mrs. Ramsay made, she is unable to provide the sympathy to Mr. Ramsay that he feels is the women's role to provide for a man. Because she can't and won't give sympathy, she is able to achieve clarity and be selfish in order to complete something that interests her. She is able to do this because she refuses to conform to her gender role, thus showing 'To The Lighthouse' as a feminist text, as Woolf gives rise to a feminist analysis of a women's situation of the female experience.

Q. A "Need of Distance and Blue": Space, Colour, and Creativity in To the Lighthouse-Write an Essay

Or

Q. Discuss the Bloomsbury aesthetics and interarts theory and then focus on space and colour, perception and composition, in To the Lighthouse.

I shall briefly revisit Bloomsbury aesthetics and interarts theory and then focus on space and colour, perception and composition, in To the Lighthouse.

According to Virginia Woolf, Roger Fry held that "Gzanne and Picasso had shown the way; writers should fling representation to the winds and follow suit. But never found time to work out his theory of the influence of Post-Impressionism upon literature". Woolf worked out the interaction herself in To the Lighthouse, which was published in 1927, the same year as Fry's Czanne: A Study of His Development. In Czanne, Fry describes "plastic colour" as a "direct exponent of form"; and in "Some Questions in Esthetics", he maintains that "our reaction to works of art is a reaction to a relation and not to sensations and objects or persons or events". Fry's formalism gave Woolf her shaping principles for To the Lighthouse; she then worked out the relation of "architectural plasticity" to verbal impressionism in composing the novel.

Woolf observes that the "arts of painting and writing lay close together and Roger Fry was always making raids across the boundaries". She herself made raids on postimpressionist painting in the experimental writing of "Kew Gardens" and "Blue & Green", where the act of looking is so intense that it dissolves content into purely visual form. In "The Artist's Vision" (published in 1919, the same year as Woolf's "Modern Fiction"), Fry says that those "who indulge in [aesthetic] vision"— as distinct from the more active "creative vision "— "are entirely absorbed in apprehending the relation of forms and colour to one another" —as Woolf is in "Blue & Green" and "Kew Gardens."

Woolf remarks that few writers met Fry's formalist standards: "they lacked objectivity, they did not treat words as painters treat paint." Her emphasis on words in relation to paint is the converse of Fry's, "many of theories held good for both arts. Design, rhythm, texture—there they were again—in Flaubert as in Cezanne". Fry saw texture as subsuming details in overall design: "The texture of the whole field of vision becomes so close that the coherence of the separate patches of tone and colour within each object is no stronger than the coherence with every other tone and colour throughout the field". This is the effect of "distance and blue" toward the end of To the Lighthouse —the effect of constructing a network of human interactions from associations of tone and colour. Woolf told Fry that she emphasized texture, which she associated with language, rather than structure, which she associated with plot. Fry admired the postimpressionist s' "attempt to express by pictorial and plastic form certain spiritual experiences", but his disjunction of "the spaceless world of psychological entities and relations" from the plastic world of "spatial relations" is the effect of extreme formalism. Woolf, in contrast, strove to invent "a system that did not shut out" and to unify psychological and spatial, vital and formal values. As distinct from the still-life painter, the "writer has to keep his eye upon a model that moves, that changes". She wanted to make the novel more like a work of art, while catching the movement of life itself.

While Fry dichotomizes art and life, he "also admit that under certain conditions the rhythms of life and of art may coincide". He concludes his study of Cezanne with the reminder that "such analysis halts before the ultimate concrete reality of the work of art". More recently, Wendy Steiner has noted that the "semiotic concreteness" of modern art "seeks a repleteness of meaning that is never fully available in art, but only in life". Woolf came to regard such purely formal experiments as "Blue & Green" as mere imitations of painting in words. For her, "creative vision" is more profoundly interactive: as objects and people are transmuted into forms, the shaping self is also reshaped, for "nothing simply one thing". Subject and object interpenetrate; the act of composition disrupts and reintegrates.

If "The Window" symbolizes creative vision and "Time Passes" a plunge into disorder, "The Lighthouse" reconstitutes vision and or der through aesthetic design. An extreme tension between life and art lies at the heart of Lily Briscoe's painting and of Woolf's writing, which seek "that razor edge of balance" between experience and form. Her problem as a novelist, mirrored in Lily's painting, is to fuse visual forms, represented in words, with vital essences transmitted by memory. Her task is to animate the spirits of the dead and unite past and present through structural rhythms that interrelate separate images and streams of In the present essay, I wish to relate Woolf's poetics of space to the psychodynamics of creativity. My approach is pluralistic, borrowing from formalism, feminism, aesthetics, psychoanalysis, and phenomenology. These critical perspectives supplement each other and enable me to draw fuller analogies between fiction, painting, and music. Aware of the instability of metaphor in interarts comparisons, I focus chiefly on textural and structural, spatial and formal elements in Woolf's style. Such comparisons accentuate the sense of difference rather than simply assimilating writing to painting; the writer draws formal concepts from art criticism only to reconstitute them in the verbal medium. To avoid the "semantic slippage" of merely metaphorical analogy, Leonard Diepeveen recommends that interart comparisons be given an ontological basis and a structural and technical focus, while Wendy Steiner maintains that the programmatic tension between artistic medium and represented world so crucial to Cezanne... has changed the meaning of the analogy [between the spatial and temporal arts]. By claiming that a poem is like a modern painting one is no longer stressing their mirroring function but their paradoxical status as signs of reality and as things in their own right.

Woolf chooses to foreground the writing/painting analogy in To the Lighthouse because she wished to vie with her sister Vanessa's more concrete and sensory art while exploring Fry's theory of formal relations. In "The Narrow Bridge of Art," she calls for a lyrical abstraction in which the writer will dramatize "the power of music, the stimulus of sight, the effect on us of the shape of trees or the play of colour". Conceiving of the novel as an "elegy" or prose poem, she achieves a complex resonance with images of space and colour. Elizabeth Abel makes some necessary distinctions between colour in poetry and in painting: words that refer to colors are not the same as pigments on a canvas. Unlike the overall harmony of colour attained by Delacroix's brushstrokes, colour words... remain much more distinct and localized; they designate precise areas bounded by the nouns they modify.

But when they are liberated from nouns, as blue can become a noun itself, colour words are not so limited and may expand beyond specific things.

In To the Lighthouse, "irst, the pulse of colour flooded the bay with blue, and the heart expanded with it and the body swam". Optically, blue opens a space for perception and meditation; as a substantive, the word blue conveys a substance as well as inviting an imaginative response. Johannes Itten describes the optical and spiritual vibrations of blue:

As red is always active, so blue is always passive, from the point of view of material space. From the point of view of spiritual immateriality, blue seems active and red passive.... Blue is a power like that of nature in winter, when all germination and growth is hidden in darkness and silence. Blue is always shadowy, and tends in its greatest glory to darkness.... In the atmosphere of the earth, blue appears from the lightest azure to the deepest blue-black of the night sky. Blue beckons our spirit... into the infinite distances of spirit.

Lily Briscoe, the painter, feels an "instinctive need of distance and blue" as she struggles to give plastic form to memories and sensations. Similarly Woolf, in "Phases of Fiction," feels a "desire for distance, for music, for shadow, for space". Like Cezanne, Lily has to transform perception into vision and design without modifying the truth of what she sees. In Woolf's stream-of-consciousness technique, with its interacting colors, the vision of space reflects the viewer. Mrs. Ramsay's vision is pervaded by blue set off by a marginal green: For the great plateful of blue water was before her; the hoary Lighthouse, distant, austere, in the midst; and on the right, as far as the eye could see, fading and falling, in soft low pleats, the green sand dunes with the wild flowing grasses on them, which always seemed to be running away into some moon country, uninhabited of men.

Christopher Reed maintains that "To the Lighthouse is Woolf's most eloquent investigation of the connections between formalism and feminism"; the gendering of space is clear here. Running away from the centre with its erect patriarchal symbol of authority are the sinuous horizontal lines of the dunes, which do not fix the eye but draw it rhythmically beyond the frame. Woolf's metonymic structuring of space consists of frontal expanse, central distance, and flowing movement to the right, where lines seem to escape structure as they are not directed to a vanishing point. Rudolf Arnheim, in Art and Visual Perception, links the vanishing point with phallogocentric and Eurocentric visual structures, as "the apex of the pyramidal world portrayed in the picture." He adds: Symbolically, such a centered world suits a hierarchical conception of human existence. It would hardly fit the Taoist or Zen philosophies of the East, which express themselves in the centerless continuum of the Chinese and Japanese lands capes.

Just as the visual field is divided between central organization and peripheral counterpoint, this feminine movement "in soft low pleats," matching right brain impulses, is opposed to masculine rationalist or geometric organization, in which the picture space is held in a static vice by the will, rather than opening out toward undefined vision and being. Arnheim observes that "central perspective portrays space as a flow oriented toward a specified end. It thereby transforms the timeless simultaneity of traditional, undeformed space into a happening in time—that is a directed sequence of events". Potentially diverging lines are pressured into "a system of converging beams." Eye movements then follow preordained linear paths, rather than slipping off to the sides or revolving like the lighthouse beams.

Intuitive movement extends beyond the visual frame composed by eye and mind, into a wild zone or "moon country, uninhabited of men" and so beyond phallogocentric control. If this were a mindscape, the zone might be called feminine intuition, but that term indicates a single function of the androgynous mind, while Woolf affirms that the "whole of the mind must lie wide open if we are to get the sense that the writer is communicating his experience with perfect fullness". The logocentricity of the "hoary," "distant, austere" tower on the rock links it with Mr. Ramsay's intellect. He finally reaches the lighthouse, only because he gives in to Mrs. Ramsay's spirit after she is dead, internalizing her will rather than expelling it beyond the margins. But in this opening panorama, two opposite views intersect within the same spatial framework, presenting the axis of vision.

The lighthouse as structure or energy appears to be linear or circular, a vertically upright tower or a horizontally revolving light. Such a marriage of opposites can be more readily understood in music, where the musician allows his attention to oscillate freely between focused and unfocused states, now focusing precisely on the solid vertical sound of chords, now emptying his attention so that he can comprehend the loose, transparent web of polymorphic voices.

Mr. Ramsay's chopped-up, sequential alphabet of thought has "solid vertical" form. But attending to the "melody" of his wife's will, he takes Cam and James on the voyage while Lily struggles to integrate fragmentary memories in her design. While her brush flickers across her canvas, scoring it with running lines, the boat travels upward on the visual plane, vanishing toward the horizon, as the sea is tilted upward like the flat surface of the picture plane. The act of reading space parallels that of listening to music. Anton Ehrenzweig observes that there "is no hard and fast distinction between vertical and horizontal listening just as there is no sharp boundary between conscious and unconscious processes". Woolf binds alternating movements together in a formal simultaneity in which textual oscillation matches the focus of attention in pictorial space.

The "normal focused type of attention" and left-brain logocentrism of Mr. Ramsay's "alphabet," with its vertical working through a mental score, contrasts with the horizontal or "scattered type of attention" that Lily practices in front of her easel. The rationalist philosopher's and intuitive artist's distinct uses of mind—purposeful focusing and "unconscious scanning" are both necessary to artistic composition. Splicing voyage and painting together in a structural rhythm that implies their interaction, Woolf links points in space by an invisible line stretching elastically from immediate foreground to distant background. The two movements intersect rhythmically until they converge at the moment the boat arrives at the lighthouse and Lily draws her final line.

Distance conveys perspective, [proportion, outline, desire, and direction; it is also a symbol of being. Distance displays what Fry calls "that characteristic feeling of Cezanne's... of the monumental repose, the immense duration of the objects represented". For Lily, "distant views seem to outlast by a million years... the gazer and to be communing already with a sky which beholds an earth entirely at rest". While stasis gives rise to thoughts of its opposite, time passing, perception of distance is relative to lighting, position, and movement:

> In the failing light they all looked sharp-edged and ethereal and divided by great distances. Then, darting backwards over the vast space (for it seemed as if solidity had vanished altogether), Prue ran full tilt into them and caught the ball brilliantly high up in her left hand.

This cameo is "sharp-edged," as if cut out from its background and framed by time and memory as well as space. The sharpness of the figures in the fading light recalls Henri Rousseau's naively magical Carnival Evening, which captures the mood of a moment.

A sudden shift of focus from point to expanse brings an overwhelming sense of space and relativity. Nancy has been playing God with the creatures of a microcosmic pool, shadowing it with her hand and then exposing it to the sun.

> And then, letting her eyes slide imperceptibly above the pool and rest on that wavering line of sea and sky... she became with all that dower sweeping savagely in and inevitably withdrawing, hypnotised, and the two senses of that vastness and this tininess... flowering within it made her feel that she was bound hand and foot and unable to move by the intensity of feelings which reduced her own body, her own life, and the lives of all the people in the world, for ever, to nothingness.

Fry describes how Cezanne, in one of his landscapes, "construct for the imagination this immensity of space filled with light and vibrating with life", while Bachelard suggests "that it is through their 'immensity' that these two kinds of space—the space of intimacy and world space—blend. When human solitude deepens, then the two immensities touch and become identical". Nancy's ontological awareness is similar to Lily's feeling of expansion and contraction while painting: "She felt curiously divided, as if one part of her were drawn out there—it was a still day, hazy; the Lighthouse looked this morning at an immense distance; the other had fixed itself doggedly, solidly, here on the lawn". The two directions of her gaze split off into space like divided aspects of herself, the long view focused centrifugally on others, the near view rooted in subjective existence.

Aesthetic and imaginative spaces loom large and demand to be filled at Mrs. Ramsay's dinner: "In a flash saw her picture, and thought, Yes, I shall put the tree further in the middle; then I shall avoid that awkward space". Here objective design is paramount; later it fuses with subjectivized space. The hostess herself sees a bowl of fruit as a microcosm "possessed of great size and depth". When the room is illuminated, the window becomes an opaque reflector, shutting out darkness, so that "the faces on both sides of the table were brought nearer by the candlelight, and composed," making interior space like "order and dry land," exterior space "a reflection in which things wavered and vanished, waterily". Mrs. Ramsay, sensing a new balance of opposites, gains poise and reaches "the still space that lies about the heart of things, where one could move or rest". Symbolically or proleptically the group around the table responds to the lighthouse beam, mediated by her in a "mo ment of being."

Woolf interweaves emotional and oneiric images' with spatial impressions: Mr. Ramsay's strenuous thoughts are metonymically entangled with red geraniums, while Lily's image of his mind as a scrubbed kitchen table is projected into the branches of a pear tree. Ten years later, the painter and surviving family members reoccupy the house on the island, resuming their unfinished projects, so that objective space, which had fallen into the vortex of raw time and nature, becomes resaturated with personal duration and association. Memory and dream fuse with present sensations, as characters readjust to the once-familiar place, recuperating dispersed or distanced parts of their selves.

Lily's search for unity among disparate, warring elements of subject and object, self and others, demands continuous effort as well as intuition. Seizing her brush, she plunges into "the waters of annihilation." Gradually, a rising-falling rhythm like that of the waves is established between her conscious ego and unconscious scanning. While she attacks her canvas, another part of her mind relives the past, so that images from the two dimensions overlap, seamlessly fusing space and time. Left alone with her painting after Mr. Ramsay's departure, Lily sees "her canvas as if it had floated up and placed itself white and uncompromising directly before her". Before she can concentrate on her design she must endure division and diffusion. The reader becomes involved in a poetics of space, in which distance modifies emotion. Lily brings her experience of self and others to bear on the virtual space of her canvas, set at the centre of surrounding space and encircling memories. "omething... in the relations of those lines cutting across, slicing down, and in the mass of the hedge with its green cave of blues and browns" reminds Lily of her formal concept. Fry explains how Cezanne constructs on "a geometrical scaffolding" and marvels at "an imagination capable of holding in so firm a grasp all these disparate objects, this criss-cross of plastic movements and directions".

Similarly, as Lily begins to paint, she activates dimensions of chaos in which her need for order is correspondingly extreme: One line placed on the canvas committed her to innumerable risks, to frequent and irrevocable decisions. All that in idea seemed simple became in practice immediately complex; as the waves shape themselves symmetrically from the cliff top, but to the swimmer among them are divided by steep gulfs, and foaming crests.

She has to cast away the control that distances her from emotion and plunge into the turbulent waters of experience: like Mr. Ramsay in the boat, she is a "castaway," sinking "beneath a rougher sea/ whelmed in deeper gulfs than he". As Ehrenzweig explains, the "first brush stroke on a white piece of paper sends a shudder right across the pictorial plane contained by the four edges of the paper. It is never possible to predict which precise shape a brush stroke will form on the paper". Internal conflict is the price the artist must pay for spontaneous rhythm: Creativity is always linked with the happy moment when all conscious control can be forgotten. What is not sufficiently realized is the genuine conflict between two kinds of sensibility, conscious intellect and unconscious intuition. Depending on intuitive structural logic, Lily moved the salt-cellar on the tablecloth and decided to put the tree nearer the centre. Now she has to reactivate her design as she starts painting, invoking once more "the diffuse inarticulate vision of the unconscious": And so pausing and so flickering, she attained a dancing rhythmical movement, as if the pauses were one part of the rhythm and the strokes another... and so, lightly and swiftly pausing, striking, she scored her canvas with brown running nervous lines which had no sooner settled there than they enclosed a space. Down in the hollow of one wave she saw the next wave towering higher and higher above her. For what could be more formidable than that space?

She feels the challenge of the empty canvas: "For the mass loomed before her; it protruded; she felt it pressing on her eyeballs". Overwhelmed at first, she manages to tap into a pulse of creativity. "Then, as if some juice necessary for the lubrication of her faculties were spontaneously squirted, she began precariously dipping among the blues and umbers," flickering her brush over the canvas until it falls into an unconscious rhythm – so that while her hand quivered with life, this rhythm was strong enough to bear her along with it on its current.... And as she lost consciousness of outer things, and her name and her personality... her mind kept throwing up from its depths, scenes, and names, and sayings, and memories and ideas, like a fountain spurting over that glaring, hideously difficult white space, while she modelled it with greens and blues.

Ehrenzweig defines, in psychoanalytic terms, three stages of the creative process that apply to Lily's painting:

- "An initial stage of projecting fragments of the self into the work";
- A " phase initiates unconscious scanning that integrates art's substructure";
- A "stage of re-introjection part of the work's hidden substructure is taken back into the artist's ego on a higher mental level". These three stages parallel manic-depressive cycles in Woolf's own creativity. In the second stage, "creative dedifferentiation tends towards a 'manic' oceanic limit where all differentia-

tion ceases" as in Woolf's composition of "Time Passes," of which she writes: "I cannot make it out... well, I rush at it, and at once scatter out two pages. Is it nonsense, is it brilliance? Why am I so flown with words and apparently free to do exactly what I like?". Ehrenzweig's "triple rhythm of projection, dedifferentiation and re-introjection" closely parallels the threefold rhythm of vision, diffusion, and design that structures To the Lighthouse.

Woolf's text also exposes parallels between the dynamics of writing and painting. Maurice Merleau-Ponty observes that "language is expressive as much through what is between the words as through the words themselves... just as the painter paints as much by what he traces, by the blanks he leaves, or by the brush marks that he does not make". In a slow-motion film of Matisse painting, the same brush which, to the eye, did not jump from one movement to another, could be seen mediting... beginning ten possible movements, performing in front of the canvas a sort of propitiatory dance, coming so close several times as almost to touch it, and finally coming down like lightning in the only stroke necessary. (Merleau-Ponty

This process matches Lily's rhythmic brushwork which, with spaces interspersing rapid bouts of activity, culminates in a visionary stroke.

Ehrenzweig describes the painter's modeling of space as a psychological as well as technical phenomenon: The pulse [of the brush stroke] contributes to the gradual emergence of a dynamic "pictorial space," the most unpredictable and at the same time the most significant result of painting. The picture plane has its own life; its elements keep heaving in and out with little regard to illusionistic realism.

In this "manic" phase of creativity, "the work of art acts as a containing 'womb' which receives the fragmented projections of the artist's self'. In Ehrenzweig's analysis, "any increase in the unconscious substructure will produce as its outward sigual... an enhanced plastic effect.... This explains why the miracle of pictorial space, its mighty pulse that heaves through the picture plane, must remain for ever beyond conscious control". In Lily's painting, the discovery of actual and virtual space, surrounding her easel and on the canvas, coincides with rediscovery of past time and its absorption into the moment. The retrieval and reintegration of memories—a temporal process associated with visual space—activate her emerging design.

While the modeling of space presents formidable challenges, it also provides the artist with opportunities to find herself. Inwardly motivated but focusing outward, Lily confronts her aesthetic problem head-on: "Heaven be praised for it, the problem of space remained, she thought... and she began to model her way into the hollow there". Woolf's "tunnelling process," in which she carved out "beautiful caves" that connect past with present in Mrs. Dalloway, is close to Seurat's "art of hollowing out a canvas" as described by Roger Fry in Transformations. "Who before Seurat," asks Fry, "ever conceived exactly the pictorial possibilities of empty space? Whoever before conceived that such vast areas of flat, unbroken surfaces... could become the elements of a plastic design?" Fry argues that "the effort of the imagination in cutting away so much material proportional to the vastness and emptiness of the space thus excavated". In Mark Rothko's canvases, with their reverberating colour and tragic vision, there is a similar sense of hollowing out a space for meditation.

As Lily tunnels back into the past, the act of painting, although outwardly focused, becomes an act of opening old wounds and achieving catharsis—an act that requires perspective. The dark space of memory expands in harmony with the sensation of physical space: "And Lily, painting steadily, felt as if a door had opened, and one went in and stood gazing silently about in a high cathedral-like place, very dark, very solemn". Traces of departed objects are inscribed on space; absence and silence, accentuated by "stalks of smoke" and distant shouts, convey an acute sense of emptiness. Past experiences leave corresponding traces in mental space, suggesting how the mind retains but transmutes its sensory sources. Looking off into the distance, Lily links space with memory. Her tenuous perception of objects suggests uncertainty about "the nature of reality": Had drawn in the air a great scroll of smoke which stayed there curving and circling decoratively, as if the air were a fine gauze which held things and kept them softly in its mesh... ometimes quite close to the shore, the Lighthouse looked this morning in the haze an enormous distance away.

The impressionist textures that support this sense of distance have epistemological or ontological overtones: the blue haze conceals an unknown reality and the trace is inscribed in an image of writing. Reality for Cezanne, says Fry, "lay always behind this veil of colour, but it was different, more solid, more dense, in closer relation to the needs of the spirit". In To the Lighthouse, sea and sky interpenetrate and perception is mirrored in the scene, fusing subject with object and space with time.

Visual surfaces are illusory, suggesting the uncertainty of the voyage and the difficulty of reaching the goal—of discovering reality. Woolf's similes the "sea is stretched like silk across the bay" underscore the artificial textures of vision that come between perceiver and perceived. As Lily looks outward, trying to follow Mr. Ramsay's voyage, her eye composes a metaphysical image of reality: "Distance had an extraordinary power; they had been swallowed up in it, she felt, they were gone for ever, they had become part of the nature of things". Distance, in a Chekovian way, makes the observer aware of almost infinite perspectives on life.

Blue is the matrix of silence and contemplation. Dipping into her blue paint, Lily seeks to revive memories of Mrs. Ramsay. Her sense of the present moment is "fertile" enough to regenerate past "moments of being":

She rammed a little hole in the sand and covered it up, by way of burying in it the perfection of the moment. It was like a drop of silver in which one dipped and illumined the darkness of the past.... And as she dipped into the blue paint, she dipped too into the past there.

The blue wavelength emanates from her memory of Mrs. Ramsay looking out the window across the sea to the lighthouse. Blue is associated with vision and contemplation;

green with aesthetic detachment and imagination. Lily combines Mrs. Ramsay's visionary blue with her own cool green: "And this, thought, taking the green paint on her brush, this making up scenes about them, is what we call 'knowing' people.... She went on tunnelling her way into her picture, into the past". Invoking the interaction of adjacent colors—the green and blue pigments have radiating spiritual powers unlike the corresponding hues in "Blue & Green"—Lily brings critical insight as well as emotion to bear on Mrs. Ramsay's vision. She revolves "the wheel of sensation" so that she can "crystallise and transfix the moment" in her design—like James, at the outset, "cutting out pictures" with his mother.

Woolf now has to bring together the "psychological volumes" of James and Lily, as each looks with desire into the blue distance which is the aura of Mrs. Ramsay's spirit. Looking simultaneously connects them across space, as "ooking along his beam add it to her different ray" united Lily and the scientist Bankes, or "looking together" at the fruit bowl united Mrs. Ramsay and the poet Canrmichael. Lily's spatial perception again has ontological overtones. Puzzled by the fluctuating mix of memories and distant views, she longs to ask Mr. Carmichael what it all means:

For the whole world seemed to have dissolved in this early morning hour into a pool of thought, a deep basin of reality... For one moment she felt that if they both got up, here, now on the lawn, and demanded an explanation... then, beauty would roll itself up; the space would fill; those empty flourishes would form into shape.

Space is bracketed with sound, motion, shape, and line in a hieroglyph of Lily's frustrated desire for form and meaning: "the whole wave and whisper of the garden became like curves and arabesques flourishing round a centre of complete emptiness". Illustrating "that razor edge of balance between two opposite forces", aesthetics is linked to metaphysics and geometric form to spiritual experience. Mark Hussey claims that the "space in the painting corresponds to one side of that tension between meaning and nothingness that is felt throughout Woolf's writing". Space also registers the tension between Woolf's attempt to contain experience within a formalist aesthetic—to lay the ghosts of her parents in a design that masters their essences through formal relations—and the cathartic need to release potentially disruptive energies of love and hate.

As she struggles to integrate long and short views in her painting, Lily has a fleeting vision of Mrs. Ramsay. This "trick of the painter's eye," superimposing being on nothingness, resembles Septimus's hallucinations in Mrs. Dalloway. The memory of Mrs. Ramsay is the catalyst that animates Lily's vision, but the vision must be perpetually remade. Now again, moved as she was by some instinctive need of distance and blue, she looked at the bay beneath her, making hillocks of the blue bars of the waves, and stony fields of the purpler spaces. Again she was roused... by something incongruous. There was a brown spot in the middle of the bay.

Ehrenzweig notes "the unique power that colour has in creating and modulating space," an optical effect that matches the spiritual intensification that Lily experiences as she concentrates on the brown boat in the blue bay. Just as Mrs. Ramsay's eye transforms the fruit bowl into a landscape, so Lily's eye transforms the smooth surface of the sea into a rougher landscape of hillocks and fields—the metaphor connecting microcosmic and aesthetic visions of space with existential reality.

Lily's "instinctive need of distance and blue," although directed outward, matches Wassily Kandinsky's "principle of the inner need" for creative expression. In his treatise on art, Kandinsky also expounds the symbolic vibrations of blue: Bass; and the darkest blue of all—an organ.

Blue can provide an overall tonality, as in Cezanne's Portrait of Mme. Cezanne, where the "basis of the whole web of colour is a blue". Response to colour is subjective and can never be fully rationalized, for "Colour expresses something in itself" as well as something peculiar to each viewer. Woolf wrote in her diary of "a 'deep blue quiet space,' into which she seemed to step, 'off the whirling world"'. The calming vibrations of deep blue are associated with recessive powers that draw the eye off into deep space. On the basis of "Andre Broca's paradox"—"To see a blue light, you must not look directly at it"—Julia Kristeva hypothesizes "that the perception of blue entails not identifying the object; that blue is, precisely, on this side of or beyond the object's fixed form; that it is the zone where phenomenal identity vanishes". This transition from phenomenal to spiritual in the perception of blue relates closely to Mrs. Ramsay's peripheral, nondifferential, all-encompassing vision that blurs the identity of objects—as "creative vision" subsumes and resynthesizes them. The conjunction of "distance and blue" that Lily needs to borrow from Mrs. Ramsay is part of a process of spiritual meditation and aesthetic design, in which the optical vibration of space corresponds with the artist's deep desire for memory, perspective, and expressive powers.

But nothing, in the creative process, is simply one thing. While focusing one part of her mind on the voyage in space and time, Lily struggles with her painting; fixed at her easel, she outwardly represents "the still point of the turning world," as Mr. Ramsay earlier represented stability amid the flux. As she opens her attention to movement in space, her unconscious mind releases scenes from the past. The image of Mrs. Ramsay, "making of the moment something permanent (as in another sphere Lily herself tried to make of the moment something permanent)", is vividly framed and highlit against a background of empty space. "Why, after all these years had that survived, ringed round, lit up, visible to the last detail, with all before it blank and all after it blank, for miles and miles?". The image stands out in memory because it signifies Mrs. Ramsay's power to harmonize conflicting emotions. It has become "one of those globed compacted things over which thought lingers, and love plays", its iconic significance guaranteed by Lily's own deep need for harmony and form.

The spatial and psychological distances of the voyage are matched by the temporal and spiritual expanses of memory. As the boat sails on, distance induces a state of reverie, signified by the arabesques Cam's hand draws in the green water and the blue aura that surrounds James's memories of his mother.

A palimpsest of temporal images is laid out metonymically in mental space: Began to search among the infinite series of impressions which time had laid down, leaf upon leaf, fold upon fold softly, incessantly upon his brain; among scents, sounds; voices, harsh, hollow, sweet; and lights passing, and brooms tapping; and the wash and hush of the sea, how a man had marched up and down and stopped dead, upright, over them.

These space/time impressions, successively formed yet co-present to the mind's eye, contain the clue to James's identity in emotional wavelengths connecting him with his father and mother. He seeks to fix his experience in a talismanic image:

Turning back among the many leaves which the past had folded in him, peering into the heart of that forest where light and shade so chequer each other that all shape is distorted, and one blunders, now with the sun in one's eyes, now with a dark shadow, he sought an image to cool and detach and round off his feeling in a concrete shape.

The psychological function of these childhood images is equivalent to the aesthetic function of forms in painting: they give concrete shape and outline to what would otherwise remain amorphous. Across space and time comes a desire to redeem those moments that radiate significance—as marked by the blue aura in James's mind or the blue paint into which Lily dips. The retrieval of such moments satisfies a need: they contain clues and latent energy for self-discovery and composition.

Walter Benjamin defines the aura of an object as "the unique phenomenon of a distance" distance combining desire with "unapproach-ability" and veneration with authenticity. The uniqueness of an artwork, its place in "the fabric of tradition," constitutes its aura.

The aura of an object is constituted by space and time; similarly, when a memory becomes irradiated it signals an emotional content that is the outcome of ritual and experience. For Bachelard, memory is ontological: "Distant memory only recalls by giving them a value, a halo, of happiness". His mother's image appears to James in "a flash of blue," just as she perceived things intuitively, "in one flash—the way of genius". The locus of James's search, with its spatial imagery of rooms, is now inside the self. So Rilke sees his childhood home as "quite dissolved and distributed inside me". Space and time fuse in memories of the childhood house that raise haunting questions of reality and identity.

James "began following her from room to room and at last they came to a room where in a blue light, as if the reflection came from many china dishes, she talked to somebody". In Woolf's musical as well as painterly form, such auras mark nodes of intensity: so James's reflected blue light signifies an unconscious association with his mother that holds a vital clue to his identity.

As the boat comes closer to the lighthouse, he readjusts his vision, combining the "silvery, misty-looking tower with a yellow eye" with "the tower, stark and straight...barred with black and white". Opposing views of the object, mediated by distance and atmosphere, are dual perspectives that do not fuse but complement each other in a balanced androgynous vision. During the voyage, perspectives alternate as characters look onward to the lighthouse on the rock, whose reality they will affirm, and backward to the island that is a spatial symbol of their past lives and memories.

The forward movement in space takes precedence over the backward movement in time; lived reality and spatial locality dissipate in a blue spell. Cam's speculation about what her father sees as he looks at the island underlines the relativity of perception. Mr. Ramsay is long-sighted, able to see clearly at a distance, but his view is often blocked by obstacles at close range. Determined to see the thing in itself, but unable to do so because he sees himself in the thing, he cannot deal with the distorting or illuminating powers of vision.

Distance and blue are spatial or plastic equivalents for memory, emotion, and vision: So much depends then, thought Lily Briscoe, looking at the sea which had scarcely a stain on it, which was so soft that the sails and the clouds seemed set in its blue, so much depends, she thought, upon distance... for her feeling for Mr. Ramsay changed as he sailed further and further across the bay.... He and his children seemed to be swallowed up in that blue, that distance. Lily's visual thinking and her more conscious reflections about the effects of distance are steeped in the blue aura that is the medium of spiritual vision.

Closeness or remoteness, sharpness or dimness, correspond with the sense of reality or unreality. James, Cam, and Lily have to sail through a hazy "limbo of being" between past and present to realise their respective visions. A sense of unreality is strong during the voyage, with its bemused retrospection countered by projection and its shifts of perspective that bring about reorientation:

> It was a way things had sometimes, thought, lingering for a moment and looking at the long glittering windows and the plume of blue smoke: they became unreal. So coming back from a journey... before habits had spun themselves across the surface, one felt that same unreality... felt something emerge. Life was most vivid then.

Habit dulls, defamiliarization revitalizes. As Lily's mind begins to bridge the gap between past and present, the space in front of her seems to gain depth and density. Through an "instinctive need of distance and blue," she revives traces of being that deepen her sense of the moment and connect it with the past.

Distance stretches Lily's imagination and exercises her sympathies in ways that impel her to complete her design:

> For the Lighthouse had become almost invisible, had melted away into a blue haze, and the effort of looking at it and the effort of thinking of him landing there, which both seemed to be one and the same effort, had stretched her body and mind to the utmost.

As the lighthouse disappears in the blue, imagination transcends reality. Subjective wavelengths fuse with objective forms, and the artist's perceptual efforts culminate in a flash of insight:

> There it was—her picture. Yes, with all its greens and blues, its lines running up and across, its attempt at something.... She looked at the steps; they were empty; she

looked at her canvas; it was blurred. With a sudden intensity, as if she saw it clear for a second, she drew a line there, in the centre. By that decisive act, she fills the empty space and gives her design its final form. For Ruddick, "Lily achieves at this moment the dark route to vision which is preparation for the light.... The brushstroke betokens the final union of the seen and unseen worlds".

Fleishman, like Ruddick, argues that the line down the centre of the canvas is the lighthouse, but it cannot simply represent that object, as Lily had 10 years earlier expounded her principles of abstraction, the "question being one of the relations of masses, of lights and shadows". I prefer Mary Ann Gaws's formalist definition of Lily's line as "the perfect minimal gesture, dividing and defining the two parts of the picture in relation to each other". The central line orchestrates lines, masses, and colors that together form an intricate series of relationships within a single design.

Lily's moment of unifying vision closes the novel off from the surrounding temporal/spatial world and seals its meanings in. But the play of imagination and reality—with its endless interrelation of signs—is released anew each time a reader's consciousness enters the text. "Subject and object and the nature of reality" are reduced to hieroglyphics in an artwork, but also illuminated by it. The centripetal tendency of closure merges with the centrifugal radiation of the art symbol to unify singularity with multiplicity, stasis with kinesis, and imagination with reality.

Space and colour are inseparable adjuncts of vision and design in To the Lighthouse. Both James and Lily have "an instinctive need of distance and blue." But the artist's need includes an inner necessity that extends her capacity for vision, feeling, and expression. Her reveries connect past and present, near and far, self and others, in a design whose composition mirrors the creative process. Through the image of painting and the consciousness of a surrogate artist, Woolf positions her implied reader within a magnetic field of distance and blue, opening imaginative spaces in the text that transcend the normal signifying power of words.

Jack stewart is professor of English at the University of British Columbia and author of The Vital Art of D. H. Lawrence: Vision and Expression. Specializing in the interrelations of literature and painting in the modern period, he is a frequent contributor to the D. H. Lawrence Review and has also published a series of essays on Virginia Woolf and the visual arts.

Chapter 13

Critical Essays

The Process of Perception: Cervantes' Don Quixote and Woolf's Lily Briscoe by John McGrath

The process of perception involves two steps: the recognition of sensory information and the interpretation of sensory information. In order for the truth to be perceived, or, in other words, for something to be perceived accurately, sensory information must be recognized or identified correctly and then interpreted faithfully according to that recognition. A faithful interpretation is one that does not negate the recognition of sensory information. Truth is not perceived if an inaccurate recognition is interpreted faithfully. An interpretation may take several forms, however, and truth still be perceived, if the recognition is accurate and if the interpretation does not negate that recognition.

In Part One, Chapter Eighteen of Cervantes' Don Quixote, when the title character enters into battle with a flock of sheep, his perception of the sheep is at first influenced by expectation. In this case the mode of perception is sight; vision is the sensory information that Don Quixote must recognize and interpret. Don Quixote and his squire Sancho at first cannot see the sheep because of the "clouds of dust they [the sheep] raised, which obscured and blinded their [Don Quixote's and Sancho's] vision". Before he can actually perceive the approaching hordes, Don Quixote expects them to be enemy armies ready to clash in battle, because, as the narrator explains, "every hour and every minute his mind was always full of those battles, enchantments, adventures, miracles, loves, and challenges which are related in books of chivalry". In other words, Don Quixote's madness, caused by literature, prompts him to expect these approaching hordes to be armies.

Yet, even after he can see the hordes of sheep, he still believes them to be armies. As the flocks grow nearer, Sancho yells to Don Quixote, who swears to defeat one of the "armies," "Turn back, Don Quixote, for I swear to God, sir, they are rams and ewes you are going to attack. Turn back!". Don Quixote, however, ignores his squire's warning and attacks the sheep as if they were an enemy army. At this point in the adventure, Don Quixote recognizes the sheep inaccurately as warriors, and interprets them as such. The first stage of his perception is inaccurate‹he does not perceive the truth—, but the second stage is accurate. He interprets his vision faithfully according to his recognition, but because the first stage of perception is inaccurate, he does not perceive truth.

The knight's perception changes, however, after the battle, when Sancho tells him, once again, "Didn't I tell you, Don Quixote, sir,...to turn back, for they were not armies you were going to attack, but flocks of sheep?". It is here that Don Quixote recognizes the truth, and he acknowledges that the hordes were, indeed, sheep. He interprets his recognition unfaithfully, though, because he goes on to claim that "an enchanter...turned the hostile squadrons into flocks of sheep". Such an interpretation negates the correct recognition, and is therefore unfaithful. In this way, Don Quixote's perception changes from inaccurate recognition and faithful interpretation to accurate recognition and unfaithful interpretation. He modifies his perception to accommodate Sancho's objection.

Another instance that illustrates Don Quixote's misperception of truth is the famous adventure with the windmills. On this occasion, unlike the battle with the sheep, in which a dust cloud at first impairs his vision, Don Quixote sees and perceives the windmills from the start, yet he still cannot perceive the truth. He says, "Look over there, friend Sancho Panza, where more than thirty monstrous giants appear". Don Quixote's command to "look," and his insistence that the giants "appear" must mean that he can see them. He recognizes the sight of the windmills inaccurately as giants, and interprets them faithfully as such. As with the sheep adventure, when, after the battle, Sancho tells Don Quixote that his perception was wrong, Don Quixote's perception changes from inaccurate recognition and faithful interpretation to accurate recognition and unfaithful interpretation. Sancho says, "Didn't I tell your worship to look what you were doing, for they were only windmills?". Once again, Don Quixote claims that an enchanter, the "sage Friston...turned those giants into windmills".

The character Lily Briscoe in Virginia Woolf's To The Lighthouse also perceives elements of the world differently from other characters. Like Don Quixote, the mode of Lily's perception is vision. Unlike Don Quixote, whose recognition of the truth changes in the sheep scene, Lily's recognition of the truth that, for instance, Mrs. Ramsay is Mrs. Ramsay, remains constant. Also unlike Don Quixote, whose interpretation takes the forms of words, as in his lengthy enumeration of the "knights" in the approaching "armies," and of action, as in his attack of the sheep, Lily's Interpretation takes the forms of thought and of representation in paint. Lily attempts, with little success, to perceive, and, thus to understand Mrs. Ramsay in all her complexity as a woman and as a human being. She uses language of "seeing" or of "vision" in order to express her frustration at such a daunting task: "Fifty pairs of eyes were not enough to get round that one woman, she thought". The interpretation for such attempts at perceiving the wholeness of people takes the form of thought. Lily's primary form of interpretation, however, is represented in her painting.

The scene Lily paints from the Ramsay's summer home in the Hebrides includes Mrs. Ramsay reading to James. Lily recognizes the form of Mrs. Ramsay to be, in fact, Mrs. Ramsay. She skews her interpretation in paint by representing Mrs. Ramsay and James as a purple triangle. It cannot be said, as it could for Don Quixote, that because her interpretation represents Mrs. Ramsay differently than she sees them, that Lily does not perceive the truth. There is a crucial difference in these characters' interpretations. Don Quixote's belief, for example, that an enchanter has changed armies into sheep belies his recognition. Although he recognizes the truth that the hordes appear as sheep, his interpretation that they are, in fact, warriors negates his recognition. Lily's artistic interpretation of Mrs. Ramsay as a triangle does not negate her recognition of Mrs. Ramsay as herself. Lily does not think that Mrs. Ramsay and James are actually a purple triangle. She tells Mr. Bankes that "she had made no attempt at likeness" in depicting Mrs. Ramsay and James as a triangular shape.

Lily's self-consciousness of interpretation, her deliberate modification of perception, marks another crucial difference between herself and Don Quixote: that Lily actively modifies her vision in order to represent truth, whereas Don Quixote modifies his vision in order to represent fantasy. Although Cervantes does not give the reader as extensive a view of the minds of characters as Woolf does, he does write that "everything that he [Don Quixote] said, thought, or did was influenced by his fantasies". As Don Quixote is enumerating the knights in the approaching hordes, even before he can perceive them, the narrator explains that he is "'carried away by his strangely deluded imagination". In this way, Don Quixote's perception, and the modification of that perception‹in response to Sancho's objections, for instance‹is in support of a fantasy, a delusion. He refuses to perceive truth.

Lily, on the other hand, is forever in search of perceiving truth. This is, perhaps, the most vital difference between her perception of the world and Don Quixote's. Her goal in changing the composition of her picture, or in representing figures abstractly is not to support a fantasy or a delusion, but, rather, to represent her "vision" or "picture." As she attempts to explain her painting to Mr. Bankes on page 53, she is described as "becoming once more under the power of that vision which she had seen clearly once and must now grope for among hedges and houses and mothers and children‹her picture". Seeing this picture, this vision, is not easy for Lily; she must strain in order to see the truth of it. As she struggles to see it, "always something...thrust through, snubbed her, waked her, required and got in the end an effort of attention, so that the vision must be continually remade". Like Don Quixote, Lily changes her perception. Unlike Don Quixote, the changes Lily makes allow her to better perceive the truth. She modifies her interpretation of the world, which she recognizes accurately, according to her sense of her changing vision. She tells Mr. Bankes thatIt was a question, she remembered, how to connect this mass on the right hand with that on the left. She might do it by bringing the line of the branch across so; or break the vacancy in the foreground by an object so. But the danger was that by doing that the unity of the whole might be broken.

Thus, her interpretation must be altered in order to support her vision. These changes in interpretation never negate her recognition of reality, however, and, thus, her perception always supports truth. She enacts changes in visual composition, favoring unity, balance of left and right, and balance of foreground and background. On the last page of the novel, when she sees "it clear for a second," she paints a single line in the centre of the painting. The novel goes on to say "It was done; it was finished. Yes, she thought,...I have had my vision". With that single line, Lily finishes her painting and is finally able to perceive the truth of her vision. Her long struggle to see and represent her vision is completed.

Tracking the recognition and interpretation of Don Quixote is rather more challenging than tracking Lily's, though, because Cervantes gives us very few glimpses into Don Quixote's mind. The progress of Lily's painting, as she struggles to "see" her vision and then to complete the painting takes place almost exclusively on a mental plane. The process of perception and its relation to truth are dependent upon the thought processes of accurate recognition and faithful interpretation. These are psychological processes. The reader sees very little of Don Quixote's psychology, and must instead rely on his words and actions, in effect, the residue and result of mental processes, in order to track his changes in perception. In Woolf, by contrast, the reader sees into Lily's thoughts, and consequently can see the actual moment of recognition and the moment of interpretation. Both characters, in the end, perceive some form of truth. Lily perceives it through active pursuit of her vision and, finally, through completion of her painting. Don Quixote perceives truth in the end when his madness abates and the goal of his perception is no longer to support a fantasy. In either case, however, the perception of truth leads the character to a better understanding of the world, and marks the completion of a journey. Don Quixote perceives truth and ends his errantry. Lily perceives truth and finishes her painting. The process of perception is the journey. Truth is the end.

An analysis of To the Lighthouse Argument

Mrs. Ramsey is triumphant over Mr. Ramsey, by her awareness and intuitive feeling of the more important things in life: the value of human relationships. Though she is submissive, with no mention of extensive educational background, she innately possesses the crucial social skills that gain: the cohesion of the family as a whole; the respect and love of her children, and the continued survival of her marriage.

Part I: The Window

"Had there been an axe handy, or a poker, any weapon that would have gashed a hole in his father's breast and killed him, there and then, James would have seized it.... grinning sarcastically, not only with the pleasure of disillusioning his son and casting ridicule upon his w:j'e, who was ten thousand times better in every way than he was." P4

"Yes, of course, if it 'sfine tomorrow, "said Mrs. Ramsey. To her son these words conveyed an extraordinary joy. P3

"Perhaps you will wake up and find the sun shining and the birds singing, "she said compassionately, smoothing.the little boy's hair, for her husband, with his caustic saying that it would not be fine, had dashed his spirits she could see. P15

"But" said his father, "it won 't be fine. " P4

"No going to the Lighthouse, James, "he said. P14

"What he said was true. He was incapable of untruth; never tampered with a fact; never altered a disagreeable word to suit the pleasure or convenience of any mortal being, least of all of his own children, who, sprung from his loins, should be aware from childhood that life is difficult. " P4

"When the great clangour of the gong announced solemnly, authoritatively, that all those scattered about, in attics, in bedrooms, on little perches of their own, reading, writing, putting the last smooth to their hair, or fastening dresses, must leave all that, and the little odds and ends on their washing-tables and dressing-tables, and the novels on the bed-tables, and the diaries which were so private, and assemble in the dining-room for dinner. P 82

"They are in the hands of the Lord"

"Yes, you were right. It 's going to be wet tomorrow. You won 't be able to go." And she looked at him smiling. For she had triumphed again. She had not said it, yet he knew.

To the Lighthouse-Bridge Between Worlds

Virginia Woolf's To the Lighthouse illustrates a bridge between the worlds of the Victorian mother and the modern, potentially independent woman. The Victorian woman was to be absorbed, as Mrs. Ramsay is, by the task of being mother and wife. Her reason for existing was to complete the man, rather than to exist in her own right. Mrs. Ramsay certainly sees this role for herself and is disturbed when she feels, momentarily, that she is better than her husband because he needs her support to feel good about himself and the life choices he has made. Yet the end of the Victorian era saw the rise of women's rights and greater freedom for women to excel without men or children. Adrienne Rich, in Of Woman Born, says that To the Lighthouse is about Virginia Woolf's need to understand her own mother and to prove, through the character of Lily Briscoe, that a woman can be "independent of men, as Mrs. Ramsay is not".

The trauma of this transition from Victorian to modern woman is portended by Mrs. Ramsay herself, at the beginning of the story. In the first chapter, as Mrs. Ramsay defends Charles Tansley against the criticisms of her children, she muses on her desire to protect men and the "trustful, childlike, reverential" attitude that her protection inspires in men. "Woe betide the girl... who did not feel the worth of it, and all that it implied, to the marrow of her bones!" she exclaims to herself, thinking of the way men respect and admire her. But Woolf shows us that as Mrs. Ramsay admonishes her children for ridiculing Charles Tansley, her daughters "could sport with infidel ideas which they had brewed for themselves of a life different from hers... not always taking care of some man or other."

The issue of the change from one concept of womanhood to another is not as simple as the newer generation revolting against the older; at the same time that Mrs. Ramsay's daughters hope to be different, they admire and worship their mother for her beauty and power. Prue, the eldest daughter, proudly watches Mrs. Ramsay as she descends the staircase and feels "what an extraordinary stroke of fortune it was for her, to have her [Mrs. Ramsay]." Although this is the closest we come to knowing the thoughts and feelings of Prue, from others' perspectives, we gather that she follows in her mother's footsteps and dies in childbirth. Does this signify the death of the old vision of womanhood? Or does it have more to do with the particular strength of Mrs. Ramsay? Perhaps it signifies the futility of the daughter trying to imitate exactly the path of the mother.

The Lighthouse of Alexandria

The lighthouse was built in 209 BC, and dedicated to Ptolemy Soter and his wife Berenice. It was used to mark the harbor using fire at night and sun rays during the day and a giant mirror that reflected these lights. When Egypt was conquered by the Arabs they took down the mirror and did not restore it. In AD 956 a small earthquake shook the lighthouse but did little damage. Later in 1303 and 1323 two stronger earthquakes shook and left the lighthouse in ruins. In 1480 Qaitbay, an Egyptian Mamelouk Sultan, used the fallen stone and marble to build a medieval fort where the lighthouse once stood.

Of the six vanished wonders the Lighthouse of Alexandria

was the last to disappear. Ancient accounts by Strabo and Pliny the Elder give a description of the tower and its marble cover. The monument was constructed of three stages: the lowest square, 183 ft. high with a cylinder core; the middle stage, an octagonal shape that stood 90 ft, and the third stage was a circular addition that stood 24 ft. high. With a total height that rose to 384 ft., equivalent to a 40 story building. The initial core was used to lift and store coal as needed to fuel the fire at night. In ancient times the statue of Poseidon, the lord of the seas, stood at the summit of this building.

Although the monument didn't last to present day, it greatly influenced the building of other lighthouses throughout the Mediterranean and as far as Spain. Thus giving its name Pharos to all the lighthouses in the world.

To the Lighthouse the Two-Dimensional Character

In the novel, To the Lighthouse, Virginia Woolf illustrates the character of Mr. Ramsay, a husband and father of eight children. As a husband, he degrades and mentally abuses his wife, Mrs. Ramsay, and as a father, he disparages and psychologically injures his children. Yet, Mr. Ramsay has another side — a second dimension. He carries the traits of a very compassionate and loving husband and a securing and nurturing father. Although Woolf depicts Mr. Ramsay as crude, brusque, and insensitive, he, nonetheless, desires happiness and welfare for his family.

Even though Mr. Ramsay frequently scolds and denounces Mrs. Ramsay, he still seeks happiness and comfort for his wife. For example, after Mrs. Ramsay lies to James about the next day's weather, "He [Mr. Ramsay] stamped his foot on the stone step. 'Damn you,' he said." Mr. Ramsay devastates his wife's emotions. Because of a little lie, the temperamental Mr. Ramsay hurts, if not kills, Mrs. Ramsay's emotions. Still, right after the incident, Mr. Ramsay self-reflects and " ashamed of that petulance [that he brought to his wife]." Mr. Ramsay understands and regrets the sorrow he brought on Mrs. Ramsay. He sympathizes with her and is "ashamed" for what he had done. Mr. Ramsay wants to appease his wife and make her happy as a result of the torment that he inflicted on her. Next, Woolf again illustrates Mr. Ramsay's insensitive dimension when Mr. Ramsay makes Mrs. Ramsay "bend her head as if to let the pelt of jagged hail, the drench of dirty water, bespatter her unrebuked." Mr. Ramsay is heartless to his wife's feelings; it is as if he enjoys "drenching" Mrs. Ramsay and enjoys seeing her in mental anguish. However, Woolf later contrasts the callous Mr. Ramsay with a more sensitive and caring Mr. Ramsay: So stiffened and composed the lines of her face in a habit of sternness that when her husband passed... he could not help noting, the sternness at the heart of her beauty. It saddened him, and her remoteness pained him.

Therefore, here Mr. Ramsay is portrayed as a sympathetic and caring husband that is "pained" by the expression of sorrow on his wife's face. Mr. Ramsay is sensitive to his wife's feelings and desires her well-being. Woolf illustrates the inconsistency of Mr. Ramsay's character through his and Mrs. Ramsay's interactions.

Next, Woolf portrays Mr. Ramsay as a brusque and callous father by his harsh interactions with his children, when his true motive is to help and secure his children's welfare. Mr. Ramsay is depicted as a father whom, "had there been an axe, or a poker, any weapon that would have gashed a hole in [Mr. Ramsay's] breast and killed him, there and then, James would have seized it," because of the Mr. Ramsay's constant, pessimistic rambling, "it won't be fine." Mr. Ramsay is depicted as a sharp, deadly, and sarcastic killjoy that destroys the anticipation and happiness of his child, James. His children regard him with the utmost rancor that they even think of stabbing him to death. However, little do his children know that, "he [Mr. Ramsay] was incapable of untruth; never altered a disagreeable word to suit the pleasure... of any human being, least of all of his own children, who... should be aware from childhood that life is difficult; [he would instill] courage, truth, and the power to endure." The main purpose for his bluntness is not to intentionally hurt his children, but instead to strengthen them. He wants his children to grow up as successful, self-sufficient people. Thus, even though Mr. Ramsay does have a crude dimension in his character, he also has a second dimension of sensibility.

Virginia Woolf pictures the character of Mr. Ramsay as an authentic human being; he has a second-dimension that allows him to have both evil and sincere attributes. She does not write about either a very humble and generous man or a very insolent and cruel man; instead, Woolf gives the readers a real character with both traits that allow readers to understand the foibles of characters like Mr. Ramsay.

Education And Thought In Virginia Woolf's to the Lighthouse

To understand Virginia Woolf's contribution to current discussions of masculine and feminine modes of thinking and living, we begin this present study by joining Mrs. Ramsay's guests at a dinner party that is described halfway through Virginia Woolf's novel To the Lighthouse. All the male guests are eagerly talking. As she listens, Mrs. Ramsay wonders:

> What did it all mean? To this day she had no notion. A square root? What was that? Her sons know. She leant on them; on cubes and squares; that was what they were talking about now; on Voltaire and Madame de Stacl; on the character of Napoleon; on the French system of land tenure; on Lord Rosebery; on Creevey's Memoirs; she let it uphold her and sustain her, this admirable fabric of the masculine intelligence, which ran up and down, crossed this way and that, like iron girders spanning the swaying fabric, upholding the world, so that she could trust herself to it utterly, even shut her eyes.

At the same time that this and other passages depict what is now known as masculine reasoning, Woolf does not narrowly render reasoning through an either/or rendition or two valenced genderized extremes. She portrays a complicated, criss-crossing of different forms of reasoning, perceiving, feeling, relating to others, and living in the world. This intricate design not only highlights the extremes of masculine and feminine reasoning, but some of the shortcomings of the present tendency to genderize theories.

To unravel Woolf's design, we first look at the reasoning of the men who are Mrs. Ramsay's dinner guests, then direct our attention to Mrs. Ramsay, and finally, look at the limitations that Woolf discerns in both these extremes.

Against the background of the rationality and reasoning that developed since the beginning of the Enlightenment, we understand Mrs. Ramsay's puzzlement about the conversation and logic of the men at her dinner table. She anticipates the present rebellion against this older type of reasoning and the positing of other ways of conceptualizing reason, one of which is dependent on gender differences.

Mrs. Ramsay muses about the features of "masculine intelligence," a reasoning as abstract as the square roots, the cubes and squares that her sons understand so well. The results of this thinking are as certain and unchanging as the solution of a square root. The image "square root" reminds us of the supremacy of the physical sciences and logic. Akin to the diagramming of an algebraic verbal problem,2 we can diagram the solution to all sorts of other dilemmas.

Remembering Andrew's comment that his father's work is like a "kitchen table," Lily Briscoe likens Mr. Ramsay's philosophic work on "subject and object and the nature of reality" to a "large kitchen table," a "scrubbed kitchen table," that was a "symbol of her profound respect for Mr. Ramsay's mind." This "phantom kitchen table" is a pregnant, but ironical image in that a kitchen table usually invokes the busyness of family life, a workplace and social meeting arena that is overrunning with the ingredients for Mrs. Ramsay's Boeuf en Daube, the many hands chopping and mixing the vegetables and seasonings, and the easy chatter and stories of the cooks. A scrubbed kitchen table is a misnomer, since even when clean, the kitchen table is not free of the flotsam and incremental remains of family life. But this is not the import of Lily Briscoe's thought of the kitchen table. Her image points to the human mind as a tabula rasa, wiped clean of every emotion and feeling, of personal interests and needs; it resonates to Mr. Ramsay's thoughts of Hume, and then, for us, out to the more recent veil of ignorance.

No matter the problem, this form of reasoning accepts that every human being including the reasoning individual is of equal worth, no better or worse than any other individual. A moral agent canna consider any special relationship with a particular human being, with A or with B. A, B, and the moral agent are actually placemarks in the moral calculus and could be replaced by any other individual. For Mr. Ramsay, James, Andrew, Prue, and Cam are not unique, his precious children, but the facts of his life, a scholar who struggles to support his family and educate his children. Yet Mr. Ramsay is troubled by his scholarly investigations. What can he know? Using linear logic, Mr. Ramsay realizes that an uncommon genius will jump from A to Z, see the whole march of knowledge in one leap. But Mr. Ramsay had to take a more difficult road, climbing from A to B, from B to C, more recently struggling from P to Q, but what of R? Will he arrive at R? Whoever undertakes this scholarly quest for knowledge, whether genius or not, will take this logical journey. For there is no other road.

Mr. Ramsay, the one reasoning, the moral agent, detaches himself from the objects of thought. The objects of thought are as psychologically separate as Voltaire, Madame de Stael, Napoleon, or the French system of land tenure are separated by time from the men at Mrs Ramsay's dinner party. Psychological, temporal, and logical detachment implies that the subject examines the problem in the same manner as William Bankes would use a microscope, dissect a specimen, or do a scientific experiment. Just as Bankes, the scientist, does not become bonded with experiment, the men talking at the dinner party do not become imbedded in the objects of their conversation. This subject-object relationship assumes that human beings can be known and understood in the same way as a table, a chair, or any other thing. Napoleon and Voltaire are not real people to be nurtured and befriended; they are the A's and B's, the X's and Y's of logical thought and calculative reasoning. They are objects, as distant as the lighthouse that Mrs. Ramsay will never visit.

In a more negative vein, some philosophers claim that this

detachment can have undesirable consequences. For Martin Buber, this form of relationship can be "the lust to make use of men by which the manipulator of 'propaganda' and 'suggestion' is possessed."6 Stuart Hampshire graphically describes negative facets of calculative reasoning as a "habit of mind has brought with it a new abstract cruelty in politics, a dull, destructive political righteousness: mechanical, quantitative thinking, leaden loveless minds setting out their moral calculations in leaden abstract prose."

In the family, we see a precursor of Buber's and Hampshire's warnings. Speaking about Mrs. Dalloway, Ellen Bayuk Rosenman states, "Underlying these external manifestions is a masculine state of consciousness, a general conception of the relationship between Self and Other. Its interpersonal imperialism dehumanizes and objectifies the Other to block out any disturbing sympathy or sense of likeness which might impede conquest." In To the Lighthouse, though he enrages James, Mr. Ramsay "block out any disturbing sympathy" and never sensing his son's feelings, bends and "tickle James's bare calf with a spring of something".

Though each man at the dinner party seems to be autonomous with his own point of view, a unique person is not speaking about Napoleon or French land tenure. Any suitably educated man would voice similar ideas, speak about the same subjects, and use the same form of argument. Mr. Ramsay might contend that impartialism is an ideal of reasoning, but impartialism often masquerades power and authoritarianism. The facts and truth are impartial for Mr. Ramsay, no matter their affect on his children. We cannot go to the lighthouse tomorrow; the weather will be bad. It is a fact. Throughout To the Lighthouse, Mrs. Ramsay completely trusts men to provide a "Heaven of security", to "upholding the world," to the extent that she can "even shut her eyes." Since the time of Plato, sight and the eyes have been metaphors to signify the attainment of knowledge and understanding. In Plato's "Allegory of the Cave," after an arduous journey, the released prisoner, the philosopher King, finally sees the stars and sun and knows the Ideal Forms of the Good, the True, and the Beautiful. Through the image of "shut eyes," Woolf metaphorically highlights Mrs. Ramsay's inability to think and know as men do and thus, her dependence on them.

Yet, Mrs. Ramsay silently thinks, she dozes, she muses. If she played the game of men and accepted their "phrase-making...she would have blown her brains out by now" Mrs. Ramsay, a personification of women's way of thinking, recognizes that men's way of thinking runs counter to women's very being. Though they adore her, men do not listen to Mrs. Ramsay; they do not take her ideas and judgments seriously; they are not concerned about her unique way of reasoning or about her picture of the world.

If we listen to Mrs. Ramsay, we hear a very different Language. Mrs. Ramsay's musings are the melody of another way of thinking:

No, she thought, putting together some of the pictures... had cut out—a refrigerator, a mowing machine, a gentleman in evening dress—children never forget For this reason, it was so important what one said, and what one did.

And then:

His arm was almost like a young man's arm, Mrs. Ramsay thought, thin and hard, and she thought with delight how strong he still was, though he was over sixty, and how untamed and optimistic, and how strange it was that being convinced, as he was, of all sorts of horrors, seemed not to depress him, but to cheer him.... Indeed he seemed to her sometimes made different from other people, born blind, deaf, and dumb, to the ordinary things.... Did he notice the flowers? No. Did he notice the view? No. Did he even notice his own daughter's beauty, or whether there was pudding on his plate or roast beef ? At the dinner party, Mrs. Ramsay glories in the Boeuf en Daube:

And she peered into the dish, with its shiny walls and its confusion of savoury brown and yellow meats and its bay leaves and its wine, and thought. This will celebrate the occasion — a curious sense rising in her, at once freakish and tender, of celebrating a festival, as if two emotions were called up in her. When describing Mrs. Ramsay and other women's thinking and how their moral reasoning develops, the literary critic, Q. D. Leavis states, "'One's own kitchen and nursery…is the realm where living takes place…and serve as a sieve for determining which values are important and genuine and which are conventional and contemptible.'" Though kitchen and nursery provide the experiences for developing both masculine and feminine reasoning, for each gender, there are different interpretations and understandings of these places and their objects. In the case of a common kitchen object, Andrew depicts his father's austere philosophic work with the image of a kitchen table, whereas Mrs. Ramsay's emotions and thinking are heightened by the image of the boeuf en daube."

Mrs. Ramsay's thoughts give us a glimpse of the contours, the objects and processes of women's thinking. These contours indicate that women see the world and life in a different way; this domain is charged with their values and what they discern as important With this view of the world, the subject matter, problems, and purposes of thinking are transformed. More recently, Sandra Harding pointed out that inquiry and thought that begins "with what appears problematic from the perspective of women's experiences" leads to "research for women…. That is, the goal of this inquiry is to provide for women explanations of social phenomena that they want and need, rather than providing…answers to questions that…[men in power] have In Three Guineas, Woolf does not just advocate education for women, but a different type of education, one that recognizes their different worlds. This different education would allow Mrs. Ramsay to solve problems that seem irresolvable, matters like the impurity of milk delivered to homes and the absence of a hospital on the island.

Mrs. Ramsay's world is directed forward by the particular and concrete, the fragrance of the Boeuf en Daube and the strength of another's arm. Each particularity, each concrete aspect of life is unique, with its own history and distinct relationship with a thinker. Even the Boeuf en Daube is no common, generalized entity. The cook's relationship to the Boeuf is not identical with Mrs. Ramsay's. The aroma and the taste vary with each person. The preparation and the memories of other times, other dinners, and other recipes contribute to each person's understanding of and relationship with the present Boeuf en Daube. Even more than the Boeuf en Daube that Mrs. Ramsay serves to her dinner guests, there is the concreteness and particularity of each person, each of the guests, each of her children as a distinct, concrete person with a life history, a narrative, with abilities, dreams and hopes, with needs, interests, feelings, and desires, with a preferred way of thinking, with different vocabularies and texts to enrich his or her life.

Knowledge of the other, whether person or object, is not based on fragmented parts, on some additive process by which separate, unconnected facts are combined. As Woolf says elsewhere, "It is no use trying to sum people up. One must follow hints, not exactly what is said, not yet entirely what is done." When she sees her children smiling, running, or playing, when she wonders whether Minta Doyle will marry Paul Bayley and the suitability of this choice, Mrs. Ramsay is not analyzing a smile, a judgment, or an instance of behaviour. A so-called instance of behaviour is akin to William Blake's epigram "To see a world in a grain of sand .... Hold Infinity in the palm of your hand." However, it is not Infinity with a capital "I" that Mrs. Ramsay sees in her child's eyes. It is a world that is James, her son.

Though this form of knowledge and thinking at first seems ephemeral and unstable, it can be described in a number of ways, as intuitive knowledge and tacit knowing. As with intuition, Mrs. Ramsay does not lack knowledge or use an incomprehensible, confused type of thought. Her knowledge and thinking are not empty or unexplainable. Though a mother's understanding of her infant's needs and desires may be called intuitive or a maternal instinct, this understanding is based on a form of knowledge and way of gaining knowledge. There is intense concentration on and involvement with the other and with the other's world. This concentration is not just hearing words and interpreting or translating their meaning into logical, propositional form. It is listening,

listening in the quietude and fullness of one's whole self. It is the leaching out, the seeing, the grasping, the feeling, the encounter. At the same time that this knowing person remains herself and retains her knowledge and values, there is a letting go of one's notions and assumptions and entering the place of the other while yet not defining that place.

Relationships form the core of the world Mrs. Ramsay inhabits. Problems requiring caring, responsiveness, communication, tangled networks of concern, emotions, and the avoidance of betrayal or isolation, and the understanding of another's life history emerge from these relationships. No relationship with another can be understood through a narrow, unitary dimension. According to Blum, for example, responsiveness involves both cognitive and affective dimensions. It includes a cognitive grasp of another's condition.... At the same time the altruistic aspect of responsiveness involves our emotional natures, in that responsiveness is not a purely rational willing of another person's good.

Each problem requiring thought consists of a unique situation in which all parties retain their personal identities, their life histories, emotions, and feelings. Caring and relationship occur between distinctive, concrete persons; moral situations exist within some particular historical and sociological context, bound by time and place. Though the language of care and response requires one to nurture and respond to the other and not to hurt either the other or oneself, it also necessitates demystification, openness, and a rejection of self-deception.

As we read To the Lighthouse, we recognize the two ways of thinking about and relating to the world, others, and ourselves. We take Mrs. Ramsay's perspective and become part of the world that she inhabits. We experience the loss and desperation of Mr. Ramsay after the death of Mrs. Ramsay. We may wonder whether his loss was the loss of Mrs. Ramsay or not having everything in its place, not having someone to take care of his mundane world, and not having the comfort of the ordinary. Mr. Ramsay never searches to know the other world and way of life that Mrs. Ramsay personified. Mr. Ramsay never questions whether at times he too should enter into this other way of knowing and thinking. Though men's language provides a "heaven of security" for ha life, Mrs. Ramsay does not presume she should speak this foreign language or enter men's world; she does not entertain the idea that this too should be ha world.

But just as the second and third sections of To the Lighthouse are fraught with darkness and foreboding, the resonance of this feeling reverberates back to expose the despair and forewarning in the first section. Even from behind the protective shield of "The Window," the melancholy, frustration, and resentment of "Time Passes" and "The Lighthouse" are felt. The foreboding and darkness emanate from below the surface and are not just based on the sudden death of Mrs. Ramsay, the shell that kills Andrew, the death of Prue in childbirth, the loneliness of Mr. Ramsay, and the bitterness of James. In the section, "The Window," we are often struck by what is not said, by what is missing. In the either-or categories personified by Mr. Ramsay and Mrs. Ramsay, we are led to recognize the uneasiness that Lily Briscoe feels and the discomfort of Bankes at having to dine with the Ramsays.

Mrs. Ramsay herself poses one of the problems that bothers us. When Bankes speaks of friends Mrs. Ramsay has not seen for many years, Mrs. Ramsay cannot believe that they still exist, that they have led their own life, throughout these years, a life she knew nothing of. Maybe, we can even say that she cannot imagine that there are other voices and themes, other moral songs and ways of living beside the one that she knows so well.She never entertains the idea that caste, social class, and economic system, race specific experiences, cultural or historical setting, and ideological differences, like language itself, may generate different, equally acceptable ways of living and thinking. Even Mrs. Ramsay's empathy with the crying chambermaid whose father is dying so far away, in Switzerland, is not a case of universality, but the nearness of the young maid. The thinness of Mrs. Ramsay's visits to the poor and needy are like the stocking she knits for the lighthouse keeper's son. They are all part of ha goodness, but it is a goodness that does not have to confront the realities of these others. Mrs. Ramsay's caring for others focuses on face-to-face encounters with those who are intimates family, friends, and all of those who are part of her daily life. Her caring, akin to Noddings' view, refers to members of constrained "concentric circles…the inner, intimate circle" being those Mrs. Ramsay loves and its bordering circles "those for whom…she has a] personal regard."Caring, response, knowledge, and thinking, for Mrs. Ramsay, focus on a very limited population, on those people, events, and occasions when she can directly affect those who hear her voice and feel her presence.

And yet, this image of Mrs. Ramsay's thinking, caring, and responsiveness are partially dissipated in what Martha Nussbaum now appropriately calls "the fragility of goodness."However, we must go beyond this idea. For in the case of Woolf's ideas, it is not just that algebraic equations or mathematical puzzles, failsafe solutions and the quest for certainty, unbridled belief in rationality and logic, in the forms that Mr. Ramsay would cherish, mask a deeply tragic element of human life. There is something equally tragic about Mrs. Ramsay's portrayal of life. Even Mrs. Ramsay herself wonders if she is too overpowering and overprotective, whether her caring at times smothers others, whether her view of what someone else's life should be is mistaken.

Do the ones she believes need caring for really need the care she gives? She orchestrates the marriage of Minta and Paul, thinks about whether Lily Briscoe and William Bankes should marry, wonders about the fate of Charles Tansley as a scholar who follows in the footsteps of ha husband, only imagines ha daughters' future in terms of marriage. But Mrs. Ramsay's dreams, her caring and responsiveness, come to naught. Minta and Paul's marriage does not measure up to the ideal match it promised to be on the day Minta lost her grandmother's brooch and became engaged to Paul. Lily Briscoe never marries, but attains ha own identity in a way Mrs. Ramsay could never imagine. And Charles Tansley during the Great War to end all wars gives speeches about love, not about logic or the scholarship Mr. Ramsay so revered. What does this tell us? To say that care, as with any other moral standard or standard of rationality, is fallible or that life has a deeply tragic vein would be to say the obvious. Instead, there is something else. With the passage of time, with the transformation of Charles Tansley and of Lily Briscoe, we also recognize how time, historical events, the vast sweep of personal and public historical events also requires us to change and reconceptualize our intellectual concepts, the way we look at reasoning and morality.

At present, a few writers suggest that covertly underlying the moral theory of the last few decades are notions of care, responsiveness, and interconnectedness. What some may call masculine reasoning and a masculine moral language are thus being reconceptualized to include aspects of the feminine. Along this line, Susan Okin argues that we must reinterpret John Rawls' theory of justice to make room for care and for a feminine language of reasoning if the theory of justice and fairness are to have any depth.The either/or categories represented by Mr. Ramsay and Mrs. Ramsay are now being shown to be partial and anemic.

Other researchers and theorists claim that it is not a matter of only women, like Mrs. Ramsay, using a feminine language and only men, like Mr. Ramsay, using a masculine language. Though each sex uses both languages that men cluster more frequently around the masculine language and women around the feminine language, as if each has its own native tongue. In one sense, this claim is misconceived and the issue is very different. The more important issue is how we conceptualize each form of reasoning and each type of moral standard.

If we accept, for example, caring, as a quality, a virtue that imbues the presence and life of someone like Mrs. Ramsay, then we must also think about what other virtues are required to give that one virtue breadth and meaning, disclose its inner its inner core. Any study of "an important range of moral virtues compassion, kindness, generosity, helpfulness, considerateness, sympathy" cannot refer to fragmented entities, each with its own set of responsibilities, each bounded by a high wall, each one a separate trait; a "bag of virtues" conceptualization s not what is required. Instead, any one moral virtue refers to a coherent set of other, interconnected virtues. For example, caring for someone requires the virtue of courage since caring for often requires acts that are out of the ordinary, that go beyond the commonplace to encounter and overcome something someone may fear. At times, we are distressed at Mrs. Ramsay's silence, at her neutrality, in the face of Mr. Ramsay's unfeeling response to his children and we wonder why Mrs. Ramsay's paralysis, why ha silence, her inability to speak, and to defend her children. Similarly, justice would be a cold, a frigid virtue, as unresponsive and austere as Mr. Ramsay often was, if it did not possess care and compassion.

In addition, feminine theorists need to provide a richer interpretation of community, instead of favoring the idea of "concentric circles," networks, and webs of relationships. One can understand the rejection of certain traditional and fundamentalist communities that autocratically and at times irrationally control and dominate not only women's lives, but the lives of men as well. However, when feminine ethical theory stresses life history and narrative, it cannot only speak of a person's life from the time of birth. Instead, these theories must recognize as Virginia Woolf did, that at the time of birth, the infant does not merely relate to caregivers, family members, and other intimates. The Ramsay family is not disassociated from some larger framework. We recognize this family as the same family described in the Godless Victorian, the biography of Leslie Stephen, Virginia Woolf's father and the model for Mr. Ramsay. This family like any other family is not a self-contained network or web of interacting relationships. Rather, in the background and within its very being, there is an explicit or tacit community that contributes to the education of the infant her life history, and the way she chooses a life narrative.

The networks of caring and loving relationships that nourish infants have tangled and at times indiscernable roots in a wide variety of communities. These communal roots contribute metaphors, symbols, meanings, skills, values, excellences, virtues, and interests to those who nourish and care for an infant. Through these caregivers, the child is inducted into a moral world that is populated by the community's moral priorities and virtues. The point here is that if we speak of particularity and concreteness and yet, dismiss rampant relativism, where do we find content for our moral virtues? The content and meaning of our interlocking system of moral virtues must then be found in the history, the memories of communal life. Let us join with feminine theorists, but let us take their findings and ideas where they are meant to go. Talk about cultural, ethnic, and religious roots and about the particular and the concrete requires that we attend to the substance of their roots and how the particular and concrete acquires meaning. When Wallace Stevens writes, "A mythology reflects its region,"he also describes how we must look at moral virtues like generosity, altruism, caring, kindness, and responsiveness. These moral virtues acquire substance and meaning through being part of a region, a community.

Bibliography

Burt, John. "*Irreconcilable Habits of Thought in A Room of One's Own and To the Lighthouse.*" ELH 49.4 (1982): 889-907. Rpt. Bloom 191-205.

Cohn, Ruby. "Art in To the Lighthouse." Modern Fiction Studies. 1962, Summer, 8.2 63-72.

Dash, Irene, Deena Kushner, and Deborah Moore. "*How Light a Lighthouse for Today's Women?*" The Lost Traditions: Mothers and Daughters in Literature. Eds. Cathy Davidson and E.M. Broner. New York; Ungar, 1980. 176-88.

DiBattista, Maria. "*To the Lighthouse: Virginia Woolf's Winter's Tale.*" Virginia Woolf: Revaluation and Continuity. Eds. Ralph Freedman and Maria DiBattista. Berkeley: University of California Press, 1980. 161-88.

Levy, Eric. "*Woolf's Metaphysics of Tragic Vision in To the Lighthouse.*" Philological Quarterly. 75:1 (1996): 109-32.

Lilienfeld, Jane. "'*The Deceptiveness of Beauty': Mother Love and Mother Hate in To the Lighthouse.*" Twentieth Century Literature. 23 (1977): 345-373.

Lilienfeld, Jane. "*Where the Spear Plants Grew: The Ramsays' Marriage in To the Lighthouse.*" New Feminist Essays on Virginia Woolf. Ed. Jane Marcus. Lincoln: University of Nebraska Press, 1981. 148-69.

Matro, Thomas G. "*Only Relations: Vision and Achievement in To the Lighthouse.*" PMLA 99.2 (1984): 212-224.

Pratt, Annis. "*Sexual Imagery in To the Lighthouse: A New Feminist Approach.*" Modern Fiction Studies. 1972. 417-431.

Stewart, Jack F. "*Color in To the Lighthouse.*" Twentieth Century Literature. 31 (1985): 439-455.

